The Russian Revolution

The collapse of the Soviet Union in 1991 has provided fresh perspectives from which to view the Revolution out of which it grew. *The Russian Revolution: 1917–1921*, by Ronald Kowalski, reviews the ever-changing debate on the nature of the Russian Revolution. This collection of documents and sources includes newspapers, memoirs and literature as well as commentary and background information for each source.

The Russian Revolution contains a narrative of the major events of the period and a re-examination of World War I in relation to the Revolution. The author also debates thematic issues such as the actions of peasants and workers.

In *The Russian Revolution*, Ronald Kowalski incorporates recent scholarship and newly available documentary material translated into English for the first time in order to address the key question of whether it was a *coup* foisted on the Russian people or a popular movement.

Ronald Kowalski is Senior Lecturer in Russian History at Worcester College of Higher Education, Worcester.

ROUTLEDGE SOURCES IN HISTORY
Series Editor
David Welch, University of Kent

OTHER TITLES IN THE SERIES
The Suez Crisis
Anthony Gorst and Lewis Johnman

Resistance and Conformity in the Third Reich
Martyn Housden

FORTHCOMING
Italian Fascism
John Pollard

The Holocaust
John Fox

The German Experience
Anthony McElligott

The Rise and Fall of the Soviet Union
Richard Sakwa

The Russian Revolution
1917–1921

Ronald Kowalski

London and New York

First published 1997
by Routledge
11 New Fetter Lane, London EC4P 4EE

Simultaneously published in the USA and Canada
by Routledge
29 West 35th Street, New York, NY 10001

© 1997 Ronald Kowalski
Typeset in Galliard and Gill by Keystroke, Jacaranda Lodge, Wolverhampton

Printed and bound in Great Britain by Biddles Ltd, Guildford and King's Lynn

British Library Cataloguing in Publication Data
A catalogue record for this book is available from the British Library

Library of Congress Cataloging in Publication Data
A catalogue record for this book has been requested

ISBN 0–415–12437–9 (hbk)
ISBN 0–415–12438–7 (pbk)

In memory of my mother

Contents

THE ISSUES OF THE REVOLUTION

OPPOSITION

CONCLUSION

Series editor's preface

Sources in History is a new series responding to the continued shift of emphasis in the teaching of history in schools and universities towards the use of primary sources and the testing of historical skills. By using documentary evidence, the series is intended to reflect the skills historians have to master when challenged by problems of evidence, interpretation and presentation.

A distinctive feature of *Sources in History* will be the manner in which the content, style and significance of documents is analysed. The commentary and the source are not discrete, but rather merge to become part of a continuous and integrated narrative. After reading each volume a student should be well versed in the historiographical problems which sources present. In short, the series aims to provide texts which will allow students to achieve facility in 'thinking historically' and place them in a stronger position to test their historical skills. Wherever possible the intention has been to retain the integrity of a document and not simply to present a 'gobbet', which can be misleading. Documentary evidence thus forces the student to confront a series of questions which professional historians also have to grapple with. Such questions can be summarised as follows:

1 *What* type of source is the document?
- Is it a written source or an oral or visual source?
- What, in your estimation, is its importance?
- Did it, for example, have an effect on events or the decision-making process?
2 *Who* wrote the document?
- A person, a group or a government?
- If it was a person, what was their position?
- What basic attitudes might have affected the nature of the information and language used?
3 *When* was the document written?
- The date, and even the time, might be significant.
- You may need to understand when the document was written in order to understand its context.
- Are there any special problems in understanding the document as contemporaries would have understood it?
4 *Why* was the document written?
- For what purpose(s) did the document come into existence, and for *whom* was it intended?

- Was the document 'author-initiated' or was it commissioned for somebody? If the document was ordered by someone, the author could possibly have 'tailored' his piece.
5 *What* was written?
- This is the obvious question, but never be afraid to state the obvious.
- Remember, it may prove more revealing to ask the question: what was *not* written?
- That is, read between the lines. In order to do this you will need to ask what other references (to persons, events, other documents, etc.) need to be explained before the document can be fully understood.

Sources in History is intended to reflect the individual voice of the volume author(s) with the aim of bringing the central themes of specific topics into sharper focus. Each volume will consist of an authoritative introduction to the topic; chapters will discuss the historical significance of the sources, and the final chapter will provide an up-to-date synthesis of the historiographical debate. Authors will also provide an annotated bibliography and suggestions for further reading. These books will become contributions to the historical debate in their own right.

In *The Russian Revolution, 1917–1921*, Ronald Kowalski reappraises the tumultuous events which gripped Russia between 1917 and 1921. The collapse of the Soviet Union has provided new source material and fresh perspectives from which to view the Russian Revolution. Much of this new material has been translated by Dr Kowalski and is incorporated in this volume. The study offers significant insights into the intense historiographical debate on the nature of the Russian Revolution. In particular, it addresses the key questions of whether the October Revolution was a *coup* foisted upon an unwilling Russian populace by a handful of fanatical revolutionaries or whether it in fact represented the wishes of the bulk of ordinary Russians. The author contends that it was a popular revolution that subsequently became hijacked by the Bolshevik minority. The text begins by presenting a primarily narrative account of the major events that affected Russia between 1914 and 1921. Specifically it re-examines the impact of World War I, before focusing on the key events of 1917 itself: the February Revolution; the July Rising; the Kornilov affair; and October itself. The narrative concludes by analysing both the evolution of the Bolshevik dictatorship as well as the causes of the Bolshevik victory in the Civil War. The author turns then to a series of major thematic issues, namely, the aspirations and actions of the peasants, workers, national minorities and soldiers during the Revolution and Civil War. The final section explores the nature of opposition to Leninist rule and concludes with an analysis of the crises that faced Communist autocracy in 1921.

This important book offers a clear and accessible introduction to the Russian Revolution. It provides a mature synthesis of recent scholarship as well as incorporating newly available documentary material that has been translated into English for the first time.

David Welch
Canterbury 1997

Acknowledgements

Several institutions and people merit special mention. The School of Humanities and Social Science at Worcester College of Higher Education provided funding for numerous visits to specialist Libraries within Britain where I was able to accumulate much of the material incorporated in this book (sadly, study leave seems largely to have vanished). The staff at numerous libraries have been unfailingly helpful, especially the Bodleian Library, Oxford; the British Museum; and Glasgow University Library. I owe a particular debt to the Baykov Library, Centre for Russian and East European Studies, University of Birmingham, which generously has allowed me use of its rich resources. My own college library has assisted, through its inter-library loan department, in the acquisition of much-needed material. Heather McCallum at Routledge has proved to be a patient editor, who coped cheerfully (I hope) with the various unintended delays in the writing of this book. Stephen White, with his typical generosity, has provided a number of the illustrations that enliven the text. Richard Sakwa has read and been supportive of sections of the manuscript. To David Saunders, a belated thanks for his critical and insightful reading of the original proposal, and a number of very useful suggestions which assisted me in the overall organisation of the book. David Welch, the Series Editor, has been a source of constant encouragement. His perceptive comments have enabled me to clarify many points that otherwise would have remained confusing to the reader. Whatever shortcomings are still to be found, they are far fewer thanks to their efforts and remain a reflection of my own foibles. Finally, I would like to thank my family (Jenny, and Anna and Helen), who have lived too long with the Russian Revolution.

Permissions

Every effort has been made to trace the owners of copyright material. If copyright has been infringed it has been done unintentionally. My gratitude, and that of the publishers, are owed to the following for permission to reproduce copyright material: Aarhus University Press for an extract from J.L. Munck, *The Kornilov Revolt. A Critical Examination of Sources and Research* (Aarhus, Denmark, 1987); Academic International Press for an extract from R.A. Wade (ed.), *Documents of Soviet History. Volume I* (Gulf Breeze, 1991); Alfred A. Knopf for an extract from R. Pipes, *The Russian Revolution, 1899–1919* (New York, 1990); Carfax Publishing Company

(Abingdon, Oxfordshire) for an extract from M. Melançon, 'Who Wrote What and When? Proclamations of the February Revolution', *Soviet Studies* (1988); Harper Collins Publishers Limited for an extract from R. Pipes, *The Russian Revolution, 1899–1917* (London, 1992); Hoover Institution Press for extracts from V.N. Brovkin (ed.), *Dear Comrades: Menshevik Reports on the Bolshevik Revolution and Civil War* (Stanford, 1991); Johns Hopkins University Press for an extract from J. Bunyan (ed.), *Intervention, Civil War and Communism in Russia. April–December 1918* (Baltimore, 1935); Lawrence & Wishart for extracts from V.I. Lenin, *Collected Works* (London, 1964–5); Ohio State University Press for an extract from H. Asher, 'The Kornilov Affair: A Reinterpretation', *Russian Review* (1970); by permission of the Oxford University Press extracts from O. Figes, *Peasant Russia, Civil War. The Volga Countryside in Revolution* (Oxford, 1989), B. Knei-Paz, *The Social and Political Thought of Leon Trotsky* (Oxford, 1979) and V. Serge, *Memoirs of a Revolutionary* (Oxford, 1967); Princeton University Press for extracts from W.H. Chamberlin, *The Russian Revolution, 1917–1921* (Princeton, 1987) and W.G. Rosenberg, *Liberals in the Russian Revolution. The Constitutional Democratic Party, 1917–1921* (Princeton, 1974); Alexander Rabinowitch for an extract from *The Bolsheviks Come to Power* (Norton: New York, 1976); Stanford University Press for extracts from D. Atkinson, *The End of the Russian Land Commune, 1905–1930* (Stanford, 1983), R.P. Browder, A.F. Kerensky (eds), *The Russian Provisional Government*, 3 volumes (Stanford, 1961) and J. Bunyan, H.H. Fisher (eds), *The Bolshevik Revolution, 1917–1918. Documents and Materials* (Stanford, 1934); and Thames and Hudson Ltd, for an extract from A. Ascher (ed.), *The Mensheviks in the Russian Revolution* (London, 1976).

Glossary and list of abbreviations

ARCWC	All-Russian Council of Workers' Control
batrak (pl. *batraki*)	landless peasant(s), farm labourer(s)
Black Hundreds	extreme right-wing, anti-Semitic mobs
CC	Central Committee (of a political party)
CCFC	Central Council of Factory Committees
CEC	Central Executive Committee
Cheka	Russian abbreviation for the Extraordinary Commission (Chresvychainnaia Kommissiia) for the Struggle against Counter-revolution and Sabotage; the Soviet secret police
chernye liudi	'the dark masses', usually meaning the peasants
chernyi peredel	Black Repartition, the equal division of all the land among the peasants
commune	village community, in Russian the *mir*, meaning 'world' or 'peace'
Council of Ministers	the Tsar's Cabinet
desiatina (pl. *desiatinany*)	land measure equal to 2.7 acres
Dual Power	the name given to the political system between the February and October Revolutions whereby the Soviet supervised the actions of the Provisional Government
Duma	national representative (but not wholly democratic) lower house of the Russian parliament, created by Nicholas II's October Manifesto of 1905; swept away by the February Revolution
glasnost'	openness, element of liberal intellectual reform introduced by Mikhail Gorbachev
guberniia (pl. *gubernii*)	province(s)
intelligenty	the intellectuals
Izvestiia	literally 'news', official Soviet newspaper, largely Bolshevik mouthpiece after October
Kadets	Party of National Freedom, the Constitutional Democrats, usually depicted as liberal party

kollegium (pl. *kollegii*)	institution of collective administration, championed by left oppositions within Bolshevik Party after October
kombedy	committees of poor peasants, created by Soviet government in June 1918 to assist in the requisition of grain and to wage (unsuccessfully) class war in the countryside
Komuch	Committee of Members of the Constituent Assembly, created by Social Revolutionaries (SRs) in June 1918 in opposition to the Bolshevik Government
kulak (pl. *kulaki*)	literally a 'fist', generally used to describe a rich peasant, more precisely referred to those peasants who acted as money lenders
Left SRs	radical wing of the Party of Social Revolutionaries, which became an independent after the October Revolution and entered a coalition government with the Bolsheviks until they abandoned it in opposition to the Brest–Litovsk Treaty
Little Russia	the Ukraine
Menshevik Internationalists	left-wing group of the moderate, Menshevik faction of the Russian Social Democratic Labour Party which opposed Russia's participation in World War I; led by Iulii Martov it attempted to act as a 'loyal' opposition to the Bolsheviks during the Civil War
Mezhraionka	the Petrograd Inter-district Group of the Russian Social Democratic Labour Party which sought to stand above the factional conflict between the Bolsheviks and Mensheviks
MRC	Military Revolutionary Committee of the Petrograd Soviet, set up after the Kornilov affair ostensibly to defend the Revolution from the forces of reaction; used by the Bolsheviks to carry out the seizure of power in October 1917
Narkomprod	People's Commissariat of Food
oblast'	region
Octobrists	party to the right of the Kadets which abandoned revolution to work for peaceful development of Russia on the basis of the principles espoused by Nicholas II in his October Manifesto of 1905 (see under Duma)
Okhrana	the tsarist secret police
pomeshchik (pl. *pomeshchiki*)	landlords, gentry, nobility
pood	measure of weight equivalent to approximately 36 pounds
Popular Socialists	right-wing splinter group which abandoned Social Revolutionaries in 1907 and favoured peaceful improvement of peasants' conditions; opposed the use of terror

Pravda	literally 'truth', main Bolshevik newspaper
RKP	Russian Communist Party, as the Bolsheviks renamed themselves at the Seventh Party Congress in March 1918; in 1922 to be renamed the Communist Party of the Soviet Union (CPSU)
RSDWP	Russian Social Democratic Workers' Party
soviet (*sovet*)	literally 'council', elected by workers, peasants or soldiers
Sovnarkom	Council of People's Commissars, in theory subordinate to the All-Russian Congress of Soviets; in practice, Lenin's government
spetsy	literally 'specialists', the term pejoratively used to describe the old managers and technicians, and officers, who served the Bolshevik regime
Stavka	military headquarters in World War I, before October Revolution
SRs	Party of Social Revolutionaries (also referred to as Socialist Revolutionaries), self-professedly the party of the peasants which sought to create an agrarian socialist society based on the commune; its majority opposed the Bolsheviks, actively or passively, after October
Trudoviki	Labour Group affiliated to the SRs
uezd (pl. *uezdy*)	district
Vesenkha	Supreme Council of the National Economy, the body set up by the Bolsheviks after October to direct the economy
Vikzhel	the All-Russian Executive Committee of the Union of Railway Workers
volost' (pl. *volosti*)	rural district, sub-division of *uezd*, comprising several communes
zemstvo (pl. *zemstva*)	elective agencies of local government at the provincial and district level created in most of European Russia in 1864; dominated by the gentry, especially after the 1890 statute which limited peasant influence over them

A note on dates and transliteration

I have employed the Russian calendar (thirteen days behind that of the West) until 1 February 1918, when it was changed to correspond to that of the West. Transliteration has been based on the Library of Congress system, except for names already widely used in a different form, e.g., Trotsky, instead of Trotskii.

Introduction

The historiography of the Revolution | **1**

The collapse of the Soviet Union at the end of 1991 was soon reflected in the ways in which the Russian Revolution has been viewed. In the West, for example, there was a resurgence of what can only be termed triumphalist writings which welcomed the fall of the Soviet Union. It was taken as vindication of the view that the October Revolution in 1917 was a malign experiment, foisted on an unwilling country by a tiny minority of Bolshevik zealots. In Russia itself there has been much soul-searching, with repeated rejections of October, and its eventual progeny, Stalinism, as alien aberrations in the course of Russian history – echoing attempts after 1945 by conservative German historians, such as Gerhard Ritter, to explain Nazism in a similar way.

But before outlining recent reinterpretations of the Russian Revolution a review of the main historiographical currents since 1917 will prove to be illuminating. In both the Soviet and Western historiography it has long been held that Lenin, and the Bolshevik Party that he created, were primarily responsible for the October Revolution (the February Revolution, as we shall see in Chapter 3, was considered to be spontaneous, a response to the sufferings and defeats inflicted on an ill-prepared and ill-led Russia in World War I). Without the Party, the so-called vanguard of the proletariat, the workers, and the other ordinary people involved in the Revolution – the peasants, sailors and soldiers – would have failed to develop the political consciousness necessary to carry out a radical revolution. In *What Is To Be Done?*, Lenin's major work on the role and organisation of the Party, published in March 1902, he had argued that the workers, in their day-to-day struggle for economic improvement, would achieve no more than a 'trade union consciousness'. To rise above this, to acquire the revolutionary consciousness required to overthrow the old order and, ultimately, to build a socialist society, external help was required. Such help had to be provided by a self-selected elite, of revolutionary-minded intellectuals, organised into the vanguard party. If such a party did not exist, then there would be no revolution.

That such an interpretation dominated Soviet historical writing from the early years of the Revolution remains unsurprising. A fundamental, and continuing, problem facing the Bolshevik-Communists was that of legitimating the monopolisa-tion of political power by the Party after 1917 **(Wolfe 1964: 63)**. The solution came to be one of stressing the leading role of the Party **(White 1994: 255–6)**. Without the Party, disciplined, centralised, obedient to Lenin, the masses would have remained insufficiently conscious and organised to seize power; without the Party, the Revolution would not have survived the Civil War; without the vanguard, the country would have failed to industrialise and hence been left at the mercy of Nazi German imperialism in World War II; and without the Party, the country would have failed to recover industrially and successfully compete in the nuclear arms race that escalated in the era of the Cold War after 1945. Moreover, the image of the Party that emerges from the pages of Soviet historiography is very much that of the archetypal (or mythical) Leninist party: tightly knit, well organised and highly disciplined, responding rapidly and obediently to the instructions which emanated from the Central Committee (CC) leadership. Dissenting voices, which highlighted the splits within the Party (Eduard Burdzhalov) or the independent political actions of the workers (Aleksandr Shliapnikov), were silenced.

Moreover, the Lenin of Soviet historiography assumes the status of a demigod. Apart from being the founding father of the Bolshevik Party, his leadership of it is depicted as infallible. For instance, in 1917 it was Lenin who alone 're-armed' the Party ideologically, his *April Theses* providing it with the programme upon which it successfully struck for power in October **(see Chapter 4)**. It was Lenin's wise caution, in seeking to restrain a premature attempt to seize power, that limited the damage inflicted upon the Party when rank-and-file hotheads staged a rising in early July **(see Chapter 5)**. It was Lenin who correctly concluded that an insurrection was ripe in the early autumn and cajoled the Party to take power into its hands **(see Chapter 6)**. It was Lenin who prevailed upon the Party to heed the wishes of the peasantry and modify its agrarian policy to secure their support **(see Chapter 9)**. Numerous other examples could be cited, but the conclusion is obvious. Lenin was the mastermind behind Bolshevik victory: no Lenin, no October Revolution! The following poster, designed by Viktor Ivanov in 1967, captures the almost divine status in which Lenin was held in the Soviet Union. The text, by the famous revolutionary poet, dramatist and artist, Vladimir Maiakovskii, reads: 'Lenin lived, Lenin lives, Lenin will Live!'

Document 1.1 Lenin's Godlike Status in the Soviet Union

[See illustration on p. 5]

Ironically, much Western historiography has painted a similar picture of the Party and its leading role (and that of Lenin) in the Revolution, albeit for different reasons. William Chase and John A. Getty described this picture in the following terms:

> The image . . . which . . . emerges from the pages of Western histories of the Party is that of highly disciplined, conspiratorial fanatics who, of necessity, operated within very well organised cohesive groups. The overwhelming majority of these people were, so the image goes, *intelligenty* [intellectuals] who had no organic links with the working masses and whose activities and ideas were simply responses to the directives of Lenin and the Central Committee.

Source: N. Baburina, The Soviet Political Poster, 1917–1980
(Harmondsworth: Penguin, 1985), p. 149

This image, they continue, was the product of ignorance of the range of evidence available, and of 'the anti-Soviet prejudices of these . . . historians' **(Chase and Getty 1978: 85)**. One might add that this 'ignorance' also was a product of the traditional emphasis, certainly within the British and American historical professions, on political history. Such an approach, unsurprisingly, led to a concentration on prominent personalities, the 'great' (or 'bad') men and women, for whom abundant, easily available evidence existed. In turn, the actions and aspirations of ordinary workers and peasants were often neglected **(Carr 1964: 9–10, 44–52)**. The prejudices alluded to by Chase and Getty were rooted in the belief that the Bolshevik seizure of power was an aberration in the course of Russian history. The Bolsheviks, playing upon the short-term exhaustion and resentments amongst the majority of ordinary Russians caused by World War I, exploited their superior organisational muscle to overthrow a socially and politically estranged Provisional Government. Thereafter, they used the power so seized to frustrate the wishes of the Russian people who, in the elections to the Constituent Assembly in November 1917, gave a majority to the Social Revolutionaries (SRs). The Bolsheviks dispersed the Assembly by force in January 1918 and then consolidated themselves in power regardless of popular will. In brief, the October Revolution and all that ensued from it were considered to be illegitimate **(Chase and Getty 1978: 85–6)**.

Let us defer this issue, of the legitimacy or illegitimacy, of the Bolshevik Revolution for the present. It remains one of the most politically contentious historical questions of the twentieth century **(Dukes 1992: 590)**. More specifically, much historical research of the last 25 years has cast considerable doubts on the stereotypes presented above. For example, Robert Service, author of a three-volume biography of Lenin, has reappraised his role in 1917. Lenin, he argued, did not create the pressures for radical 'socio-political and economic change in Russia'. It was the product of war-weariness, industrial decline and unemployment, food shortages and peasant impatience for land reform. Lenin too, he continued, made a number of potentially disastrous political interventions. In April, his advocacy of soviet power led to rank-and-file demonstrations that might have precipitated the suppression of the Party. His tardiness in preventing his followers from attempting to seize power in early July again threatened the survival of the Party. Most of all, his call for an insurrection in mid-September would in all likelihood have resulted in the Mensheviks and SRs mobilising sufficient support behind Aleksandr Kerenskii, head of the Provisional Government, to crush the Bolsheviks. Service's Lenin is no infallible demigod. Yet he did play a vital role in determining the outcome of 1917. His insistence that the Bolsheviks act independently to assume power precluded the formation of a coalition socialist government in the autumn and set in motion the train of events that led to the creation of a one-party state **(Service 1990: 16–19)**, as we shall see in Chapters 6 and 7.

Similar revisions have been made to our understanding of the role of the Party in the Revolution. In his studies of the Bolshevik Party in Petrograd, Alexander Rabinowitch has demonstrated that it was far from monolithic, disciplined and well-organised, and that in many instances the leadership lagged behind rank-and-file aspirations. Moreover, the new 'social' history of the revolutionary period, in particular the studies of the working class of Petrograd and Moscow by Victoria Bonnell, Laura Englestein, Diane Koenker, David Mandel and Steven Smith, have demonstrated that the Russian workers were not merely 'irrational, poorly educated, and incapable of independent participation in the political process' **(Smith 1984: 288)**. Indeed, Engelstein has gone further. In her analysis of the Moscow workers during the 1905 Revolution, she concluded that they were not simply 'malleable', that is, manipulable and manipulated by the radical intelligentsia. On the contrary, frequently many of the more skilled and literate workers displayed considerable hostility to such attempts at manipulation on the part of the intellectuals **(Engelstein 1982: 2, 14)**. This distrust was the product of bitter disappointment with the very conduct of the radical intelligentsia. In the 1890s intellectuals (including students) had played their part in setting up workers' educational circles and the rudiments of a revolutionary party organisation. In the face of severe police repression, in large part they abandoned the revolutionary movement, leaving the workers to bear the brunt of prison and exile **(Pipes 1963: 185)**. After 1905 itself, the intellectuals who had swarmed to support the revolutionary cause again deserted it to avoid the iron heel of reaction, so confirming many workers in their suspicions of them. But on this occasion the workers were not left virtually leaderless as by then they had developed their own 'organic' intellectual stratum **(Gramsci 1971: 6)**.

Similar revisions have been made to our understanding of the role of the peasantry in the Revolution. Far from being simply 'immured in the idiocy of rural life', to use Marx's famous phrase, recent studies emphasise the ability of the peasantry to organise itself, within the confines of a revitalised village commune, and, on its own initiative and with its own goals in mind, to revolutionise the countryside **(Figes 1989: especially chs. 2, 3; Gill 1979: 170–3)**. Moreover, recent research on the 'peasants in uniform', the army, has confirmed this conclusion. Allan Wildman has stressed that the rank and file were not simply pawns manipulated at will by the Bolsheviks but active agents with their own 'vision of land and peace, of their definitive social liberation, but above all of their own collective power to attain such results' **(Wildman 1987: 403)**.

This new 'social', or revisionist, history has two important implications. First, it goes a considerable way to support the thesis controversially proposed by Teddy Uldricks some 20 years ago. Russia in 1917, he argued, confirmed that popular mobilisation was a 'key element in the revolutionary process', but with a crucial twist. Rather than the elite mobilising the masses, 'in this instance . . . the masses mobilised an elite [the Bolshevik Party]' **(Uldricks 1974: 412)**. Arguably, this conclusion too is rather one-sided, as it appears that both the elite and the masses were split on what should be done. It also minimises, if not neglects, the role of the intelligentsia in framing different political solutions to the problems gripping Russia during 1917. Second, the picture that emerges from these recent works also substantiates the proposition put forward almost 30 years ago by Leopold

Haimson. He then argued that a fundamental split in *Weltanschauung*, or world views, existed between educated society and the 'dark masses' (*chernye liudi*). Many in educated society welcomed a limited political revolution that would usher in an era of constitutionalism – and, for the small but growing urban bourgeoisie, capitalism. The latter, however, embraced a different vision of revolution, one that would produce a fundamental transformation of power relations within the economy and society as well **(Haimson 1964; 1965)**. For the peasants in particular revolution was synonomous with Black Repartition (*chernyi peredel*), that is, with the appropriation and equal division of all the land of the hated gentry.

However, the so-called revisionists have not swept all before them. Indeed, events of recent years, in particular the break-up of the Soviet Union at the end of 1991, have fanned the flames of controversy again. Whether this new hothouse of debate has enhanced scholarship is a moot point since, as Alan Wood commented, it appears to have produced a tendency, both in Russia itself and the West, 'to attribute all the country's problems to the Revolution itself' **(Wood 1992: 484)**. Let us begin with the triumphalist current in Western historiography referred to at the outset, briefly yet aptly caught in a series of articles in the *Times Literary Supplement* of November 1992, many of which rejoiced in the collapse of the Soviet Union. That doughty cold-warrior, Richard Pipes, set the ball rolling. He reiterated his long-standing belief that October was a *coup d'état*, conducted 'by a band of fanatical intellectuals' with no 'popular mandate'. He unequivocally condemned the idea 'that the Bolsheviks rose to power in the wake of an explosion of popular fury' as simply an 'entrenched myth'. He venomously castigated the 'revisionist' school as virtual simpletons who had been duped into accepting the approved Soviet view that 'October was indeed a genuine mass revolution driven from below'. He rather intemperately concluded: 'Academic monographs intended to establish this view, filled with statistics and for the most part as unreadable as they were irrelevant for the understanding of the subject, and silent on its political and ideological dimensions, poured forth from the pens of these historians and their pupils' **(Pipes 1992b: 3–4)**. Somewhat more temperately, Michael Howard argued that during 1917 'power slipped into the hands of inexperienced ideologues determined to create a new, just and rational new [*sic*] order by getting rid of everyone who did not fit in' **(Howard 1992: 5)**. Leszek Kolakowski categorised October as 'a calamitous accident', caused by the Bolshevik Party's skill in manipulating 'a largely spontaneous, genuinely mass movement . . . in order to impose dictatorial power of its own' **(Kolakowski 1992: 5)**. Martin Malia was in broad agreement. He claimed that 'October was indeed a *coup d'état*, but made possible only by a revolutionary social collapse; the workers were not the Bolshevik Party's "social base", but they were its indispensable social springboard to power' **(Malia 1992: 9)**. The picture is clear. And, of course, it was this *coup* that was to lead to the horrors of Stalinism and ultimately to the collapse of the Soviet Union and the chaos afflicting its successor states – with no gleam of a silver lining in sight!

Within the old Soviet Union itself, haltingly in the era of historical *glasnost'* begun by Mikhail Gorbachev, and later much more vigorously in the new Russia, reappraisals of the Revolution were also evident, despite the bitter rearguard action fought by the old party historical hacks **(Shishkin 1992: 520; Volobuev 1992: 568)**. At a historians' conference organised by the Russian Academy of Sciences in November 1992, P.V. Volobuev, a distinguished scholar of the Revolution, conceded that, despite the massive literature on 1917 and the plethora of documentary publications, Soviet historiography had remained flawed and required substantial revisions **(Iurchenko 1993: 566)**. But attempts by Soviet 'revisionists' to undertake their own *perestroika* in the historical profession, to create a more balanced and nuanced picture of events, were overtaken by the collapse of the old regime. Volobuev's plea, for a considered evaluation of the costs and benefits of 1917, in particular regarding the extent to which it facilitated the modernisation of society, has met with little response **(Volobuev cited in Iurchenko 1993: 212)**. As Kornev subsequently remarked, the study of history in Russia has remained deeply politicised, with 'a new dogmatism' replacing the old dogmas of the Soviet period:

> Its ideological foundation is the rejection of anything positive in Marxism-Leninism, in the concept of socialism. In practice it means presenting the entire domestic history of the Soviet period only in a negative light. New stereotypes began to be created: the idealisation of the pre-Soviet period, the canonisation of Nicholas II, the idealisation of the Russian Orthodox Church, the complete rejection of the progressive significance of the October Revolution, of class struggle, etc.
>
> **(Kornev 1994: 93)**

Indeed, many former Soviet historians underwent a 'magical transformation' into great democrats overnight and, as Pipes, came to depict October – and Lenin himself – as the source and architect of all the sufferings the country had experienced since 1917. The Bolsheviks are now frequently characterised as, at best, Utopian intellectuals, bent on the creation of a just and 'rational' social order, and at worst simply as 'destructive demogogues' **(Buldakov 1992: 213–14; Shishkin 1992: 525)**. However regarded, it is their intolerance that is held to be responsible for the failure of a democratic order to emerge in 1917. And their attempts to restructure Russia totally led to the mobilisation of a self-seeking, careerist *lumpenproletariat* which created an evil totalitarianism, even more terroristic than its Nazi counterpart **(Igritskii 1993: 15; Ioffe 1992: 154)**.

While there has been a vigorous resurgence of what Edward Acton has described as 'the liberal view' of the October Revolution, one which essentially stresses its conspiratorial nature **(Acton 1990: 35–9)** and is perhaps best exemplified by the two lengthy studies by Richard Pipes, *The Russian Revolution, 1899–1918* **(1992a)** and *Russia under the Bolshevik Regime, 1919–1924* **(1995)**, the work of revisionist historians continues to stimulate much fruitful discussion. In his recent, judicious reappraisal of the contribution made by the social historians, John Marot has graciously conceded that their 'enduring social-scientific achievement . . . has been to annihilate the conventional view of the masses as invariably acting impulsively, anarchically and shortsightedly' **(Marot 1994: 114)**. However, he criticises them for their neglect of politics *per se*. In particular, he rejects the idea that reference to the deepening economic crisis in urban Russia in itself is sufficient to explain the gravitation of the workers towards a second political revolution (the first was the February Revolution), one which would transfer power into the hands of the soviets. Critical to this outcome were the political programmes presented by the various parties which remained dominated by the intelligentsia. Crucially, it was the Bolsheviks, Lenin and his allies, who provided a political focus, initially unpopular in April, for the satisfaction of the material demands of the workers (and peasants and soldiers) by linking it to the establishment of soviet power. In a subsequent article he concluded:

> For party-political competition functioned as a selection mechanism by means of which workers chose from among rival political solutions, advanced by competing political parties, to economic crisis, and responded, as workers, to the associated potential for the transition from one type of society to another, from capitalism to socialism, for example.
>
> **(Marot 1995: 263)**

Steve Smith, author of a path-breaking study of the Petrograd workers during the Revolution, *Red Petrograd*, accepts that social historians 'have failed to think of the autonomy of politics with sufficient rigour' **(Smith 1995: 113)**. Yet he still believes that Marot has placed too much weight on politics *per se*, on 'the action of parties', especially of the Bolshevik Party, as the fundamental determinant of October. Mass political action, he insists, can only be understood in a broader context, one which takes into account rapidly changing economic and social conditions as well as the cultural beliefs of the Russian workers (and, one must add, peasants too). The need to understand the role of belief patterns in the shaping of the Revolution may well lead historians to address the methodological implications of the 'linguistic turn' provoked by postmodernism. To date, relatively little has been done in this regard. As Ron Suny commented, '[T]he discourses of language and culture, their impact on class formation, demand further exploration' **(Suny 1994: 178–82; also Kolonitskii 1994: 188, 195)**.

The debate on the dynamics and meaning of the Russian Revolution remains far from finished, as the Marot–Smith dialogue suggests. Moreover, much new evidence has become available in the last decade, the product first of the publication of hitherto suppressed materials in the era of *glasnost'* and then of the opening of the archives after 1991. Till now, it appears that few, if any, earth-shattering discoveries have been made. Rather, access to the archives has tended to substantiate existing knowledge. Historians of quite different political persuasions at least agree on this. Richard Pipes again recently wrote:

> Acquaintance with this material [the personal archive of Lenin and that of his Secretariat, as well as the archives of Stalin, Dzerzhinskii, and others] enabled me to modify and amplify certain parts of my narrative, but not in a single instance did it compel me to revise views which I had formed on the basis of printed sources and archives located in

the West. This gives me a certain degree of confidence that no new and startling information from other, still secret, archival repositories – notably the so-called Presidential Archive, which contains minutes of the *Politburo*, and the files of the *Cheka*/KGB – is likely to invalidate my account.

(Pipes 1995: xviii)

Steve Smith too remains 'rather sceptical that dramatic revelations await us in the archives'. While welcoming their opening, he cautions us not simply to become 'archive rats', at the expense of 'creative, innovative thinking' **(Smith 1994: 567)**. Moreover, even should the archives become fully opened to all serious scholars (the reality appears to be that access remains limited, either to those favoured by Yeltsin's entourage or to foreign institutions which can afford to buy extensive sections of them), problems in studying the Revolution will persist. As A.M. Kulegin commented, an indeterminate, yet considerable, amount of material, especially that produced by non-Bolshevik parties or organisations, has been 'cleansed' from the archives **(Kulegin 1993: 91–2)**. But a new era in the history of the Revolution has certainly arrived, one that promises to be both fascinating in itself and stimulating, not least for those of us who have engaged in the historical battles of the last 25 years.

A final, personal, statement, however, is perhaps appropriate. While still doubtful of the validity of many of the claims made by postmodernism there is one proposition, I think, that historians should consider seriously. As Keith Jenkins remarked, the least that any historian can do is to reflect on the political values that influence, often implicitly, his or her work and declare them **(Jenkins 1995: 176)**. Consequently, it seems prudent to outline, briefly, my own perspectives on the Revolution. The October Revolution, in my opinion, cannot simply be dismissed as an aberration in the course of Russian history. All was not well in the Russian Empire before 1917, nor 1914 for that matter. As we shall see **(Chapters 2 and 3)**, a combination of war-weariness, economic hardship, political oppression and numerous other factors precipitated the collapse of the widely hated autocracy. The hopes that the new regime, of Dual Power **(see Chapters 4 and 5)**, would bring peace and economic well-being were soon to be confounded. Disillusion with this regime, and those parties that supported it, rapidly grew. The Bolshevik Party, prompted by Lenin, adapted its policies to correspond with popular demands, summarised in the now famous slogans of 'Peace, bread and land' and 'All Power to the Soviets!' Whether this is viewed as opportunism or realism arguably remains more of a political than a historical judgment. While never formally supported by a majority of the population, as the results of the elections to the Constituent Assembly demonstrated **(Chapter 7)**, the October Revolution was accepted by most ordinary citizens. In that sense it may be seen as legitimate. But while peace, a costly peace, was concluded and land was redistributed amongst the peasants, widespread opposition quickly emerged. In part, this was the product of the continued economic disintegration of the country which the Bolsheviks could not halt (and of their own solutions to this problem, particularly forcible grain requisitioning). In part, it was a response to their increasing suppression of all dissenting voices. In other words, they lost whatever legitimacy they had in October and clung to power by dictatorial means. The outbreak on a broad scale of civil war in the summer of 1918 arguably reinforced the drift to authoritarianism (whether it caused it is an important question to which we shall return in the Conclusion). By 1921, when this study of the Revolution concludes, the foundations of what we now term 'Stalinism' appear to have been firmly laid. Some historians would dispute this (here students could usefully refer to the powerful arguments presented by Stephen Cohen, especially in his biography of Bukharin). My own feeling is that the degeneration of the Revolution into a Stalinist-type dictatorship was in all probability determined by 1921. Previous research on the early opposition movements in the Bolshevik Party (no other opposition could hope to survive by then) led me to conclude that at the very core of Bolshevik ideology, of the allegedly more democratic Left Communist opposition as much as of Lenin himself, were contradictions or *lacunae*, 'democratic deficits' if you like, that would have made the creation of a democratic socialist society, even in a Panglossian best of all possible worlds, impossible **(Kowalski 1991: 183–8)**. Such a conclusion, however, does not mean that I believe that the October Revolution, and all the horrors that followed, both during the Civil War and later under Stalin, can be simply laid at the door of a handful of fanatical intellectuals who illegitimately seized power in October. For Russia did not exist in the best of all possible worlds. It was still a backward, peasant society, encircled by much more advanced, militarily stronger and potentially hostile powers. A retrospective glance at the course of the twentieth-century history demonstrates that it has been neither easy, nor painless, for backward peasant societies to survive, let alone prosper, in an increasingly competitive global economy and polity. As Barrington Moore has reminded us, it is not simply revolutions that exact high human costs. The failure to modernise also produces massive human suffering **(Moore 1967: 410)**.

However, the purpose of this volume is not to present my own defences of, or attacks on, the Russian Revolution, though my own views no doubt influenced the documents selected and their interpretation. Rather, it is an attempt to introduce students, through the use of sources, to the debates that exist over the many, diverse facets that made up the Revolution. The structure of the book is almost self-explanatory. First, it seeks to present a narrative of events, from Russia's entry into World War I, through the tumultuous year of 1917, until final Bolshevik victory over the White (if not Green) armies in late 1920. Then it attempts to consider the aspirations, and actions, of those who made up the majority of this vast society. The exclusion of any sustained treatment of women in the Revolution was a belated decision, in part determined by the fact that I failed to uncover any significantly new material on them. Moreover, as Christopher Reed has commented in his recent book, *From Tsar to Soviets. The Russian People and Their Revolution, 1917–1921*, it was class rather than gender issues that were the major driving forces of the revolution. It ends by examining the nature of the opposition to the Bolshevik dictatorship that emerged after October, including that within the

Party itself, that of the rival socialist parties which (barely) survived after 1917, and, finally, that of ordinary peasants, workers, soldiers and sailors which seemingly threatened to topple the regime in the winter of 1920–1. I have sought to incorporate as far as possible new archival material that has been recently published. Other material is less unfamiliar, but its inclusion was warranted by the purposes of this book. It remains inconceivable, to give but one classic example, to omit Lenin's *April Theses* from a source-based text on the Revolution.

The course of the Revolution

The impact of war | **2**

In 1914 the Russian Empire found itself in the midst of a political crisis. It was most obvious in the strike wave that had escalated rapidly after the bloody repression of striking miners in the Lena goldfields of Siberia in April 1912, with 4,098 strikes (officially) recorded in 1914 **(McKean 1990: 193)**. Moreover, a growing section of educated, liberal society found itself increasingly alienated from the autocracy as the Tsar, Nicholas II, urged on by the reactionary elements dominant in the court and the country, reneged on the modest commitment to constitutionalism conceded in the October Manifesto of 1905. He sought to restrict the powers of the state Duma, the representative assembly (with real, if limited, legislative powers) created after 1905 **(Pearson 1977: 16–19)**. Some, such as the Moscow industrialists P.P. Riabushinskii and A.I. Konovalov, leaders of the liberal Progressist Party, had become so embittered that, incredibly, they were even prepared to help finance the Bolsheviks' revolutionary activities **(Thurston 1987: 187)**. Within the peasantry, too, resentments festered. Continued dissatisfaction at not receiving all the land when they had been freed from serfdom in the Emancipation of 1861 was exacerbated by the the agrarian reforms of the recently assassinated Prime Minister, P.A. Stolypin, which, in seeking to create a wealthy, independent and loyal peasant class, threatened to destroy the village commune. These resentments became manifest in a series of agrarian disturbances, 17,000 of which were recorded in European Russia between 1910 and 1914 **(Channon 1992a; 117)**.

Whether these challenges amounted to a revolutionary crisis temporarily diverted by the wave of patriotism precipitated by the outbreak of World War I, as the Bolsheviks later were to claim, remains questionable. The so-called 'general' strike of July 1914 reveals the reasons for doubt: it was limited to the then capital, St Petersburg (renamed Petrograd on the outbreak of war with Germany), where little more than one-quarter of the work-force participated, compared to the four-fifths in February 1917; it failed to attract support from liberal and professional quarters; and the army, in particular the city garrison, remained loyal to the auto-cracy **(McKean 1990: 315–17)**. However, they do bring into question the view that the reforms precipitated by the 1905 revolution – limited constitutionalism; the legalisation of trade unions; and Stolypin's efforts to recast the countryside along capitalist lines, to create a new social basis for the autocracy – had ushered in an era of peaceful, liberal evolution **(Mendel 1971: 17–26)**. In a seminal article Leopold Haimson cast scorn on this optimistic prognosis, arguing that the existence of two unbridgeable splits in Russian society – between the autocracy and educated society, and between the latter and the worker and peasant 'dark masses' – precluded the harmonious development of Russia along liberal, democratic lines **(Haimson 1964; 1965)**.

Haimson's conclusions echoed those of P.N. Durnovo, formerly Minister of the Interior and a leading Russian conservative. In his now justly famous Memorandum of February 1914 to Nicholas II he warned the Tsar of the disastrous consequences for Russia of a future war with Germany, emphasising in particular the different aspirations of the 'dark masses' and the Liberals.

Document 2.1 Durnovo's Warnings of the Impact of War on Russia

. . . Certainly Russia, where the masses without doubt instinctively profess to socialist principles, represents an especially favourable soil for social tremors. Notwithstanding the oppositional attitude found in Russian society, itself as instinctive as the socialism of the broad masses of the people, a political revolution is impossible in Russia, and any revolutionary movement inevitably will degenerate into a socialist revolution. Nothing stands behind our opposition; it has no support among the people, which sees no difference between a government official and an intellectual. The Russian plebeian, the peasant and worker alike, does not seek political rights, which he does not need or understand. The peasant dreams of being alloted gratuitously some-one else's land, the worker of expropriating all the capital and profits of the factory owner, and their horizons do not extend beyond this longing. . . . The opposition in Russia is nothing but intellectual and this is its weakness, since between the intelligentsia and the people there is a deep gulf of mutual misunderstanding and mistrust. . . . However much the members of our legislative institutions harp upon the trust that the people have in them the peasant sooner will believe the landless government official than the Octobrist landowner who sits in the *Duma*: the worker regards the factory inspector who works for a wage with more trust than the factory owner who also acts as legislator, even though the latter professes all the principles of the Kadet party . . .

. . . If the war ends in victory, the suppression of the socialist movement will not pose any difficulties. . . . But in the case of defeat, the chance of which in a struggle with such an opponent as Germany it is impossible not to foresee, social revolution inevitably will manifest itself in its most extreme forms. As was already indicated, it will start with the Government being held responsible for all the failures and misfortunes. In the legislative institutions a furious campaign against it will begin, as a result of which revolutionary actions will commence throughout the country. These actions immediately will advance socialist slogans, the only ones which are capable of stirring up and rallying the masses: the initial slogan will call for Black partition [the division of all the land among the peasants], followed by the call for the complete division of all valuables and property. The defeated army, by then having lost in the course of the war its regular and most reliable troops, in its greater part seized by the elemental peasant yearning for the land, will be found to be too demoralised to act as a bulwark of law and order. The legislative institutions and the opposition parties of the intelligentsia, devoid of real authority in the eyes of the people, will be unable to turn back the waves of uncontrollable popular protest stirred up by themselves, and Russia will be plunged into hopeless anarchy, the end of which cannot even be foreseen . . .

Source: E. Tarle, 'Germanskaia orientatsiia i T.N. Durnovo v 1914g'., Byloe, 19, 1922, pp. 172–4.

Durnovo's prognosis, that the Liberals' desire for measured constitutional reform would be swept away by an elemental peasant and worker revolution, proved to be an uncannily prescient (and came to be shared by leading Liberals, as Document 2.10 reveals). However, this warning was ignored by the autocracy. It had already suffered a loss of credibility when it had backed down in 1908 in face of the annexation of Bosnia–Herzegovina by Austria–Hungary. Afraid that a similar surrender would intensify the domestic challenges facing it, in the summer of 1914 it resolved to mobilise to assist Serbia resist the threat to its independence posed by Austro-German machinations **(Lieven 1983: 153)**. The outbreak of war, and the patriotism that it engendered, initially muted the challenges that had faced the autocracy, no doubt facilitated by the mobilisation of many militant workers to the front and the exile of others **(Gaponenko 1970: 124)**. But whether all of Russia was seized by patriotism and the desire for unity is more doubtful. Many peasants and workers, if not educated society, appeared at best passively to have accepted their lot, while British consular reports from the non-Russian periphery of the Empire suggested a marked lack of enthusiasm for war **(Hughes 1996: 79; Rogger 1966: 105–9)**. Moreover, whatever unity had emerged in 1914 did not survive for long. As the Russian army experienced repeated defeats the Liberals revived their criticisms of the autocracy, its alleged incompetence and corruption, as they sought, in vain, to exploit the country's plight to extort political concessions from Nicholas.

In part, Liberal criticisms of the government, especially its failure to provide adequate supplies of war materials, were supported by General A.A. Polivanov (in the view of Alfred Knox, British military attaché to the Russian army, 'undoubtedly the ablest military organiser in Russia, but dismissed by Norman Stone as "the Duma politicians'" friend'), who had replaced General V.A. Sukhomlinov, the scapegoat for Russia's defeats, as Minister of War in June 1915 **(Stone 1975: 191)**.

Document 2.2 Report of General A.A. Polivanov, Minister of War, to the Council of Ministers on the Military Situation, July 16, 1915

I consider it my civic and official duty to declare to the Council of Ministers that the country is in danger.

Enjoying an enormous superiority in artillery and an inexhaustible supply of shells the Germans forced us to retreat by artillery fire alone. As they were firing almost on their own our batteries had to remain silent even during serious clashes. Thanks to this, having the opportunity not to use its infantry, the enemy suffered hardly any losses, while our soldiers were killed in their thousands. Naturally our resistance daily grew weaker while the enemy onslaught grew stronger. Only God knows where to expect the retreat will end . . . . The soldiers are without doubt exhausted by the continued defeats and retreats. Their confidence in final victory and in their leaders is undermined. Ever more threatening signs of impending demoralisation are evident. Cases of desertion and of voluntary surrender to the enemy are becoming more frequent. It is difficult to expect enthusiasm and selflessness from men sent into battle unarmed and ordered to pick up the rifles of their dead comrades.

. . . there is yet one other development especially fraught with danger about which it is no longer possible to keep silent. There is growing confusion at General Headquarters. It is also seized by the fatal psychology of retreat and is preparing to retreat deep inside Russia . . . . Back, back back – that is all that is heard from there. No system, no plan is evident in its conduct and orders. Not one boldly conceived manoeuvre, not one attempt to exploit the mistakes of an over-confident enemy. Moreover, Headquarters continues jealously to guard its authority and prerogatives. In the midst of a growing catastrophe it does not consider it necessary to consult close colleagues. Neither army commanders nor commanders-in-chief of the fronts once have been summoned to Headquarters to discuss the situation, or possible ways out of our difficulties . . . . General Ianushkevich rules over everyone and everything. Everyone must silently carry out orders issued by him in the name of the Grand Duke. No initiative is permitted. Silence, no discussion – this is Headquarters' favourite cry. But the blame for our present troubles falls not on HQ but on everyone else . . . . The generals, the regimental and company commanders are to blame . . . the Minister of War to blame, the government is to blame . . . the rear is to blame. In a word, everyone is guilty, except for the one body which bears any direct responsibility.

Source: A.N. Iakhontov (ed.), 'Tiazhelye dni. (Sekretnye zasedanii Soveta Ministrov 16 Iiulia–2 Sentiabria 1915 goda)', Arkhiv russkoi revoliutsii, XVIII (1926), pp. 15–16

Notwithstanding Polivanov's alleged political sympathies, a shortage of munitions did contribute to the reverses that Russia suffered in the first year of war. However, its impact has been much exaggerated. Contrary to continued Liberal accusations, it was resolved by 1916 when the government, at the cost of expenditure well in excess of tax revenue, had succeeded in mobilising state and private industry sufficiently well to supply the army adequately. Equally, if not more important in explaining the defeats that befell Russia, were the other causes adduced by Polivanov: poor military leadership; falling morale; and the administrative confusion and in-fighting that permeated the General Staff and also bedevilled relations between the army and the government **(Gatrell 1994: 234; Stone 1975: 12–13, 94–5)**.

In the summer of 1915 the Liberals within the Duma sought to take advantage of Russia's parlous military situation, which had left the government vulnerable to renewed political challenges. For a time it appeared ready to appease the Liberals. Sukhomlinov was dismissed, and the conservative Minister of the Interior, N.A. Maklakov resigned, as did the reactionary V.K. Sabler from the Holy Synod and I.G. Shcheglovitov from Justice **(Pipes 1992a: 220–1)**. Conciliation was urged by more moderate figures in the government, most notably A.V. Krivoshein, the Minister of Agriculture. He hoped to create a coalition of moderate conservatives and Liberals within the Duma which would support him as head of government. His objective was to rally educated society behind the government in order to revive the war effort. Equally, such an alliance would act to check the baneful influence of the Tsarina, Alexandra. Her politicial power, it was feared, would rise when, in August, Nicholas decided to depart the capital to take charge of the army. These developments prompted a majority of Duma members (up to 70 per cent), ranging from Progressive Nationalists on the Right to the Progressists on the Left, to coalesce into what came to be known as the Progressive Bloc **(Pearson 1977: 39–56)**.

Document 2.3 The Programme of the Progressive Bloc, August 25, 1915

The undersigned representatives of factions and groups in the State Council and State Duma, convinced that only a strong, firm and active government can lead our country to victory, and that such a government can only be one that is based upon the confidence of the people and is capable of organising the active cooperation of all citizens, have come to the unanimous conclusion that the most important and urgent task of creating such a government cannot be fulfilled unless the following conditions are met:

1 The formation of a united government of individuals who enjoy the confidence of the country . . .
2 A radical change in the methods of administration employed to date, which have been based on a mistrust of public initiative, in particular:

(a) strict observance of the principles of legality in government;

(b) abolition of the dual authority of the military and civil authorities in questions which have no immediate bearing on the conduct of military operations;

(c) the renewal of the personnel of local administration;

(d) a rational and consistent policy designed to maintain civil peace and the elimination of discord between nationalities and classes.

To realise these policy ends the following measures, both administrative and legislative, must be adopted.

1 By means of an Imperial amnesty the termination of all actions against those accused of purely political and religious crimes . . . , their release . . . and the restoration of their rights, including participation in elections to the State Duma, *zemstvo* and municipal institutions . . .

2 The release of those administratively exiled for political and religious offences.

3 A complete and definite end to religious persecution on whatever pretexts . . .

4 A solution to the Russo-Polish problem, namely: the abolition of all limits on the rights of Poles throughout Russia, the rapid preparation and introduction in the legislature of a bill granting autonomy to Poland, and, at the same time, the revision of the laws relating to Polish landownership.

5 A beginning made to abolish the restrictions on the rights of Jews, in particular, further steps toward the abolition of the Pale of Settlement, the easing of [Jewish] entry to educational institutions and . . . to a variety of the professions. Restoration of the Jewish press.

6 A conciliatory policy toward Finland should be adopted, in particular, changes in the composition of the administration and the Senate, and an end to the persecution of officials.

7 The Little Russian press is to be restored; the immediate review of cases of Galician inhabitants under arrest or exiled and the release of those who have been subject to wrongful persecution.

8 The restoration of trade unions' activity and the end to the persecution of the workers' representatives in the sickness funds on suspicion of them belonging to an illegal party. Restoration of the workers' press.

9 Agreement between the government and the legislative bodies on the early introduction of:

a) All bills closely related to national defence, the supply of the army, the care of the wounded, the improvement of the lot of refugees, and other problems directly connected with the war.

b) The following programme of legislation, designed to organise the country to contribute to victory and to preserve internal peace:

equal rights for peasants with those of other estates;

introduction of *volost' zemstva*;

revision of the *zemstvo* law of 1890;
revision of the municipal law of 1892;
the creation of *zemstva* in the border regions;
legislation on cooperative societies;
legislation on rest days for shop workers;
material improvements for postal and telegraph workers . . .

For the Progressive Nationalist faction	V. Bobrinskii
For the Centre faction	V. L'vov
For the Zemstvo–Octobrist faction	I. Dmitriukov
For the Union of October 17 Group	S. Shidlovskii
For the Progressist Party	I. Efremov
For the People's Freedom (Kadet) Party	P. Miliukov
For the Centre Group of the State Council	V. Meller-Zakomel'skii
For the Academic Group of the State Council	D. Grimm

Source: B.B. Grave, Burzhuaziia nakanune fevral'skoi revoliutsii
(Moscow–Leningrad: Gosudarstvennoe izdatel'stvo, 1927), pp. 27–8

The most striking feature of Document 2.3 is its moderation. Fearful of alienating its more conservative supporters, the Progressive Bloc had rejected the demand of its more radical Progressist members that a government responsible to the Duma must be created. If met, this demand would have transformed the autocracy into a constitutional monarchy. More cautiously, it simply sought the opportunity to participate in government by seeking the formation of a 'ministry of public confidence', one in which its members were strongly represented. Such a ministry, it was hoped, by introducing what remained of a programme of civil liberties, regardless of class, nationality or religion, would mobilise popular support for a revitalised war effort. Sadly for the Liberals, their aspirations were dashed by the intransigence of Nicholas who, urged on by I.L. Goremykin, chairman of the Council of Ministers, refused to compromise. To their anger and chagrin, he simply dismissed the Duma in September **(Pearson 1977: 57–8)**. The reforms that they outlined had to await the February Revolution and the formation of the Provisional Government before they could be implemented (see Document 4.1).

The summer of 1915 also witnessed growing dissatisfaction with the war and its consequences among the working class, as the following document illustrates.

Document 2.4 Reports of the Council of Ministers on the Revival of Worker Unrest, August 11, 1915

Shcherbatov [Minister of the Interior]: The Council of Ministers knows that there were disturbances in Moscow which ended in bloodshed . . . . There were even more serious disorders at Ivanovo-Voznesensk when it was necessary to fire on the crowd with the result that sixteen were killed and thirty wounded. There was a critical moment when it was uncertain what the garrison would do.

Shakhovskoi [Minister of Trade and Industry]: I have the most disturbing evidence from the factory inspectors about the workers' mood. Any spark will be enough to start a fire.

Shcherbatov: The Minister of the Interior is taking all measures which . . . the present circumstances permit. I have often called your attention to the abnormal position . . . in which the Minister of Internal Affairs is placed. Almost half of European Russia has been taken out of his jurisdiction, with power in the rear generally in the hands of the governors who have despotic leanings and little understanding of their duties . . . even in Petrograd, which sets the tone for the whole of Russia, the Minister of the Interior is a mere resident whose actions are constrained by the fancies of the military authorities . . . . How do you wish me to fight the growing revolutionary movement when I am refused the support of the troops on the grounds that they are unreliable . . . when the ranks of the police are being thinned out not daily but hourly, and every day the population is being stirred up by speeches in the Duma, by lies in the newspapers, by endless defeats at the front and by rumours of disorders in the rear . . . . I also agree that action must be taken. But how, when on the one hand there is no support and when responsible officials are not heard on questions which threaten the fate of the state . . . the flood of refugees and German settlers and Jews evicted by the military authorities is forever growing. The population is so agitated at these newcomers that it is beginning to attack them on arrival with clubs. There already have been several cases of severe wounding and even deaths.

In conclusion, General Ruzskii [Commander-in-Chief of the Northern Front] touched upon the condition of labour in the Petrograd factories, pointing out that labour is bearing an extremely heavy burden and is suffering under the weight of the high cost of essential goods. Meanwhile the plants' employers are not implementing new rates of pay and in order not to starve the workers must work overtime, which exhausts them. Serious attention must be given to this question and measures introduced speedily to deal with it since strikes and attendant disorders are possible. Then the prosecution of the war will become hopeless.

Source: A.N. Iakhontov (ed.), 'Tiazhelye dni. (Sekretny zasedanii Soveta Ministrov 16 Iiulia–2 Sentiabria 1916 goda)', Arkhiv russkoi revoliutsii, XVIII (1926), pp. 63–6

These reports, based on information presented to the Council of Ministers by the police and factory inspectors in the towns and cities of the Empire, quite accurately reflect growing and widespread worker unrest in the summer of 1915. The revival of worker militancy noted in Document 2.4 in large part was initially motivated by concerns with rising inflation (only workers in the metal and chemical industries received wage increases above inflation); long hours; harsh labour discipline; and increased overcrowding in the cities as women and youths flocked from the countryside to the burgeoning war industries, and refugees fled from the threatened west of the Empire, often to the very hostile reception depicted by the Minister of the Interior. However, the heavy-handed response of the authorities, for example, the shooting of striking workers in Kostroma on 5 June and in Ivanovo-Voznesensk in August, proved to be counter-productive **(Gaponenko 1970: 125)**. They transformed what began as primarily economic strikes aimed at improving material conditions into a more overtly political, anti-autocratic movement **(Fleer 1925: 6–7)**. Equally noteworthy, Shcherbatov's criticism of the 'despotic inclinations' of many provincial governors was not simply an attempt by the government to wash its hands of the bloodshed that had occurred. The 'Statute on measures to safeguard state security and public order', enacted in the wake of the assassination of Alexander II in 1881, had led to the increasing devolution of effective power from the government in St Petersburg to these self-same governors who often acted in an arbitrary, brutal and uncontrollable manner **(Waldron 1995: 21–3)**. But wherever responsibility in fact lay, it was the government that was culpable in the eyes of the population.

Yet little was done to appease growing opposition as Nicholas himself remained stubbornly intransigent throughout 1916. Encouraged by better news from the front, which had stabilised, he made no effort to conciliate educated society. The government became ever more the preserve of reactionary and often incompetent, if not corrupt, figures: the highly unpopular B.V. Sturmer replaced I.L. Goremykin as chairman of the Council of Ministers in January; on March 9, Polivanov was sacked as Minister of War in favour of General D.S. Shuvaev, in Miliukov's view, 'honourable but uneducated and completely unfit for this post' **(Miliukov 1921: 31)**; S.D. Sazonov was ousted from the Ministry of Foreign Affairs in July; and the 'renegade' Octobrist, A.D. Protopopov, was promoted to Minister of Internal Affairs in September **(White 1994: 55)**. Growing disillusion prompted the Liberals to attack the government with increasing bitterness. This often slanderous campaign even embraced hitherto moderate figures, such as P.N. Miliukov, the Kadet leader. Under pressure from the left wing of his party and from the Progressists, in the autumn he launched a violent assault on the government **(Katkov 1969: 261)**. His particular target was the hapless Sturmer **(Pearson 1977: 114–15)**.

Document 2.5 P.N. Miliukov's Speech to the Fourth Duma, November 1, 1916

We now see and know that we can no more legislate with this government than we can lead Russia to victory with it. (Voices from the left: 'True.') We tried earlier to prove that it was impossible to use all the country's strength to fight a war against an external enemy if a war was going on inside the country, for popular support is vital in achieving the nation's aims . . . it is useless when fear of the people of one's own country grips the government and when the fundamental task becomes to put an end to the war, at any cost, so that the government can distance itself as quickly as possible from the need to find popular support. (Voices from the left: 'True.') On February 10, 1916, I finished my speech by saying that we had decided to pay no more attention to the 'wisdom of the authorities' and that I did not expect any answer from a cabinet in its present form to these alarming questions. My words sounded a little too gloomy then. We can now go further and perhaps these words will sound too optimistic. We say to this government, as the declaration of the [Progressive] Bloc stated: we will fight you, we will fight by all legal means until you go. (Voices from the left: 'true.') It is said that one member of the Council of Ministers . . . hearing that on that occasion the Duma was going to talk about treason, excitably exclaimed, 'I may be a fool, but I'm no traitor.' (Laughter) The predecessor of this Minister was undoubtedly intelligent, just as the predecessor of the Minister of Foreign Affairs was honourable. But they are no longer in the Cabinet. And surely it has bearing on the actual result whether we are dealing with stupidity or with treason?

When the Duma declares again and again that the home front must be organised for a successful war and the government continues to insist that to organise the country means to organise a revolution, and consciously chooses chaos and disorganisation – is this stupidity or treason? (Voices from the left: 'treason.') Moreover, when on the basis of this general discontent the government deliberately busies itself with provoking popular outbursts – for the involvement of the police in the spring disturbances in the factories is proven – when provocation is used to incite disturbances, knowing that they could be a reason for shortening the war – is this done consciously or not?

You must understand why we have no other task than to get rid of this government. You must ask why we are carrying on this struggle in wartime. It is only in wartime that they are dangerous. They are dangerous to the war . . . and in the name of the war, in the name of that which has united us, we now fight them. (Voices from the left: 'Bravo.' Applause.)

We have many different reasons for being discontented with this government . . . but all these reasons boil down to one general one: the incompetence and evil intentions of the present government. This is Russia's chief evil, and victory over it will be equal to winning an entire campaign. (Voices from the left: 'true.') And therefore in the name of the millions of victims and of their spilled blood, in the name of our achieving our national interests . . . in the name of our responsibility to those people who elected us, we shall fight until we get a responsible government which is in agreement with the three general principles of our programme. Cabinet members must agree unanimously as to the most urgent tasks, they must agree and be prepared to implement the programme of the Duma majority and they must rely on this majority not just in the implementation of this programme, but in all their actions. A Cabinet which does not satisfy these conditions does not deserve the confidence of the Duma and should go.

Source: Gosudarstvennaia Duma. *Stenograficheskie otchety. suzyv IV, session V, cols. 46–8, in M. McCauley (ed.),* Octobrists to Bolsheviks: Imperial Russia 1905–1917 *(London: Edward Arnold, 1984), pp. 88–9*

Miliukov's speech, as Pearson argued, was designed to maintain unity within the Progressive Bloc: the radicals would be appeased by the violence of Miliukov's attack on the government, while posing the charge of treason as a question would prevent its right wing becoming irretrievably alienated **(Pearson 1977: 114–17)**. Yet the speech misrepresented the real state of affairs, as no evidence existed, then or since, to suggest that Sturmer, or anyone else in the government, was seeking to 'betray' the country by deliberately undermining the war effort or negotiating a separate peace with Germany (Shuvaev was justified in denying being a 'traitor'). By pandering to the prejudices of his audience, however, many of whom loathed Sturmer, Miliukov scored a cheap victory, but not without unintended costs. His subsequent claim that his own belief, in the stupidity, not treason, of the government, was misinterpreted by his audience seems to be rather disingenuous, an attempt to absolve himself of its devastating impact **(Miliukov 1921: 33)**. Despite government censorship, unofficial copies of his speech were widely disseminated and it hastened considerably the erosion of whatever faith was left in the autocracy in all strata of society, even in the former bastions of reaction **(Pipes 1992a: 253)**. The recently published memoirs of V.S. Arsen'ev, Deputy Governor of Pskov between October 1915 and May 1917, testify to the opposition towards Nicholas growing at the highest levels of Russian society.

Document 2.6 Memoirs of V.S. Arsen'ev, Deputy Governor of Pskov

All sorts of rumours and gossip had reached their apogee; the appointment of Protopopov, speeches in the State Duma against German influence, the role incorrectly assigned to Rasputin, his murder, the punitive actions against his murderers . . . and the hubbub of all sorts of congresses poured oil on the flames of dissatisfaction. The situation had reached the stage that Guards officers seriously intended to carry out a palace revolution, that the Grand Duchess Mariia Pavlovna . . . who read certain left-wing newspapers, in December, after the assassination of Rasputin in which her brother had taken part, openly spoke to me, the governor of a province, of the need for a revolution, and to my objections that the fate of the Emperor was closely linked to the fate and life of Russia, of the dynasty, of everything, received the answer that Russia would never forget the services rendered by her brother. Count A.A. Bobrinskii who had investigated the activity of the Union of Zemstva in the summer of 1916, told me that unequivocal evidence of its revolutionary activity existed, concealed behind expressions of loyalty and goodwill.

Source: V.S. Arsen'ev, *"Sud'by rodiny kazalis' v kakom-to tumane".*
Vospominaniia V.S. Arsen'eva. 1917g', Istoricheskii arkhiv, *2 (1994), pp. 91–2*

There is much truth in Arsen'ev's account, as by November 1916 even the nobility, 'the staunchest pillar of the monarchy', had come to support the Progressive Bloc. Yet the nobility still thought that the autocracy could be saved if it was 'purified' by the removal of the influence of Rasputin and the *nemchka* ('German woman'), the Empress Alexandra, who allegedly were preventing Nicholas from compromising with the Duma **(Pipes 1992a: 256)**. Members of the royal family held similar views. The Grand Duke Nikolai Mikhailovich, for one, had written to Nicholas in December to warn him to liberate himself from 'the persistent interference of dark forces in all matters.' (*The Times*, 24 March 1917, where the letter is translated in full), while Grand Duke Alexander Mikhailovich urged him to bow to the demands of educated society and establish 'a government of public confidence' (*Arkhiv russkoi revoliutsii*, V, 1922: 333–4).

The growth of opposition within the royal family and educated society was matched in late 1916 by profound and widespread disenchantment amongst the 'dark masses'. The following police report indicates the extent of popular dissatisfaction.

Document 2.7 Summary Report of the Chief of Police (Petrograd Province), October 1916

The gradually growing disruption of the rear . . . at the present moment has reached such high and monstrous levels which . . . promises in the very near future to plunge the country into the destructive chaos of catastrophic and elemental anarchy.

The systematically growing disorganisation of transport; the unrestrained orgy of pillaging and swindling of every kind by shady operators in the most diverse branches of the country's commercial, industrial and socio-political life; the unsystematic and mutually contradictory orders of representatives of local government; the unconscientiousness of minor and lower agents of the government in the provinces; and . . . the irregular distribution of food products and essential goods, inflation that is growing immeasurably, and the lack of . . . food among the presently hungry populations of the capitals and large population centres . . . all this, taken together . . . categorically and definitely points to the fact that a dire crisis is already upon us which inevitably must be resolved one way or another.

The above summary may be confirmed by the particularly troubled mood now observable among the masses of the people. By the beginning of September . . . an exceptional intensification in the mood of opposition and animosity was markedly evident among broad sections of the populations of the capitals. There were more and more frequent complaints against the administration and harsh and relentless condemnation of government policies.

By the end of the month the mood of opposition . . . had reached such exceptional levels which it had not . . . even in 1905–6. Open and un-constrained complaints about 'the venality of the government', against the enormous burdens of the war, and against the intolerable conditions of daily life began to be heard. The calls from radical and left-wing elements on the need 'first of all to defeat the Germans at home, and then deal with the Germans abroad', have begun to meet with more and more sympathy.

The difficult material position of ordinary people, consigned to a half-starved existence and seeing no hope of improvement in the near future, has made them regard with sympathy . . . any sort of plans and projects promising to improve conditions of life. As a result, a situation has been created which greatly favoured any sort of revolutionary propaganda and actions, a situation which was correctly evaluated by the active leaders of left-wing and other anti-government groups . . .

. . . Despite the great increase in wages, the economic condition of the masses is worse than terrible. While wages . . . have risen 50 per cent, and only in certain categories 100–200 per cent (metal workers, machinists, electricians), the prices on all products have increased 100–500 per cent. . . . Even if we accept that a worker's wage has risen 100 per cent, the prices of goods on average have risen 300 per cent. The impossibility of even buying many food products and necessities, the time wasted standing in queues to receive goods, the increased incidence of disease due to mal-nutrition and unsanitary living conditions (cold and dampness because of lack of coal and wood), and so on, have made the workers as a whole prepared for the wildest excesses of a 'hunger riot'.

Inflation is felt in the country no less than the towns: in the country as well it brings with it incredible rumours even more fantastic than those heard in the towns. The peasants willingly believe rumours about the export of leather, grain, sugar, etc. to the Germans, and about Count Frederiks selling off half of Russia to those same Germans. Everything makes the atmosphere in the countryside very troubled.

The attitude of the countryside to the war from the outset has been extremely unfavourable, for conscription had a much greater effect there than in the towns. Now in the country there is no belief that the war will be successful; in the words . . . of the 'rural intelligentsia', 'everyone wants the war to end, but no one expects that it will'. The peasantry willingly talk about politics, something which was hardly ever heard between 1906–14, and say the 'Sukhomlinov should be hung', 'hang ten or fifteen generals and we might start to win'. The atmosphere in the country has become one of sharp opposition not only to the government, but to other classes of the population: workers, civil servants, the clergy, etc.

... In the villages one sees revolutionary ferment, similar to that of 1906–7: everywhere political questions are discussed, resolutions are passed against landowners and merchants, cells of various organisations are being established . . . . Of course, there is no organisational centre to this, but it seems as if the peasantry are uniting through the cooperatives which are growing by the hour throughout Russia. In this way the peasantry will undoubtedly be an active participant in a new and inevitable movement.

Source: B.B. Grave, Burzhuaziia nakanune febral'skoi revoliutsiia *(Moscow–Leningrad: Gosudarstvennoe izdatel'stvo, 1927), pp. 128–34*

Document 2.7 indicates that Liberal accusations of corruption, even treason, had widespread resonance amongst the workers and peasants of Russia. Moreover, it illustrates well the ever-deepening deterioration in the material conditions of the workers: accelerating inflation; and ever greater shortages of food as the peasants increasingly refused to market their surpluses in exchange for a rapidly depreciating currency and the railway system failed to cope with the demands placed upon it; all fuelled popular opposition within the towns and cities and a marked increase in strikes. Even more disturbing for the autocracy, growing war-weariness as well as shortages of manufactured goods (Russian industry was insufficiently developed to produce for the war and at the same time satisfy the demands of the peasants) were at the root of an ever-widening dissatis-faction in the countryside which hitherto had remained relatively quiescent **(Rogger 1983: 258–9)**.

Confirmation of the difficulties facing the majority of ordinary Russians as a result of inflation can be gleaned from the following table. In the absence of official government statistics, it was compiled from data provided by the unions of *zemstva* and towns.

Document 2.8 Inflation of Food Prices, July 1914–July 1916

	July 1915	December 1915	July 1916
Wheat	113	161	182
Rye	189	176	183
Wheaten flour	121	154	183
Rye flour	144	183	199
Oats	193	225	251
Barley	109	142	154
Average rise for breadstuffs	137	174	**189**

Sugar	131	146	147
Meat	121	168	332
Butter	114	233	224
Salt	228	401	583

(1913–14 price = 100)

Source: S.O. Zagorsky, State Control of Industry in Russia during the War *(New Haven: Yale University Press, 1928), pp. 60–1*

Statistics, of course, do not speak for themselves and three qualifications must be taken into account when considering the table above. First, as Document 2.7 indicated, wages also rose, in the case of skilled workers in the defence industries (chemical, engineering and metal plants), in excess of inflation until the middle of 1916. The majority of workers, however, became considerably worse off as their wages failed to keep pace with prices **(Andrle 1994: 117)**. Second, the issue of the availability of food is not addressed in the table, and as the war dragged on so the urban Russia suffered increasing shortages (see Document 2.7). Third, by ending in July 1916 it fails to reveal the sharp increase in inflation in the winter of 1916–17. The following table illustrates the rapid rise in food prices in the months immediately preceding the February Revolution.

Document 2.9 Percentage Increase in Food Prices, December 1916–February 1917

Potatoes	25	Bread	15
Carrots, turnips	35	Chocolate	100
Cabbage	25	Sugar candy	75
Meat	20	Cookies, sweet rolls	100
Sausage	50	Apples	70
Ham	60	Pears, oranges	150
Butter	15	Cheese	25
Eggs	20	Milk	40

Source: from T. Hasegawa, The February Revolution: Petrograd 1917 *(Seattle: University of Washington Press, 1981), p. 200*

Fear that rapidly deteriorating living standards would incite the workers to erupt into an elemental, uncontrollable revolution that would put the 'dark masses', not educated society, into power prompted some Duma politicians to seek an alternative solution. In particular, A.I. Guchkov, a leading figure in the Octobrist Party and then chairperson of the War Industries Committees, who shrewdly foresaw the probable political outcome of such a revolution from below, began to seek to engineer a 'palace *coup*'. The objective was to depose Nicholas, in favour of his son (with the Tsar's brother, Grand Duke Mikhail, as regent), and transform Russia into a constitutional monarchy that would be better able to prosecute the war and fend off radical revolution from below. The rationale of Guchkov and his fellow thinkers is revealed in the following extract, taken from interviews conducted between November 1932 and February 1933 by N.A. de Basily, head of the diplomatic chancellery at Headquarters during the war. (They were published in full for the first time in 1991.)

Document 2.10 The Origins and Objectives of the Guchkov Plot

Guchkov: From the very beginning it was clear that any prospects of successfully creating a new government could only be realised at the price of the abdication of the Tsar. Of course there were people of republican inclinations, such as the Kadets, but no one raised the question of the character of the regime because at heart everyone was decided that it must remain monarchic.

At Fedorov's a copy of the Fundamental Laws was unearthed. We found the law which provided for the dismissal of the Tsar and the article regarding a regency which said who becomes regent . . . . We all then had the distinct desire to shake the foundations of the system as little as possible.

de Basily: This was before Miliukov's speech?

Guchkov: After.

de Basily: At that time Miliukov stopped at nothing.

Guchkov: He failed to consider the consequences because he was possessed by fear, or, more correctly, dread of all the dangers that would be posed by a revolutionary explosion. He remained . . . [an advocate] of revolutionary action, as before. But during the war he realised that the time was not propitious for this.

de Basily: Yet there is one thing I fail to understand. You see, Miliukov's speeches were one of the major factors that revolutionised public opinion. How did he see the situation himself? You know, if he was afraid of an explosion, then the character of his speeches contradicts this fear.

Guchkov: He intended to shake the foundations of the government but not to topple it, only to influence it. He thought that above all his speeches would shake morale there, at the top, and that there they would realise that a change of personnel was necessary. The struggle was not for the sort of regime itself but for executive power. I am convinced that a combination of Krivoshein, Ignat'ev and Sazonov would have been quite satisfactory. I took little part in these debates. I did not object, but made only one observation which served as the catalyst for certain future steps and events: it seems to me, gentlemen, we are mistaken when we assume that certain forces will carry out the Revolution while other forces will be called upon to establish the new government. I fear that those who carry out the Revolution will remain in charge of this revolution. These were my words. They were not a call to associate ourselves with revolution but simply pointed out that of those two possibilities about which we were talking (the possibility, so to speak, of a collapse of authority under the impact of revolutionary pressure, or of the summoning to power of responsible political figures) I saw only the second. I was convinced that if the government was overthrown the streets would rule, in which case the collapse of authority, of Russia, of the front, would result.

There were two such meetings. Once again we met, but then I was ill, in bed, when suddenly I was told that Nekrasov, who had never visited me, had arrived. He approached me and spoke: from your statements that only those who have a hand in the Revolution might find themselves called upon to create a government, it seemed to me that you have your own particular ideas . . . . Then I told him that in fact I had considered this question, that it was impossible to allow the growth of anarchy, to allow a change of government by revolutionary means, that responsible politicians themselves must undertake these tasks, because, if not, it would be carried very badly out by the spontaneous force of the streets. I said that I was considering the question of a palace revolution as the only solution.

My conversation with Nekrasov made it clear that he too had come to the same conclusion that it was quite impossible by normal means to bring about a radical change in government policy and that a violent revolution was inevitable. The fear presented itself that the blind, spontaneous forces of the street, the workers, the soldiers . . . would take this task upon themselves and from this emerged the definite conclusion that responsible politicians must undertake this task themselves . . . . And from here was born the idea of a palace revolution, the result of which would be that the Tsar would be compelled to abdicate and hand over the throne to his legal heir. Within these limits the plan quickly took shape. With the agreement of Nekrasov within the next few days Mikhail Ivanovich Tereshchenko joined us, the two initial conspirators, and so the group was formed which shouldered the burden of carrying out the plan.

Source: A.I. Guchkov, 'Aleksandr Ivanovich Guchkov passkazyvaet', Voprosy istorii, 7–8 (1991), pp. 204–13

Guchkov added that Prince D.L. Viazemskii, a close associate of the former Supreme Commander, Grand Duke Nikolai Nikolaevich, soon was co-opted to join the conspiracy, with the task of seeking support among the officer corps. However, the continuing ill-health of Guchkov, and of the army Chief of Staff, General M.V. Alekseiev, whose support would have been critical to the success of the plot, delayed any more definite preparations. The seriousness of this plot remains subject to differing interpretations. Richard Pipes has argued that it made little 'headway because it failed to secure a broad base of support, especially among senior officers' **(Pipes 1992a: 269)**. George Katkov, however, claims that it was instrumental to the success of the February Revolution. By seeking to involve both key figures of the general staff (Guchkov had a close relationship with

Alekseiev) and especially officers of the Petrograd garrison it 'may well have undermined the morale of the whole officer corps' and contributed to the almost indecent haste with which they were ready to ditch Nicholas when revolution did come' **(Katkov 1969: 554; White 1994: 59)**. In the event, whatever prospects for success it may have had soon became academic, as the autocracy was overthrown by revolution from below **(Pearson 1977: 129)**.

Before proceeding to the February Revolution itself, it is necessary to consider Guchkov's account more carefully. As many memoirists do **(Tosh 1992: 36)**, arguably he was seeking to justify his plans for a palace revolution in retrospect. Yet his fears of the outcome of revolution from below expressed in Document 2.10 were not simply the product of hindsight. On the contrary, as early as 9 March 1917, he had written to Alekseiev, bemoaning the fact that real power in fact resided with the Soviet, which represented the forces (workers and soldiers) that had carried out the Revolution **(Shliapnikov 1923–5: 236–7)**.

The February Revolution and the origins of Dual Power

In her seminal work, *States and Social Revolutions* Theda Skocpol argued that revolutionary strength in itself was neither 'the ultimate [nor] sufficient condition for revolution'. No regime, she concluded, will be overthrown until its 'administrative and military power . . . break[s] down' **(Skocpol 1979: 16, 285)**. Her argument has particular relevance in understanding the February Revolution.

The threat to the autocracy, as the preceding chapter has shown, came not simply from the growth of popular opposition but the fact that it was expanding to embrace hitherto loyal sources of support, including elements within the army and the government itself. By the beginning of 1917 the concern raised in the summer of 1915 by the then Foreign Minister, S.D. Sazonov, that the regime would find itself 'hanging in the air', had become the case: educated, liberal society had been alienated; worker militancy continued to rise, evident in the mass strikes (of 140,000 and 84,000 respectively) in Petrograd, on 9 January to mark the anniversary of Bloody Sunday and on 14 February to greet the re-opening of the State Duma **(McKean 1990: 498)**; the nobility itself was becoming increasingly disillusioned; and even elements within the tsarist court were prepared to urge political change upon Nicholas himself. Little wonder, then, that when a serious challenge emerged on the streets of Petrograd in late February the autocracy found itself vulnerable.

The dithering of the Council of Ministers and especially the Petrograd district military leadership during the critical days of late February contributed to the rapid, and relatively bloodless, success of the February Revolution. A.P. Balk, Governor of Petrograd at the time of the Revolution, reveals that it was only on the third night of the ever-growing demonstrations on the streets of the capital that the decision was taken to curb them by force if necessary. Document 2.1 is an extract from his recently published memoirs (the title of which translates as *The Last Five Days of Tsarist Petrograd*), written in the form of a diary in 1929.

Document 2.1 Indecision within the Government

February 25

During the entire period of our service together General Khabalov struck me as an affable fellow, industrious, composed, not lacking in administrative experience, but . . . without any ability to command the respect of his subordinates and . . . of his troops.

The absence of Lieutenant-General Chebykin who knew the entire Guards' officer staff of the Petrograd garrison well . . . a strict officer, able to talk to the soldiers and influence them, made itself felt.

One must concede that February 25 convinced those intent on the spread of disorder that the absence of a popular, energetic military leader enhanced their chances of successfully conducting propaganda amongst the exhausted troops, the more so as the reserve battalions, overloaded with local conscripts . . . were led by sick or wounded officers or inexperienced young men, who had only just completed accelerated military training courses.

February 25 was a total defeat for us. Not only were the leaders of the revolutionary actions convinced that the troops were acting without spirit, even unwillingly, but the crowd also sensed the weakness of the authorities and became emboldened. The decision of the military authorities to impose control by force, in exceptional circumstances to use arms, not only poured oil on the fire but shook up the troops and allowed them to think that the authorities . . . feared 'the people'.

At an evening meeting of the military at which reports of the heads of the military districts were heard everyone supported the energetic application of force the next day against even the slightest disturbance.

Without hesitation General Khabalov agreed and hastened to compose a very firm proclamation to the citizens.

At midnight I was summoned urgently to the Chairman of the Council of Ministers, Prince Golitsyn . . . where all the Ministers and the director of the Department of Police, State Counsellor A.T. Vasil'ev, were already sitting behind the table.

General Khabalov said nothing new, adding that for tomorrow he had ordered decisive measures to be taken to suppress the disorders . . . . Orders to the troops and a warning to the citizens of the capital that any attempt to create disturbances would be mercilessly suppressed were being printed and would be posted in large quantities in the streets before dawn. General Khabalov spoke, as was his habit, calmly but his words betrayed a lack of conviction in the success of such action.

General Beliaev also spoke without conviction, without confidence. He had the air of a man who feared responsibility and concluded with the words: 'Yes, certainly, it is necessary to take energetic measures.'

Protopopov, the Minister of Internal Affairs, began with a sketch of the existing political parties and their influence on events . . . . The conclusion of the Minister was: to take immediate and decisive measures to suppress the disorders in the capital before it was too late.

Rittikh, the Minister of Agriculture . . . concluded that only adamantine energy and the resolve to accept whatever sacrifices were necessary could re-establish . . . authority and order tomorrow. Everyone had to be fully conscious of the need to accept bloodshed, however horrible it was, since if the opportunity were missed now a sea of blood would be demanded later . . . .

Then Pokrovskii, the Minister of Foreign Affairs, took the floor. Until now he had sat indifferently on the sofa without uttering a word: listless, often closing his eyes, he gave the impression of being exhausted, only just fighting off sleep. Yet with his first words one sensed candour, a total lack of confusion, and the conviction that there was only one solution.

'Gentlemen,' the Minister said, 'in my opinion we are left with only one way out: immediately to go to the Emperor and entreat His Majesty to replace us all with other people. We have not gained the trust of the country and by remaining in our posts we shall achieve absolutely nothing.

Pokrovskii's statement rang true. I suppose that the majority realised this in their heart of hearts but also felt that to lay down their portfolios when the mob was rising in revolt in the capital was untimely and criminal.

The views expressed by the other Ministers offered nothing special. Everyone, except Pokrovskii, demanded decisive measures. Accordingly, the timid General Beliaev and the indecisive General Khabalov became convinced of general support for such action, a decision at which they arrived unfortunately only on the night of February 26.

Source: A.P. Balk, 'Poslednie piat' dnei tsarskogo Petrograda (23–28 fevralia 1917g.)', Russkoe proshloe, (1991), pp. 38–41

Balk's account is correct in emphasising that the vacillations of the authorities in the capital had allowed the demonstrations to develop considerable momentum. By 26 February over 200,000 workers were on the streets. Yet on February 26 itself there was no conclusive evidence that an attempt to put the demonstrations down by force would fail, although the hitherto reliable Cossacks had already shown a reluctance to use force. Military units did fire on the demonstrators, inducing some revolutionary leaders to seek to retreat before bloodshed on a massive scale occurred **(Hasegawa 1981: 368–71)**. However, Balk's pessimistic conclusion that action to restore order was taken too late was soon vindicated. The garrison, itself diluted by the presence of numerous disgruntled casualties of the war and by reservists over 40 who had taken part in the suppression of the 1905 Revolution, ultimately proved unwilling to shoot down the insurgents. Ironically, the unintended consequence of Khabalov's orders to repress the demonstrations by force was to provoke an almost full-scale mutiny of the Petrograd garrison by 27 February **(Wildman 1980: 136–7)**.

At the same time, the High Command itself had failed to act promptly and decisively. In part, the lack, or conflict, of information regarding the gravity of the situation in the capital might have contributed to its inaction. Initially, both the Minister of War, General M.A. ('dead-head') Beliaev and the commander of the Petrograd Military District, General S.S. Khabalov, had minimised the seriousness of the events. On 27 February, when they belatedly requested the Stavka to send loyal troops to the capital to suppress the revolutionary movement, the President of the Duma, M.V. Rodzianko, informed General N.V. Ruzskii, Commander-in-Chief of the Northern Front (the nearest to Petrograd) that now the only possible solution to the crisis was the formation of a government of public confidence **(Browder and Kerensky, I, 1961: 83–4)**. More plausibly, its inaction can be better explained by its growing doubts about the capacity of an unreformed autocratic system to prosecute the war effectively. P.N. Miliukov recalled the growing disillusion of many of Russia's leading generals at the start of 1917.

Document 3.2 General A.I. Krymov's Plea for a *coup d'état*

At the beginning of January General Krymov arranged a meeting with members of the Duma at Rodzianko's. Having pointed out that, in the opinion of the army, victory could not be achieved without a change of course, he declared: 'the mood of the army is such that everyone will welcome the news of a *coup* with joy. If you decide on this extreme measure we will support you. Everything else has been tried but the baneful influence of his wife is stronger than the honest words addressed to the Tsar. It is obvious that there is no other way.' Prince G.E. L'vov informed me that General Alekseiev also shared this view and that before his illness he had intended to arrest the Tsarina if she had visited the Stavka.

Source: P.N. Miliukov, Rossiia na perelome: Bol'shevistskii period russkoi revoliutsii, *volume 1 (Paris: Voltaire, 1927), pp. 21–2*

That Krymov should have urged the Duma politicians to stage a palace *coup* remains unsurprising in light of the fact that he had been made privy to the plans of Guchkov, an old acquaintance of his. Whether M.V. Alekseiev was as active in the plot, as Miliukov claimed, remains a matter of dispute. He did sympathise, however, with the creation at the very least of a ministry of public confidence **(White 1994: 59; Wildman 1980: 126)**. However, many of Russia's leading generals (Miliukov cites Ruzskii and A.A. Brusilov, Commander-in-Chief of the South-western Front) arguably sought to exploit the revolutionary crisis in Petrograd in late February to achieve this goal. Alexeiev himself, in a telegram of 1 March urged Nicholas to accept this solution.

Document 3.3 Alekseiev's Telegram to Nicholas II, 1 March 1917

The danger that is growing by the minute of anarchy spreading all over the country, of the further disintegration of the army, and the impossibility of continuing the war in the present circumstances urgently demand the immediate publication of an imperial act which could still settle the situation. This is possible only by summoning a responsible ministry, assigning the President of the State Duma with its formation.

The news which reaches us gives us reason to hope that the Duma politicians, led by Rodzianko, can still prevent general disintegration, and that it is possible to work with them. But the loss of every hour reduces the last chances to preserve and restore order and fosters the seizure of power by extreme Left elements. In view of this, with all my heart I implore your Imperial Majesty to deign to the immediate publication from Stavka of the following manifesto:

We declare to all our faithful subjects:

A terrible and cruel foe is straining its last forces for the struggle against our fatherland. The decisive hour is approaching. The fate of Russia, the honour of our heroic army, the welfare of the people, the whole future of our dear fatherland demand the prosecution of the war to a victorious conclusion whatever the costs.

Desiring more strongly to unite all the forces of the people for the speediest achievement of victory, I have acknowledged it to be necessary to summon a Ministry responsible to the representatives of the people, entrusting to Rodzianko . . . its formation from people who enjoy the confidence of all Russia.

Source: 'Dokumenty k "Vospominaniiam" gen. A. Lukomskago', Arkhiv russkoi revoliutsii, III (1922), pp. 253–4

Alekseiev clearly was prompted by the desire to contain the Revolution lest it undermine Russia's war effort. Many senior generals supported him, as their replies to his telegram of 2 March outlining his strategy confirmed **(Arkhiv russkoi revoliutsii 1922, III: 260–2)**.

The Duma politicians themselves initially had failed to respond decisively to the events in the streets of Petrograd and put themselves at the head of the movement. They were finally shaken from their torpor on 26 February by the suspension of the Duma by N.N. Golitsyn, the chairman of the Council of Ministers. On 27 February they set up a Temporary Committee which felt compelled by the pressure of events to assume authority from the crumbling government.

Document 3.4 Resolution of the Temporary Committee of the State Duma

Under the difficult conditions of internal chaos brought on by the measures of the old regime, the Temporary Committee of the State Duma has found itself compelled to take the responsibility for restoring national and public order. Conscious of the vast responsibility it has assumed by this decision, the Committee expresses its assurance that the population and army will assist it in the difficult task of forming a new government that will correspond with the desires of the population and will be capable of commanding its confidence.

Source: R.P. Browder and A.F. Kerensky, The Russian Provisional Government, *I (Stanford: Stanford University Press, 1961), p. 50*

Document 3.4 reveals the immediate objective of the Duma politicians: to control the Revolution. Their broader aims, however, are not expressed in it. As the generals, they feared that the Revolution, if unchecked, would prove fatal to the effective prosecution of the war. Politically, they also sought the agreement of Nicholas to transform himself into a constitutional monarch.

However, the hopes of the military and the Duma politicians alike were to be confounded. Unprepared to surrender his autocratic powers and act as a constitutional monarch, on 2 March Nicholas, to the chagrin of his critics in the military, and the Duma, resolved to abdicate. Moreover, he also, with dubious legality, abdicated on behalf of his son, Aleksei, and proposed to hand the throne over to his brother, Mikhail. However, the weight of anti-Romanov sentiment amongst the revolutionary workers and soldiers of Petrograd precluded such a solution. As the American, Frank Golder, who was conducting research in Petrograd at the time, recorded in his diary on 3 March 1917: 'Agitation for a republic is strong' **(Golder 1992: 39)**. During a telephone conversation early in the morning of 3 March Rodzianko explained to Ruzskii, Commander-in-Chief of the Northern Front, that Mikhail's accession to the throne would provoke further, more radical and threatening disturbances. His reference to the possible future restoration of the dynasty seems, with the benefit of hindsight, to have been sanguine.

Document 3.5 Telephone Conversation of Rodzianko to Ruzskii, 5.00 a.m., 3 March 1917

[Rodzianko on the telephone] . . . . Unexpectedly for all of us, a mutiny of soldiers has broken out, the like of which I have not seen. Of course, they were not soldiers but simply peasants taken from their ploughs, who found it useful to announce their demands now. All that could be heard in the crowd was 'Land and Freedom', 'Down with the Dynasty', 'Down with the Romanovs', 'Down with the Officers', and in many units a massacre of officers had begun. Workers joined this movement and anarchy had reached its climax. After lengthy negotiations with the workers' deputies we managed . . . to come to a certain agreement, the essence of which was that a Constituent Assembly should be convened within a certain time so that the people could express their views on the form of government. Only then Petrograd breathed freely and the night passed relatively calmly.

Little by little the troops are being brought to order during the night, but the proclamation of Grand Duke Mikhail Aleksandrovich as Emperor will pour oil on the flames and a merciless extermination of everything that can be exterminated will begin.

. . . all power will slip from our hands and no one will remain to pacify the popular unrest.

In the proposed formula, the return of the dynasty is not excluded, and it is desirable that approximately until the war's end the Supreme Council and the now functioning Provisional Government should continue to act . . . under these circumstances, a rapid restoration of order will be guaranteed . . . there is no doubt that a resurgence of patriotic feeling will occur . . . and victory, I repeat, can be guaranteed.

Source: 'Dokumenty k "Vospominaniiam" gen. A. Lukomskago', Arkhiv russkoi revoliutsii, *1922 (III), pp. 266–7*

The Revolution clearly had gone far beyond what the High Command had envisaged, but the majority swiftly conceded that any monarchical solution now was impossible. The restoration of order in the interests of continuing the war to a victorious conclusion remained the paramount objective and could only be achieved, it seemed, by abandoning the dynasty. The majority of the newly formed Provisional Government came to the same conclusion. Guchkov, Minister of War, and Miliukov, Minister of Foreign Affairs, alone argued that without the symbol of monarchical authority the new government would be doomed. But to no avail, and Mikhail himself, aware of the intensity of anti-Romanov sentiment, declined the throne on 3 March **(Miliukov 1921: 50–1)**.

While it is relatively straightforward to chart the breakdown of the administrative and, in particular, the military power of the autocracy, it remains a much more complex task to determine the influence of the various revolutionary organisations in the February Revolution. Indeed, for long historians accepted that, in W.H. Chamberlin's memorable words, '[t]he collapse of the Romanov autocracy . . . was one of the most leaderless, spontaneous, anonymous revolutions of all time' **(Chamberlin, I, 1987: 73)**. Yet, for many historians, this has remained an unsatisfactory explanation. As Paul Dukes aptly remarked: 'There has been much discussion concerning the "spontaneity" of the February Revolution, and direction and leadership were certainly not as visible then as they were in October. But too much emphasis on "spontaneity" would render impossible any form of explanation' **(Dukes 1979: 87)**.

Such dissatisfaction has led to the elaboration of many, frequently dubious, hypotheses concerning who in fact did instigate and lead it. The late George Katkov, in his often tendentious study of February, unequivocally rejected all notions of spontaneity. He considered a range of possible suspects for the dubious honour of organising it, merely to dismiss them: the generals, while prepared to accept a constitutional monarchy, did not precipitate in February; the Duma politicians, fearful of revolution from below, certainly did not initiate a popular rising (Guchkov's palace *coup* apparently had been scheduled for mid-March); and the secret police, contrary to later demonology, had laid no plans to incite the workers on to the streets in order simply to suppress them (ironically, an allegedly competent observer writing in *The Times* of 21 April 1917 gave currency to the myth of the Protopov machine guns by arguing that '[t]he one certain thing is that the Reactionaries led by the Empress and M. Protopoff, the Minister of the Interior, were bent upon promoting disturbances in Petrograd and elsewhere'.) Despite a self-professed lack of hard evidence, Katkov himself gave his 'unreserved support' to the proposition that German agents had fomented the Revolution in order to disrupt Russia's war effort **(Katkov 1969: 551–64)**.

This conclusion is simply untenable. As Robert McKean, drawing upon abundant material compiled by the Okhrana (secret police), has convincingly demonstrated, German involvement in the revolutionary movement in Russia had been minimal since 1916 **(McKean 1990: 387–8)**. And, one can easily add, it was not Lenin, in Switzerland at the time, nor any other prominent Bolsheviks, also in exile, nor the leading Bolshevik organisation in Russia, the Russian Bureau headed by Aleksandr Shliapnikov, who precipitated the February Revolution. The other socialist parties, the Mensheviks and Social Revolutionaries (SRs), according to Nikolai Sukhanov, himself a Menshevik Internationalist and an active participant in the tumultuous events of 1917, equally failed to provide effective leadership in February.

Document 3.6 Sukhanov on the Absence of Leadership in the February Revolution

Meanwhile it is necessary to recall and underline right now the very peculiarity of the conditions of the parties at that time and what precisely distinguished the St Petersburg party centres from those which arose during the Revolution: to wit, *there were no authoritative leaders on the spot* in any of the parties, almost without exception. They were in exile, in prison or abroad. In the positions of the responsible leaders of the great movement, at its most criticial moments, were people who were absolutely second rate, perhaps clever organizers but nevertheless routine party hacks . . . . It was impossible to expect of them, in the great majority of cases, a proper political perspective on the new situation or any real political direction of events, in a word, to expect them in reality to rise to the occasion. In the ranks of such leaders . . . I felt competent and useful. But I was cut off from the work they were doing. And at the time of my conversation with Sokolov there was nothing in my mind but a consciousness of my inability to influence events in any way.

Source: N.N. Sukhanov, Zapiski o revoliutsii, *volume 1 (Moscow: Izdatel'stvo politicheskoi literatury, 1991), p. 60*

Sukhanov's conclusions, however, have not gone unchallenged. As early as 1923 they were disputed by Shliapnikov himself, who argued that Sukhanov's own isolation from the illegal revolutionary organisations in Petrograd deprived him of any knowledge of what they might have done after 23 February **(White 1994: 263)**. Recent research too has returned to the question of the spontaneity of the February Revolution and has gone some way to illuminating its potential leaders. There appear to be two main strands to this admittedly complex and unfinished debate. The first strand, the clash of opinions between David Longley and Michael

Melançon, focuses directly on the origins of the Revolution, and their different readings of the following leaflet, issued by the Mezhraionka (the Petersburg Inter-district Committee, comprising both Bolsheviks and Mensheviks opposed to the split in the ranks of Russian Social Democracy) on 23 February, International Women's Day.

Document 3.7 The Printed Leaflet of the St Petersburg Mezhraionka Committee, February 23, 1917

Comrade working women. For 10 years women in all countries have commemorated February 23 as International Women's Day . . . . On this day meetings and assemblies are organised where attempts are made to explain the causes of our burdensome conditions and to indicate the solution to them. For a long time now hunger has driven women to the plants and factories . . . [where] millions of women work at their machines all day on an equal footing with men. The factory owners and masters wring just as much sweat from us as from our male comrades, and then they throw us in jail for striking . . . . But women . . . in many cases are still afraid and do not know what they must demand . . . . The bosses always have taken advantage . . . of their ignorance and timidity. On this day, comrades, let us especially consider how we can defeat our enemy, the capitalist, as quickly as possible. Let us remember our near ones at the front, let us remember what a difficult struggle it was to wring from the bosses every additional ruble of pay, every hour of rest, every freedom from the government. How many of them found themselves at the front, in prison or in exile for their courageous struggle. You have replaced them . . . in the factories and plants, and your duty is to continue their great cause . . . . Comrade working women, you must not hold back your remaining male comrades but yourselves join them in a united struggle with the government and factory owners in whose interests the war is now being conducted . . . . Our fathers, husbands and brothers are dying. Our dear ones return home . . . crippled. The tsarist government sent them to the front, maimed and killed them and cares nothing about their well-being. Without end it has shed and continues to shed workers' blood. It shot down workers on January 9, on April 4 during the Lena strike, recently it has shot them in Ivanovo-Voznesensk, Shuia, Gorlovka and Kostroma [see Document 2.4]. Workers' blood is being shed on every front . . . . And in the rear the plant and factory owners under the cover of war want to turn the workers into serfs. A terrible inflation is growing in all the towns and hunger is knocking on every door. In the villages the last grain and cattle are being taken for the war. For hours we stand in queues. Our children grow hungry . . . . How many children toil till late in the evening at their machines at work beyond their strength. Everywhere there is grief, and tears . . . . Everywhere the war brings disaster, inflation and the oppression of the working class. For whose sake, working women? For what is the war being waged? . . . It is being waged for gold, shining in the eyes of the capitalists. Ministers, factory owners, bankers . . . profit in wartime while after the war they will not pay war taxes, the workers and peasants will bear all the sacrifices and pay all the costs . . . . The government is guilty, it began this war and cannot end it. It is tearing the country apart, it is its fault that you are going hungry. The capitalists are guilty – it is being waged for their profit . . . . Enough! Down with the criminal government, and all its gang of plunderers and murderers. Long live peace. The day of reckoning is already approaching. For long we have ceased to believe the cock-and-bull stories of the Ministers and masters. Anger is growing in all countries. Everywhere workers are beginning to understand that their own governments will not bring an end to the war. If they conclude peace then they will try to take foreign lands, plunder another country, and this will lead to a new war. Workers do not need plunder from abroad. Down with the autocracy! Long live the Provisonal Revolutionary Government! Down with the war! Long live the democratic republic! Long live the international proletarian solidarity! Long live the united RS–DRP.

Source: A.G. Shliapnikov, Semnadtsatyi god, *volume 1 (Moscow: Gosizdat, 1923), pp. 240–1*

The material roots that led to the worker demonstrations that developed into the February Revolution are well captured in Document 3.7: the human toll taken by the war; the long hours of work; inflation; food shortages; and the often heavy-handed repression of protesting workers. But, as Longley has pointed out, this leaflet, while summarising these grievances, did not call explicitly for a strike, or any other specific revolutionary action on 23 February itself. The Mezhraionka, and all the other underground socialist organisations (Bolsheviks included), he continues, were fearful of using International Women's Day as the spark for revolutionary actions lest they be premature, uncontrollable and hence vulnerable to repression **(Longley 1989: 625, 633)**. The implication is clear: for Longley, the February Revolution began spontaneously.

Melançon, however, disputes Longley's argument, on the grounds that the evidence itself may be incomplete. First, he questions whether the text of the leaflet reproduced above is wholly authentic, claiming that contemporary police reports indicate that it did specifically call on the workers to strike on 23 February. He surmises that as 'the only text we have of this document' was that reprinted in 1923 by Shliapnikov, in February 1917 the leader of the Bolshevik Russian Bureau, it may have been edited to minimise the role of the Mezhraionka in the February Revolution. Second, additional evidence (in particular, he cites the memoirs of the Menshevik-Internationalist, O.A. Ermanskii) suggests that other, as yet undiscovered, socialist leaflets were also published on 23 February, implying that they might have called for radical action **(Melançon 1990: 584–6)**. In the absence of further evidence it remains impossible to determine how tenable Melançon's inferences are.

While the debate on who, if anyone, sought to start a revolution on 23 February remains unresolved, there is considerably more substance to the argument that once the movement had begun the revolutionary organisations in Petrograd did seek to impart direction to it. The various leaflets issued from 24 February by the Mezhraionka, the SRs and the Bolsheviks, urging the workers to continue their demonstrations, encouraging the garrison to join the workers, and even advocating the election of soviets, bear witness to this fact **(Melançon 1988: 480–96)**. What remains contentious, however, is which organisation was the most influential in achieving this end. The following proclamation, issued on 27 February, illustrates this strand of the debate.

Document 3.8 To the Finland Station

Comrades, the long-awaited hour has arrived! The people are taking power into their own hands, the Revolution has begun; do not lose a single moment, create a Provisional Revolutionary Government today! Only organisation can strengthen our forces. First of all, elect deputies, have them make contact with one another and create, under the protection of the armed forces, a Soviet of Deputies. Bring over to our side all soldiers still lagging behind, go to the barracks themselves and summon them. Let the Finland Station be the centre where the revolutionary headquarters will gather. Seize all buildings that can serve as strongholds for our struggle. Comrade soldiers and workers! Elect deputies, forge them into an organisation for the victory over the autocracy! THE ORGANISING SOVIET OF WORKERS' DEPUTIES

Source: Reproduced in M. Melançon, 'Who Wrote What and When? Proclamations of the February Revolution in Petrograd, 23 February–1 March 1917', Soviet Studies, XL, 3 (1988), p. 489

The purpose of this leaflet is not at issue. While Melançon and White dispute who issued it, they concur that it was directed against the moderate Right socialist intelligentsia. Eventually, stirred into action by the spread of the Revolution throughout Petrograd, it began to establish a soviet in the Tauride Palace. Those who issued the Finland Station leaflet, suspecting (correctly) that the Right socialists would be prepared to make any compromises for the sake of an agreement with the Liberals, sought to create their own independent soviet, in order to ensure that the Revolution was not betrayed: hence the call to the Finland Station, situated in the radical workers' district of Vyborg. The controversial question remains precisely who composed 'the organising soviet of workers' deputies'. For White (and other historians of February, such as Tsuyoshi Hasegawa and the late Eduard Burdzhalov) it was of Bolshevik provenance, issued by the worker activists who composed the Vyborg District Committee of the Party. Melançon, however, demurs, speculating that it was jointly produced by Mezhraionka, Anarchist and Bolshevik activists **(Burdzhalov 1987: 185; Hasegawa 1981: 314, 333;**

Melançon 1988: 492–3; White 1979: 499–501). Again, gaps in archival evidence (should any such survive), combined with the politically tendentious character of memoir and other historical material published in the Soviet Union after the Revolution, have made it impossible to date to attribute it to any group with certainty.

Whatever its origins, this proclamation failed in its purpose. The Tauride Palace, not the Finland Station, became the site of the Soviet as the centre of gravity of the revolutionary movement moved inward, from the working-class districts to the heart of the city where the crucial levers of power were located. Its authors, however, had been correct in their suspicions. The socialist intelligentsia did prove ready to compromise with the Liberals. Rather than create a Provisional Revolutionary Government based on soviet power, as more radical socialists desired, the Menshevik and SR leaders surrendered power into the hands of the Temporary Committee of the Duma, soon to be transformed into a new Provisional Government. In his memoirs, published in France after he had died while in emigration, I.G. Tsereteli, a leading Menshevik, explained the reasons for this action.

Document 3.9 Irakli Tsereteli's Analysis of the Character of the February Revolution

The fundamental question was: what were the tasks and social content of the Revolution? . . . In Social Democratic ranks the answer to this question . . . did not provoke any disagreements. The huge amount of theoretical work undertaken by Marxism in the last three decades and the experience of the 1905 Revolution had brought us to understand that revolution in Russia could not make the leap from a semi-feudal to a socialist system and that what it could hope to achieve was limited to the complete democratisation of the country on the basis of bourgeois economic relations. Before the Revolution not only the Mensheviks but also the Bolsheviks firmly defended this position. In Siberia we received the platform of the Bolshevik Central Committee where Lenin, at the height of the war . . . advanced socialist revolution as the slogan of insurrection for West Europe, but democratic revolution for Russia. In the SR programme, it is true, the idea of the socialisation of the land figured but they considered it compatible with a bourgeois-democratic system, the consolidation of which in the first instance was at the heart of their practical programme.

But the Revolution occurred in conditions which again raised this question . . . . The army and the working class were the mainsprings of the Revolution and gave the socialist parties such power that the most radical experiments became possible. The danger of the socialist proletariat over-estimating its strength was great because there was no organised force capable of suppressing an attempt by the socialists to seize power and to implement their maximum programme. But such an attempt inevitably would have led to the defeat of the Revolution in a roundabout way – by the outbreak of civil war and the disruption of the economy. Therefore, in our view, one of the main tasks of the socialist parties was to teach the masses to assess soberly the significance of the events that had just taken place. The starting point of revolutionary politics had to be the understanding that the Revolution at the present moment could be consolidated only on the basis of social transformations that corresponded to the will of the majority . . . and to Russia's level of economic development; that an attempt to transcend these limits and, by force, to impose on the country the will of the socialist minority would bring about the collapse of the Revolution and the loss of the basic gains that it could objectively secure. We explained that the creation of the Provisional Government, agreed by the Committee of the Duma and the Soviet, was the acknowledgement by both parties . . . of the bourgeois-democratic tasks of the Revolution. We did not see the soviets . . . as organs in competition with the government . . . but as centres for the organisation and political education of the toiling masses, created to ensure the influence of these classes on the future course of the Revolution.

Source: I.G. Tsereteli, Vospominaniia o fevral'skoi revoliutsii *(Paris: Mouton, 1963), pp. 22–3*

This evaluation of the objectives of the February Revolution, Tsereteli hastened to add, was not simply that of the Mensheviks but also of the majority of the SR Party, especially its right wing led by A.R. Gots. The essence of their argument is lucidly outlined in Document 3.9: any attempt to pursue socialist objectives would be fatal. Politically, it would provoke the opposition of the military elites, the industrialists, the landlords and most of educated society, who, they imagined, would be able to mobilise sufficient force to wage the 'civil war' that Tsereteli so feared. Even if the counter-revolutionaries failed to re-impose an authoritarian regime, the costs of such a war would be ruinous for the country and the Revolution. Ideologically, their thinking was shaped by Marxist theory (as then widely understood) which posited that all societies must pass through definite, and economically determined, stages of development. Accordingly, socialist revolution was practicable only in fully developed capitalist societies where the proletariat was in the majority. In economically backward – 'semi-feudal' – societies such as Russia, the next stage of development was that of capitalism itself. Only after capitalism had matured in Russia would socialism be possible. Meanwhile, during this bourgeois-democratic revolution, the task of socialists was not one of government. The logic of this analysis led to what became known as 'Dual Power': the Soviet accepted the Provisional Government, on the condition that it acted in ways consistent with the democratic transformation of the country, and created its own commission to monitor its actions. Finally, the argument advanced by Tsereteli in Document 3.9, that Lenin subscribed to the same views as he did, is borne out by the following document.

Document 3.10 Lenin's Analysis of the Tasks of the Russian Revolution, Autumn 1916

The social revolution cannot be the united action of the proletarians of *all* countries for the simple reason that most of the countries and the majority of the world's population have not even reached, or have only just reached, the capitalist stage of development . . . . *Only* the advanced countries of Western Europe and North America have matured for socialism.

The *un*developed countries are a different matter. They embrace the whole of Eastern Europe and all the colonies and semi-colonies . . . . In those areas, as a rule, there *still* exist oppressed and capitalistically undeveloped nations. *Objectively*, these nations still have general national tasks to accomplish, namely, *democratic* tasks.

Source: V.I. Lenin, Collected Works, *23 (Moscow: Progress, 1964–5), pp. 58–9*

Document 3.10 (an extract from *A Caricature of Marxism*, written in the late summer and early autumn of 1916) was directed against those on the Left of the Bolshevik Party who anticipated that socialist revolution would sweep across the world in one mighty united wave. Unpublished at the time, its contents nevertheless became widely known in Bolshevik ranks. It typifies the thinking of Lenin (and the great majority of leading Bolsheviks) before 1917. Its political message is unequivocal: the forthcoming revolution in Russia will be bourgeois-democratic, not socialist. As late as January 1917 Lenin reiterated this conclusion. In March, when Lev Kamenev and Joseph Stalin had returned to Petrograd from their Siberian exile, they acted on the basis of this analysis, urging the Party to support, as the Mensheviks and SRs had, the bourgeois Provisional Government that had emerged from the Revolution. By then, however, Lenin himself had revised his own views on the nature of revolution in Russia, as we shall see in the next Chapter.

The first official act of the newly formed Provisional Government was to issue its programme, following intensive negotiations during the night of 1–2 March between the Temporary Committee of the Duma and the Executive Committee of the newly formed Petrograd Soviet.

Document 4.1 The Programme of the Provisional Government, March 3, 1917

The Cabinet will be guided in its actions by the following principles:

1 An immediate general amnesty for all political and religious offences, including terrorist acts, military revolts, agrarian crimes, etc.

2 Freedom of speech and press; of trade unions; of assembly; and to strike. These political liberties should be extended to the soldiers in so far as war conditions permit.

3 The abolition of all restrictions based on social, religious and national grounds.

4 Immediate preparation for the calling of a Constituent Assembly, elected by universal, equal, secret and direct suffrage, which will determine the form of government and the Constitution of the country.

5 The replacement of the police by a national militia with elective officers, subject to the organs of local self-government.

6 Elections of the organs of local self-government to be carried out on the basis of universal, direct, equal and secret suffrage.

7 The military units which took part in the revolutionary movement will not be disarmed or removed from Petrograd.

8 While strict military discipline will be maintained for soldiers on duty and in active military service they will be granted the same civil rights as other citizens.

The Provisional Government considers it its duty to add that it has no intention of taking advantage of war conditions to delay the realisation of the above-mentioned measures of reform.

Source: N. Avdeev (ed.), Revoliutsiia 1917 goda (Khronika sobytii), *volume I,* ianvar'–aprel' *(Moscow, Petrograd: Gosudarstvennoe izdatel'stvo, 1923), pp. 189–90*

This programme was issued in the names of M.V. Rodzianko, Chairman of the State Duma, G.E. L'vov, the new Prime Minister, and the Ministers of the Provisional Government: P.N. Miliukov (Foreign Affairs); A.I. Guchkov (War); M.I. Tereschenko (Finance); A.A. Manuilov (Education); A.I. Shingarev (Agriculture); N.V. Nekrasov (Transport); A.I. Konovalov (Industry); V.N. L'vov (Holy Synod); and the sole socialist, A.F. Kerensky (Justice). In effect, this programme instituted the civil liberties demanded by the Progressive Bloc in August 1915 **(see Document 2.3)**, and more! Under pressure from the workers and soldiers, and their representatives in the Soviet, the Liberals conceded reforms that they had not envisaged. Despite their preference for a constitutional monarchy, point 4 was tantamount to the *de facto* transformation of Russia into a democratic republic. Moreover, they were compelled to grant extensive civil rights to the soldiers (point 8) and (point 7) bow to the wishes of the triumphant Petrograd garrison not to be sent to the front (see Chapter 12). Of equal importance was what was absent from this programme. No precise measures of economic and social reform, with respect to the land or working conditions, were outlined, nor was there any indication what revolutionary Russia's future role in the war would be **(Liebman 1970: 117–18)**.

These lacunae soon provoked tensions between the Provisional Government and the Soviet. Many workers, in both Petrograd and Moscow, remained disgruntled. Their major bone of contention was the fact that the long-sought eight-hour working-day had not been enacted. The Soviet itself called for a return to work, fearing that its implementation day would allow the bourgeoisie to drive a wedge into revolutionary ranks by claiming that the self-interested action of the workers was jeopardising the position of the soldiers at the front. In many factories and plants they continued to strike until the eight-hour day in effect was implemented **(Mandel 1983: 87; Burdzhalov 1971: 33–4)**. A compromise of sorts was reached when the workers, persuaded by Soviet emissaries, agreed to work overtime, where necessary, to ensure that the army remained adequately supplied **(see Document 10.1)**.

The issue of the war, however, proved to be a more serious cause of conflict. As its *Declaration to the Peoples of the World* of 14 March made clear, the Petrograd Soviet, with a stunning disregard to the intransigent bellicosity of both Russia's allies and the Central Powers, sought the speedy conclusion of a general, democratic peace. In the interim it was prepared to continue the war, to defend the Revolution from the threat posed by reactionary German imperialism. The driving-force behind this policy, of revolutionary defencism, was the Menshevik leader, Irakli Tsereteli. For its part, the Provisional Government had hoped that the Revolution would have united the country sufficiently to enable it to prosecute the war to a victorious conclusion, thereby securing the territorial gains (in particular, control of the Dardanelles) conceded by Russia's allies in the secret treaties of 1915. Under pressure from the Soviet it was compelled formally to renounce any annexationist objectives.

Document 4.2 Provisional Government's Declaration of War Aims, March 27, 1917

Leaving to the will of the people, in close union with our allies, the final solution of all questions linked with the world war and its end, the Provisional Government considers it its right and duty now to declare that the objective of free Russia is not the domination of other nations, nor the expropriation of their . . . property, nor the forcible seizure of foreign territories, but the ratification of a stable peace on the basis of national self-determination. The Russian people is not seeking the reinforcement of its external power at the expense of other nations. It does not intend to enslave or humiliate any of them. In the name of the highest principles of justice it has removed the fetters on the Polish people. But the Russian people will not allow its native land to emerge from the great war humbled and sapped of its life strength.

These principles will be established as the basis of the foreign policy of the Provisional Government, unswervingly carrying out the will of the people and protecting the rights of our country in strict observance of the commitments adopted with respect to our allies.

Source: Revoliutsionnoe dvizhenie v Rossii posle sverzheniia samoderzhaviia *(Moscow: Izdatel'stvo akademii nauk SSSR, 1957), pp. 444–5*

At first sight, Document 4.2 appears to commit the Provisional Government to the Soviet's Declaration in favour of peace with no annexations or indemnities, on the basis of the independence of all nations. As evidence of its honourable intentions, the Provisional Government cited its recognition of Poland's just claims for independence. In fact, this cost it nothing, as by then the territories of Russian Poland had been lost to the Germans, whereas Finland, which remained in Russian hands, was not granted the independence it sought. The sting of this document, however, was in its tail. This soon became clear when the Foreign Minister, Miliukov-Dardannelski (Miliukov of the Dardanelles), as Victor Chernov, one of the SR leaders, dubbed him, reaffirmed the Provisional Government's fidelity to Russia's existing treaties with Britain and France, with all their annexationist implications **(see Document 4.4)**.

In the meantime, Vladimir Lenin, who had returned to Russia on 3 April, was quick to dismiss the *Declaration* as mere rhetoric **(see section 3 of Document 4.3)**. His very presence exacerbated the tensions between the Provisional Government and the Soviet and hastened the end of the 'honeymoon' period of the Revolution. Bitterly opposed to any collaboration with the Provisional Government, he berated Kamenev and Stalin for aligning the Bolshevik Party behind the Soviet's policy, in support of Dual Power and revolutionary defencism. In Document 4.3, *The April Theses*, Lenin outlined the objectives that he wished the Bolsheviks to pursue.

Document 4.3 The Tasks of the Proletariat in the Present Revolution, 4 April 1917

1 In our attitude towards the war, which under the new government of Lvov and Co. unquestionably remains on Russia's part a predatory imperialist war owing to the capitalist nature of that government, not the slightest concession to 'revolutionary defencism' is permissible.

The class-conscious proletariat can give its consent to a revolutionary war, which would really justify revolutionary defencism, only on one condition: (a) that power pass to the proletariat and the poorest sections of the peasants . . . (b) that all annexations be renounced in deed and not in word; (c) that a complete break be effected . . . with all capitalist interests.

In view of the undoubted honesty of those broad sections of the mass believers in revolutionary defencism . . . in view of the fact that they are being deceived by the bourgeoisie, it is necessary with particular thoroughness, persistence and patience to explain their error to them, to explain the inseparable connection existing between capital and the imperialist war, and to prove without overthrowing capital *it is impossible* to end the war by a truly democratic peace.

The most widespread campaign for this view must be organised in the army at the front.

Fraternisation

2 The specific feature of the present situation in Russia is that the country is *passing* from the first stage of the Revolution – which, owing to the insufficient class consciousness and organisation of the proletariat, placed power in the hands of the bourgeoisie – to its *second* stage, which must place power in the hands of the proletariat and the poorest sections of the peasants.

This transition is characterised . . . by a maximum of legally recognised rights (Russia is *now* the freest of all the belligerent countries . . .) . . . by the absence of violence towards the masses, and, finally, by their unreasoning trust in the government of the capitalists, those worst enemies of peace and socialism.

This peculiar situation demands of us an ability to adapt ourselves to the *special* conditions of party work among unprecedently large masses of proletarians who have just awakened to political life.

3 No support for the Provisional Government; the utter falsity of all its promises should be made clear, particularly of those relating to the renunciation of annexations.

4 Recognition of the fact that in most of the Soviets of Workers' Deputies our party is . . . a small minority, as against *a bloc of all* the petty-bourgeois opportunist elements, from the Popular Socialists and the Socialist-Revolutionaries down to the Organising Committee (Chkeidze, Tsereteli,

etc.) . . . who have yielded to the influence of the bourgeoisie and spread that influence among the proletariat.

The masses must be made to see that the Soviets of Workers' Deputies are the *only possible* form of revolutionary government, and that therefore our task is, as long as *this* government yields to the influence of the bourgeoisie, to present a patient, systematic, and persistent *explanation* of the errors of their tactics, an explanation expecially adapted to the practical needs of the masses.

As long as we are in the minority we carry on the work of criticising and exposing errors and at the same time we preach the necessity of transferring the entire state power to the Soviets of Workers' Deputies, so that the people may overcome their mistakes by experience.

5 Not a parliamentary republic – to return to a parliamentary republic from the Soviets of Workers' Deputies would be a retrograde step – but a republic of Soviets of Workers', Agricultural and Peasants' Deputies throughout the country, from top to bottom.

Abolition of the police, the army and the bureaucracy.

The salaries of all officials, all of whom are elective and displacable at any time, not to exceed the average wage of a competent worker.

6 The weight of emphasis in the agrarian programme to be shifted to the Soviets of Agricultural Labourers' Deputies.

Confiscation of all landed estates.

Nationalisation of *all* lands in the country, the land to be disposed of by the local Soviets of Agricultural Labourers' and Peasants' Deputies. The organisation of separate Soviets of Deputies of Poor Peasants. The setting up of a model farm on each of the large estates . . . under the control of the Soviets of Agricultural Labourers' Deputies and for the public account.

7 The immediate amalgamation of all banks in the country into a single national bank, and the institution of control over it by the Soviet of Workers' Deputies.

8 It is not our *immediate* task to 'introduce' socialism but only to bring social production and the distribution of products at once under the *control* of the Soviets of Workers' Deputies.

9 Party tasks:
  (a) Immediate convocation of a Party Congress
  (b) Alteration of the Party Programme, mainly:
      (1) On the question of imperialism and the imperialist war;
      (2) On our attitude towards the state and *our* demand for a 'commune state';
      (3) Amendment of our out-of-date minimum programme;
  (c) Change of the Party's name.

10 A new International:
We must take the initiative in creating a revolutionary international, an
international against the *social-chauvinists* [socialists, such as the Menshevik,
Georgii Plekhanov, who enthusiastically supported the war against
Germany] and against the 'Centre'.

Source: V.I. Lenin, Collected Works, *24 (Moscow: Progress, 1964–5),
pp. 21–4*

Document 4.3 is one of the seminal documents of 1917. Published in *Pravda*,
the Bolshevik Party newspaper, on 7 April 1917, it became the heart of Bolshevik
strategy until the October Revolution. Contrary to his previous views, that given
its backwardness Russia could only anticipate a bourgeois-democratic revolution
(Document 3.10), now Lenin was advocating a socialist revolution. While the
Theses remained a statement of general principles rather than a programme of
precise measures necessary to begin the transition to socialism **(Service 1991:
159)**, on two key issues Lenin was quite adamant. First, there was to be no
support for the Provisional Government, nor any sort of 'parliamentary republic'.
Instead, a new 'commune state' was to be created, a Republic of Soviets in which
all would participate in government, equally and for equal pay, without specialised
and highly paid bureaucrats in charge. This was the political blueprint for socialist
revolution that he had come to believe Marx, reflecting upon the experiences
of the short-lived Paris Commune of 1871, had bequeathed. Second, as Russia,
Provisional Government or not, remained essentially an imperialist state there
could be no support for revolutionary defencism.

His volte-face provoked great consternation amongst the overwhelming
majority of Russian socialists, leading Bolsheviks included. They regarded him as a
'madman', arguing that he had failed to offer any analysis of the objective economic
conditions that made socialism now possible in a still backward and predominantly
peasant Russia. There is considerable merit in their critique, as it was only later in
1917 that Lenin sought to provide a theoretical justification for socialist revolution
in Russia **(Kowalski 1991: 53–6; Document 6.4)**. Yet, whatever deficiences
the *Theses* may have possessed, they became the basis upon which the Bolshevik
Party, in Leon Trotsky's memorable phrase, was re-armed ideologically. The
considerable opposition that he initially faced soon was overcome through a
combination of Lenin's own persuasive logic, of the return of radical Bolsheviks
from exile, and the influx into the Party of new recruits itching for a more radical
revolution to resolve their material difficulties **(Rabinowitch 1991: 41)**. No
doubt he also gained the support of many lower-ranking Bolsheviks, those of the
Vyborg district among others, who since February had been advocating a similar
strategy. Perhaps Lenin's success was also eased by the fact that his critique of the
Provisional Government was given credibility by the crisis over foreign policy that
erupted on 20 April. It was precipitated by the publication in the Russian press of
Miliukov's note of 18 April to the Allies.

Document 4.4 Miliukov's Note to the Allies

Recently our enemies have been striving to disrupt relations amongst the Allies by disseminating absurd reports alleging that Russia is ready to conclude a separate peace with the Central Powers. The text of the attached document best of all refutes such falsehoods. You will note . . . that the general principles expressed by the Provisional Government fully correspond with those lofty ideas which have been constantly expressed . . . by many eminent statesmen in the allied countries. . . . The government under the old regime was, of course, incapable of grasping and sharing these ideas of the liberating character of the war, of the establishment of solid foundations for the peaceful existence of nations, of self-determination for oppressed peoples . . . . But free Russia, however, can now speak in a language that will be comprehensible to the leading democracies . . . and she now hastens to add her voice to those of her allies. Imbued with this new spirit of a free democracy, the Declaration of the Provisional Government cannot, of course, give the slightest cause to think that the Revolution has entailed any weakening of Russia's role in the common struggle of the Allies. Quite the contrary, the aspiration of the entire nation to conduct the world war to a decisive victory has only been strengthened . . . . This striving has become even more active, since it is concentrated on the immediate task which touches all – to repel the enemy who has invaded our country. It goes without saying, as stated in the communicated document, that the Provisional Government, while protecting the rights of our own country, will observe fully the obligations assumed towards our allies.

Source: N. Avdeev (ed.), Revoliutsiia 1917 goda (Khronika sobytii), *volume II,* aprel'–mai *(Moscow–Petrograd: Gosudarstvennoe izdatel'stvo, 1923), pp. 247–8*

With its emphasis on prosecuting the war to a victorious conclusion rather than seeking a speedy democratic and non-annexationist peace, this note provoked mass demonstrations of workers and soldiers, in Moscow as well as Petrograd. They saw the note as confirmation that Miliukov (and others) within the Provisional Government had not abandoned their imperialist ambitions. On 21 April, as the protestors clashed with those who supported Miliukov, the Soviet was compelled to intervene to prevent mass bloodshed. It ordered all military units to remain in their barracks, unless commanded to the contrary by itself, and banned all street demonstrations. To the chagrin of the the Provisional Government, the success of the Soviet in mediating this crisis revealed where real power and authority lay **(Wade 1969: 38–43)**. This outcome to the April crisis increased Guchkov's pessimism about Russia's future, as the following document illustrates.

Document 4.5 Guchkov's Response to the April Crisis

My entire plan was to do away with the Soviet of Workers' and Soldiers' Deputies. I thought that if we managed to form a united and strong government, free and responsible to itself and not to others, then even in face of all the ruin which enveloped both the country and the front there was the possibility of restoring order. Some very bloody action was necessary, there was no alternative to violence. Sometime later Miliukov and I reflected on the situation. He said: 'Aleksandr Ivanovich, I blame you for one thing: why did you not arrest the Provisional Government?' I could have arrested it but I did not know how the country would react to this.

The demonstrations at the end of April made one thing clear: in the Soviet . . . they realised that they would not find it as easy to seize power as they assumed. Accordingly, two or three days later the Soviet demanded from the government that the authority of the commander of the Petersburg district to call out the troops was to be subject to . . . the agreement of a delegation from the Soviet. They thought to assign . . . two or three people to the staff of the Petersburg military district so that any order of the Commander-in-Chief regarding the mobilisation and use of the troops would be acted upon only if they had countersigned it. I answered that I disagreed with this and insisted that it be rejected.

We resigned. But one feature was striking: for all his qualities, Kornilov urged me to agree to this. You see, such intelligent men did not comprehend the situation, they sought some sort of concilatory solution, they tried to put off the moment of conflict . . . . He was very insistent on conciliation, thinking he would be able to come to some agreement with those delegated by the Soviet. I opposed this, considering that this would simply be capitulation, and for that very reason would tie our hands materially and physically. A military demonstration against the Provisional Government took place at that time. Highly inflammatory propaganda was being conducted – at this time Lenin was making speeches in Kseshinskaia's palace [Bolshevik headquarters at the time] and this was producing a harmful influence on the army, on the troops in Petrograd . . . . I don't remember the details.

I remained firmly convinced that until we achieved a united government, as long as Dual Power continued (while the Soviet of Workers' and Soldiers' Deputies issued orders at its own behest) – until then we would not be able to deal with our problems, would not be able to restore order either in the country or in the army. To me the question of a *coup* seemed perfectly clear.

When I became convinced that the difficulties, while great, could be overcome, but for one remaining insuperable obstacle – the categoric refusal of the majority of the Provisional Government to take decisive military measures – then my mission was at an end. I did not give up, generally speaking, all my efforts, but it seemed to me that it was necessary to shift their focus to the front. There, perhaps, some healthy units could be made ready with which it would be possible to march upon Petersburg to cleanse it. From the very beginning I had come to the conclusion which Kornilov later developed, without success.

Source: A.I. Guchkov, 'Aleksandr Ivanovich Gruchkov rasskazivaet', Voprosy istorii, 9–10 (1991), pp. 208–9

Document 4.5 reaffirms Guchkov's conviction **(see Chapter 2)** that Dual Power had deprived the Provisional Government of real authority. His despair reached breaking-point and he resigned when the majority of his fellow Ministers rejected his proposed solution to the April crisis: the forcible dissolution of the Soviet of Workers' and Soldiers' Deputies. The viability of his proposal remains questionable. It is doubtful whether the majority of rank-and-file soldiers would have tolerated it, as the fate of Kornilov's subsequent attempt to create an authoritarian government (which Guchkov supported) seems to confirm **(see Chapter 5)**. Two other points in this document, however, require clarification. First, Guchkov misrepresented the aspirations of the Soviet. Its Menshevik and SR majority had no intention 'to seize power'. In fact, it was reluctant even to enter a coalition, as we shall shortly see. Second, General Lavr Kornilov, Commander of the Petrograd Military District, was not as 'conciliatory' as Guchkov suggested. He had been prepared to deploy force against the demonstrators. But his orders were countermanded by the Soviet, with the tacit consent of the Provisional Government, whereupon he resigned and was appointed to command the Eighth Army on the South-western Front. The final casualty of this crisis was 'Miliukov-Dardannelski' himself, who resigned rather than continue in government as the Minister of Education. The contemporary cartoon opposite, from *New Satirist*, ironically depicts Miliukov being swept away by the Straits that he desired so much. The caption reads: 'In these straits, the current *is* swift.'

Document 4.6 The fall of Miliukov

[See illustration on p. 58]

Illustrated satirical journals only emerged in the Russian Empire in the second half of the nineteenth century. The Revolution of 1905 in particular stimulated the publication of cartoons critical of the autocracy and its policies. Between 1905 and 1907 alone, according to Stephen White, more than 3,000 such cartoons appeared. In the face of increased government repression and censorship after 1907 it became necessary for satirical journals to moderate their attacks if they were to survive. *Satirikon*, founded in 1908, pursued such a strategy, to the dismay of the more radical members of its staff who set up *Novyi Satirikon* in 1913. While defending the democratic objectives of the February Revolution, it remained suspicious of the Bolsheviks' aims and did not support their actions in October. It did not survive long and was closed down in 1918. However, many who had

Source: A. Nenarokov, An Illustrated History of the Great October Socialist Revolution *(Moscow: Progress, 1987), p. 43*

contributed to it (most famously, Vladimir Maiakovskii) did serve the Bolshevik regime and helped to develop the Soviet political poster **(White 1988: 7–11)**. In part inspired by earlier satirical cartoons (another major source was the icon), poster art became the main medium of political propaganda during the Civil War used both by the Bolsheviks and their opponents. In what remained a largely illiterate country striking (often highly colourful) visual images were deployed, in tens of millions of copies, in an attempt to rally support **(Brown, Kaser and Smith 1994: 186)**.

The eventual outcome of the April crisis was not a dictatorship. Instead, the Provisional Government sought to strengthen itself by the inclusion of representatives of the majority socialist parties, the Mensheviks and SRs. While hesitant to assume any governmental responsibility in what they continued to regard as a bourgeois revolution, their reluctance was overcome by a combination of grassroots support for a Coalition Ministry and, in particular, G.E. L'vov's threat that the Provisional Government would resign (and leave the country prey to anarchy) if a coalition was not created **(Wade 1969: 44–8)**. After lengthy negotiations the First Coalition was formed on May 5 and issued the following programme.

Document 4.7 Programme of the First Coalition Provisional Government

The Provisional Government, reorganised and strengthened by representatives of revolutionary democracy, declares that it will with the utmost determination put into practice the ideas of liberty, equality and fraternity under the banner of which the great Russian Revolution arose.

1 In its foreign policy the Provisional Government, rejecting, in agreement with the whole people, any thought of a separate peace, openly adopts as its aim the establishment of a general peace which shall not have as its objective either domination over other nations, or the seizure of their national property, or the violent seizure of their territories – a peace without annexations or indemnities, based on the rights of nations to self-determination . . . the Provisional Government will take steps to secure an agreement with its allies on the basis of its declaration of 27 March.
2 Convinced that the defeat of Russia and her allies would not only be the source of the greatest disasters . . . but would postpone or make impossible the conclusion of a general peace on the principles indicated above, the Provisional Government firmly believes that the Russian Revolutionary Army will not permit the German troops to destroy our allies . . . and then attack us with the full force of their arms.
3 The Provisional Government resolutely and decisively will combat the economic disorganisation of the country by the planned introduction of state . . . control of production, transport, exchange and distribution

of goods, and where necessary will have recourse to the organisation of production.

4 Measures for the comprehensive protection of labour will be energetically developed.

5 While assigning to the Constituent Assembly the resolution of the transfer of land to the toilers yet carrying out the preparatory work for this, the Provisional Government will adopt all necessary measures to guarantee the greatest possible production of grain needed by the country and to regulate the use of the land in the interests of the economy and the working population.

6 . . . the Provisional Government will pay particular attention to the increase in direct taxation on the propertied classes (death duties, taxation of war profits, property tax, etc.).

7 Work on the introduction and strengthening of democratic organs of local government will be continued with all possible speed.

8 Equally, the Provisional Government will apply all its energies to the convocation of the Constituent Assembly as soon as possible.

Source: Revoliutsionnoe dvizhenie v Rossii v mae–iiune 1917g.: Iiunskaia demonstratsiia *(Moscow: Izdatvel'stvo akademii nauk SSSR, 1959), pp. 229–30*

At first sight, this programme went considerably beyond that of 3 March **(Document 4.1)**. The unequivocal support for a general, democratic peace (section 1) appeared to signal a major concession to the demands of the Soviet. Moreover, the Provisional Government also sought to reassure the workers and peasants that their socio-economic aspirations would be addressed (points 4 and 5), though these proposals arguably remained general statements of intent, not precise policy statements. It was still committed to the principle that the resolution of all fundamental economic and social questions must await the decision of the Constituent Assembly. But contrary to its promise to hasten elections to it, those scheduled for 17 September, again were to be deferred. Schapiro suggests that the delay was the product of the difficulties involved in framing the Electoral Statute, compounded by 'administrative incompetence'. More plausibly, Radkey explains the delay by reference to the fear of the government, in particular the Kadets within it, that once elected it would refuse to prosecute the war vigorously **(Radkey 1990: 92; Schapiro 1985: 70)**.

This programme, in practice little more than a vague promissory note, failed to temper the tensions growing within Russian society. The urban economy continued to decline, provoking a sharp deterioration in relations between the industrialists and the workers **(see Chapter 10)**. In the countryside the peasants became increasingly restless in the absence of any effective measures of land reform **(see Chapter 9)**. However, rather ironically given the commitment expressed in section 1 of Document 4.7, they first became most manifest over the issue of war and peace. The goverment's decision to launch a major offensive in June proved to be a significant turning point. Many high-ranking officers claimed that an offensive was vital to maintain discipline and prevent the disintegration of the army **(Feldman 1968: 532–3)**. More surprisingly, the socialist Ministers and the majority of the Soviet supported this action, in the naive (and vain) belief that a demonstration of Russian military strength would enable them to exert greater pressure on the Allies and compel them to pursue a general, democratic peace **(Wade 1969: 56, 70–1)**. This policy was ill-conceived and ill-executed. First, while the majority of soldiers (and workers) may still have accepted revolutionary defencism, they had absolutely no enthusiasm for an offensive campaign. Second, there were no substantial grounds to suppose that a successful offensive would compel the Allies, their confidence in victory reinforced by the entry of the United States into the war in April, to seek a negotiated peace **(Wade 1969: 72–3)**. The offensive itself, badly planned and launched without a simultaneous assault by Allied forces in the West, rapidly turned into an ignominious rout, exposing Russia's military weakness, not its strength **(Feldman 1968: 535–40)**.

Whatever patriotism the offensive may have engendered was short-lived as advance rapidly turned into defeat. More ominously, even before it began on 18 June radical voices of protest increasingly were heard. The leading Bolshevik organisations – the Central Committee (CC), the Petersburg Committee and the Military Organisation – vied to mobilise this growing opposition. The CC called for a demonstration on 10 June in favour of an end to the war and the transfer of power to the Soviets. However, under pressure from the Soviet, a majority of the CC at the last minute agreed to abandon it. Rather it successfully hijacked the Soviet's own demonstration on 18 June, which passed off largely under Bolshevik slogans. Thereafter, grassroots radicalism swiftly mounted, culminating in a rising against the Provisional Government that began on 3 July.

At the Sixth Congress of the Bolshevik Party, which convened in secret in the Vyborg district on 26 July, Stalin provided the following explanation of the Bolsheviks' role in the July Days.

Document 4.8 Stalin's Report on the July Days

The end of June and the beginning of July witnessed a political offensive. There were rumours of the restoration of the death penalty, of the dissolution of whole regiments, of a whole series of brutal punishments at the front. Delegates arriving from the front spoke of arrests and beatings . . . . The Grenadier and Machine-gun Regiments informed us of the same . . . . I will now move on to the events of July 3–5, which interest you most. At three in the afternoon of July 3 in Kshesinskaia's palace an all-city conference was taking place . . . . Suddenly two delegates of the Machine-gun Regiment burst in and interrupted us: 'They want to dissolve our regiment, they are taunting us. We cannot wait any longer and have resolved to take action for which purpose we have already sent our delegates to the plants and factories.'

The chairman of the conference, Volodarskii, declared that the Party had decided not to act. It was clear to the Central Committee (CC) that both the bourgeoisie and the Black Hundreds would like to provoke us into action in order to make it possible to shift the responsibility on to us for the failure of the offensive. We had resolved not to respond to provocation, not to take any action while the offensive was continuing, but to wait until it finally discredited itself in the eyes of the masses and the Provisional Government exhausted its credibility . . . . members of the Party in their regiments must obey this decision. The representatives of the regiment departed, protesting.

At 4 p.m. a meeting of the CC convened in the Taurida palace. The CC resolved to refrain from any action. At a session of the Central Executive Committee (CEC), on the instructions of the CC, I declared that our Party had decided not to act. I presented it with all the facts and reported that the delegates of the Machine-gun Regiment had sent their own representatives to the plants and factories. I proposed that everything should be done to prevent this demonstration and demanded that our proposal be minuted. The SRs and Mensheviks who now accuse us of planning the demonstration, forget this fact. At 5 p.m. the all-city conference resolved not to take action. All its members dispersed to their districts and plants to restrain the masses from demonstrating. At 7 p.m. two regiments approached Kshesinskaia's palace, displaying banners with the slogans: 'All power to the Soviets' . . . . Lashevich and Kuraev tried to convince the soldiers not to act and to return to their barracks. The soldiers responded by shouting 'Down with them!', which had never happened before. At the same time a workers' demonstration appeared, under the slogan of 'All Power to the Soviets'. It became clear to us all that it was impossible to stop the demonstration. Then an unofficial meeting of the CC resolved to take part in the demonstration, to propose to the workers and soldiers to act in an organised manner and to proceed peacefully to the Taurida palace, to select delegates and through them to present their demands . . . . At 10 p.m. . . . there was a meeting of the CC, delegates to the city conference and representatives from the regiments and plants. It was resolved to reverse our policy and to take part in and control the movement that had already begun. It would have been a crime if the Party then had washed its hands of the whole affair.

Source: Shestoi s″ezd RSDRP (Bol'shevikov) avgust 1917 goda: Protokoly, *(Moscow: Gosizdat, 1958), pp. 17–18*

Document 4.8 refutes the accusations levelled against Lenin and the Bolshevik leadership by their opponents at the time, by memoirists such as Sukhanov, and subsequently by hostile historians, most recently Richard Pipes, that the CC initiated the rising against the Provisional Government **(Pipes 1992a: 419)**. The weight of evidence suggests that Stalin's denial that this had been the case in large part was true, if overlooking the extent to which the Bolsheviks' political attacks on the government had stirred up grassroots resentments against it. However, the spark that ignited the July Days came from below, in particular from the First Machine-gun Regiment, which feared it was about to be sent to the front. Its call for an insurrection to overthrow the Provisional Government found a ready response among many soldiers opposed to the offensive and workers disgruntled at inflation and food speculators. The pleas of the moderate majority in the CC, ironically now including Lenin, that the time was not yet ripe for an insurrection, were ignored. It found itself unable to control its subordinate organisations, especially the Military Organisation and the Petersburg Committee, a failure which casts doubt on the much-vaunted myth of Bolshevik discipline and unity during 1917 **(Rabinowitch 1991: 232–3)**. Belatedly recognising that its policy of restraint had been in vain, the CC reluctantly resolved to take charge of the demonstrations. Its rationale for so doing is not fully explained in Document 4.8. First, convinced that the rising would end in defeat, it sought to control it in order to minimise the damage that the Bolsheviks would suffer as a result. Second, inaction would cast doubt on the Party's radical credentials, already challenged by the Anarcho-Communists, and threaten it with a loss of support **(Rabinowitch 1991: 100–2, 176)**.

As the rising rapidly disintegrated in face of slanderous charges that the Bolsheviks were agents of Imperial Germany bent on subverting the Revolution and of the imminent arrival of frontline troops loyal to the government, the CC called for it to end on 5 July. In retrospect, its prospects for success appear to have been limited, as Lenin had warned. Provincial Russia, including Moscow, failed to support it. A counter-offensive against the Bolsheviks was launched. Many were imprisoned and, in fear for his life, Lenin fled the capital 'to think again'. Not for the first, or last, time in his career Lenin radically revised his political strategy. Embittered by the readiness with which the Mensheviks and SRs had condoned the repression of the Bolsheviks he abandoned his call for 'All Power to the Soviets!'

Document 4.9 Lenin against the Soviets

The present Soviets have failed, have suffered complete defeat, because they are dominated by the Socialist-Revolutionary and Menshevik parties. At the moment these Soviets are like sheep brought to the slaughterhouse and bleating pitifully under the knife. The Soviets *at present* are powerless and helpless against the triumphant and triumphing counter-revolution. The slogan calling for the transfer of power to the Soviets might be construed as a 'simple' appeal for the transfer of power to the present Soviets, and to say that, to appeal for it, would now mean deceiving the people. Nothing is more dangerous than deceit.

V.I. Lenin, Collected Works, *25 (Moscow: Progress, 1964–5), pp. 189–90*

After protracted debate within the Party its Sixth Congress eventually endorsed Lenin's about-face on the Soviets. Yet those Bolshevik defenders of the Soviets who argued that pressure from below, from the mass of workers and soldiers, would restore their revolutionary zeal soon were to be proved correct. But not before another political crisis had seized the country.

The Kornilov affair | 5

The seminal political event of the summer of 1917 was the Kornilov affair, the attempt to re-establish an authoritarian government in Russia. Despite the importance of this affair its history remains unclear, the result of remaining gaps in the evidence and the often anecdotal and selective, if not biased, nature of that which is available **(Munck 1987: 16–39)**. However, the context within which it took place is more certain. The collapse of the June offensive and the increasing radicalisation of the 'dark masses' moved those conservative forces opposed to any further deepening of the Revolution to mobilise to prevent it. They thought to take advantage of the rout of the Bolsheviks during the July Days to put pressure on the Provisional Government to introduce measures to reimpose discipline, both at the front and in the rear.

The July Days themselves had coincided with the collapse of the First Coalition, precipitated by the resignation of the Kadet Ministers on 3 July. The ostensible reason for their resignation was their rejection of the limited autonomy granted to the Ukraine by Kerensky, Tereshchenko and Tsereteli **(see Chapter 11)**. However, equally important was their opposition to Viktor Chernov, the SR Minister of Agriculture. His proposal to ban the sale of land pending the final resolution of the agrarian question by the Constituent Assembly was seen by them as pandering to the desires of the peasants to seize the land **(Radkey 1958: 254–61; see Chapter 9)**. The growing conservatism of the Kadets, fortified by the influx of Octobrists into the Party since March, was reinforced by the Declaration of Principles. This Declaration was issued on 8 July by the socialist-dominated rump of the government, now headed by Kerensky after G.E. L'vov's resignation on 7 July.

Document 5.1 The Declaration of Principles of the Provisional Government, 8 July 1917

The first fundamental task of the Provisional Government is to exert all its energies in the war against the external enemy and in the preservation of the new political order against all sorts of anarchist and counter-revolutionary attack . . . . With respect to its foreign policy, the government again reaffirms that the revolutionary army can go into battle with the firm belief that not one drop of a Russian soldier's blood will be shed in pursuit of aims alien to the ideals of Russian democracy . . . the Provisional Government intends to propose to the Allies that they convene a conference during August to determine the general direction of their foreign policy and to coordinate their actions in order to implement the principles proclaimed by the Russian Revolution.

The Provisional Government will take all measures to ensure that elections for the Constituent Assembly take place on time (17 September) . . . . In terms of domestic policy a primary objective of the government is the most rapid introduction of a system of urban and rural self-government on the basis of universal, direct, equal and secret suffrage.

In order to combat economic disorganisation and to introduce further legislation for the protection of labour, the Economic Council and the main Economic Committee established under the Provisional Government must quickly get down to elaborating a general plan for the organisation of the economy and labour, to drawing up laws . . . for the regulation of economic life and control of industry . . . . In terms of labour policy laws dealing with the freedom of trade unions, labour exchanges and arbitration boards have been drawn up and will be implemented within the next few days. Laws on the eight-hour day, comprehensive labour protection, all kinds of social insurance . . . are being drawn up.

The agrarian measures of the Provisional Government . . . are founded on the conviction that the idea of transferring the land into the hands of the toilers should be the basis of future land reform . . . . On this basis a land reform law is being prepared which will be put before the Constituent Assembly.

Source: Revoliutsionnoe dvizhenie v Rossii v iiule 1917g.: Iiul'skii krizis (Moscow: Izdatel'stvo akademii nauk SSSR, 1959), pp. 295–6

Document 5.1 in general terms restated the objectives contained in the programme of the First Coalition **(Document 4.7)**, one implication being that in the intervening period little had been done to implement them. Reaffirming the government's commitment to a democratic peace and the speedy election of the Constituent Assembly (again to be postponed!), it elaborated in greater detail the character of the economic and social reforms that the workers and peasants could expect. In particular, it now was prepared to concede the eight-hour day and the principle that the land should be divided amongst the peasants. It drew a rapid and intransigent response from the Kadets who, in their desperation to form a coalition just two months earlier, had agreed to much of the above.

Document 5.2 Kadet ultimatum to Kerensky, July 15, 1917

1 All members of the Government are to be responsible only to their conscience regardless of their party affiliations, and their actions and presence in the Cabinet are no reason for interference in the direction of state affairs by any kind of committee or and organisation.

2 In matters of internal policy, the Government is to limit itself to guarding the conquests of the Revolution, and not undertake measures that might lead to civil strife. All basic social reforms and all questions relating to the form of government are to be left absolutely to the Constituent Assembly.

3 In matters of war and peace, the Government is to be guided by the principles of complete union with the Allies.

4 Steps are to be taken to develop a strong army by restoring strict military discipline and putting a definite stop to interference by soldier committees in questions of tactics and strategy.

5 As a fundamental of internal administration, an end is to be made to the pluralism of government authority; order re-established in the country; a vigorous fight waged against anarchistic, anti-governmental and counter-revolutionary elements; and a stable local administration organised as soon as possible.

6 State courts are to be brought back to a position from which they might carry on their funtions properly. Prosecuting attorneys and judges are not to be interfered with by politicians.

7 Elections to the Constituent Assembly are to be conducted so that the people might express the true national will.

Source: W.G. Rosenberg, Liberals in the Russian Revolution: The Constitutional Democratic Party, 1917–1921 *(Princeton: Princeton University Press, 1974), p. 184*

The architect of Document 5.2, according to Rosenberg, was Paul Miliukov. Apparently ignoring the lessons of the April crisis and the disastrous June offensive, the Kadets reaffirmed their commitment to war to a victorious conclusion, albeit in Aesopean language ('complete union with the Allies'). This objective explains their demand in section 4 that the power of the soldiers' committees, in their eyes the main cause of the disintegration of the army, had to be severely curbed, if not destroyed. Moreover, their insistence on deferring all fundamental reforms until the Constituent Assembly convened put them at odds with the majority of workers and peasants whose impatience at the lack of tangible economic and social reform was growing rapidly.

Their refusal to enter a new coalition precipitated a crisis of authority which, in Rosenberg's opinion, fatally undermined the power of the Provisional Government **(Rosenberg 1974: 191)**. It was resolved, after a fashion, by Kerensky's own abrupt resignation on 21 July. The Mensheviks and SRs, still unwilling to assume sole governmental responsibility (the plea of Julius Martov, leader of the Left – Internationalist – wing of the Mensheviks for the socialists to do so went unheeded), felt compelled to grant Kerensky virtually a 'blank cheque' in the formation of a new government. He accepted the Kadets' demand that all Ministers were to act as individuals, not as party members; even the socialist Ministers were not responsible for their actions to the Soviet. Subsequently, the Second Coalition formed on 25 July.

However, its formation failed to resolve the growing political crisis. The ultimatum of the Kadets reflected the aspirations of other powerful forces for 'strong government': the Petrograd industrialists, who organised in the Society for the Economic Rehabilitation of Russia (most Moscow industrialists, with the notable exception of Guchkov, did not join it); the gentry; and sections of the old officer corps (e.g., the Union of Officers and the Union of St George Cavaliers, among others); and the Republican Centre, composed of representatives of finance and industry and the military. The old officers were particularly vociferous in demanding the restoration of discipline and order, both at the front and the rear. Their demands were put bluntly to Kerensky and Tereshchenko, Minister of Foreign Affairs, when they met with the High Command at the Stavka on 16 July. General A.I. Denikin, Commander-in-Chief of the Western Front, spoke for most of Russia's senior officers. He bitterly accused the Provisional Government of undermining discipline within the army, and hence its combat capability. He also presented his own measures to restore the fighting capacity of the army.

Document 5.3 Denikin's Proposals to Restore Military Discipline

The Army has been falling to pieces. Heroic measures are needed to place it on the correct rails:

1 The Provisional Government, which has not understood and estimated the noble and sincere impulse of the officers who had greeted the news of the Revolution with joy, and had sacrificed innumerable lives for their country, should recognise its mistakes and its guilt.

2 Petrograd, completely detached from the Army, and ignorant of its life and of the historical foundations of its existence, should cease to introduce military regulations. Full power must be given to the Supreme Commander-in-Chief, who should be responsible only to the Provisional Government.

3 Politics should be eliminated from the Army.

4 The *Declaration* [Document 12.2] must be abolished in its fundamentals. Commissars and Committees must be eliminated.

5 Authority must be restored to commanding officers. Discipline and the outward form of order and good conduct must be re-established.

6 Appointments to senior posts must be made . . . according to . . . military and administrative experience.

7 Special law-abiding units . . . must be placed at the disposal of commanding officers as a bulwark against mutiny.

8 Military Revolutionary Courts must be established and capital punishment introduced in the rear for the troops and civilians guilty of the same crimes.

Source: A.I. Denikin, Ocherki Russkoi Smuty, *I (Paris: Povolozky & Co., 1921), pp. 185–6*

As we have seen in Chapter 3, Denikin's claim that many officers had welcomed the February Revolution (if not the collapse of the monarchy) contained much truth. What they had not envisaged was the fact that it would fail to rekindle the patriotic fervour necessary to enable them to conduct the war to a victorious conclusion. Denikin's explanation of this unintended consequence of the Revolution had much in common with that of the Kadets, and others on the Right. The Provisional Government was culpable. By recognising the soldiers' committees and accepting the Declaration of Soldiers' Rights **(see Document 12.2)** it had left the rank and file of the army vulnerable to politicisation, and revolutionary propaganda, which had corroded its discipline and morale. The solution then was simple: do away with the committees and the Declaration and restore traditional forms of authority and discipline, if necessary by use of the death penalty which the February Revolution had abolished. However, Denikin's analysis was very one-sided: many committees, as Wildman has stressed, sought to help maintain discipline, often against the wishes of the rank and file whom they represented. The root of the problem, one the old officers could not comprehend, was that the soldiers *en masse* had no desire to sacrifice themselves for 'victory'. Their objective was peace (and land) **(Wildman 1992: 79–83)**. In these circumstances it was highly probable that any attempt to implement the measures proposed by Denikin would have precipitated mass opposition amongst the soldiers rather than restoring discipline in the Russian army.

Within the Provisional Government itself support for the restoration of order was strong, with Kerensky and Tsereteli even prepared to defend the death penalty. On 12 July Kerensky yielded to Kornilov's request that it be reintroduced at the front in order to maintain discipline (three days after the latter, on his own initiative, had ordered retreating troops on the South-western Front to be shot). A week later he promoted Kornilov to the post of Commander-in-Chief. He replaced the hapless Aleksei Brusilov, held to be culpable for the failure of the offensive (Kornilov had cautioned against it) and also seen by many officers as too conciliatory towards the soldiers' committees **(Munck 1987: 56–7)**.

The promotion of Kornilov, rather than a general with stronger liberal credentials, such as A.V. Cheremisov of the Eighth Army or A.I. Verkhovskii of the Moscow Military District, requires some explanation. His military record was not particularly distinguished, nor were his intellectual capacities for military leadership. Moreover, he too demanded strong measures to restore discipline within the army **(Rabinowitch 1976: 97–103)**. However, unlike Denikin, he seemingly was prepared to tolerate the soldiers' committees, assigning them a limited role in 'economic and other matters'. The telegram sent in his name to the conference at the Stavka on 16 July suggested so, although in fact it was composed by the Petrograd industrialist, V.S. Zavoiko, who had volunteered to serve as Kornilov's orderly **(Munck 1987: 62–3; White 1994: 137, 139)**. But there were reasons to doubt Kornilov's apparent moderation. On occasion he clearly had favoured a Draconian approach to unrest and indiscipline: during the April crisis, as we have seen in Chapter 4; and his independent reintroduction of the death penalty during the June offensive. Denikin's recollection that Kornilov wholeheartedly had supported his own proposals for restoring order in the army **(Document 5.3)** is confirmed by the following letter.

Document 5.4 Kornilov's Letter to Denikin, 27 July 1917

Dear Anton Ivanovich!

It was with sincere and deep satisfaction that I read your speech delivered at the conference held at Stavka on 16 July. I would sign such a report with both my hands. I respect you deeply for it and I admire your courage and your resolution. I firmly support the measures you have proposed for bringing the army and the rear to a normal state. I am insisting categorically that the Provisional Government pass a whole series of resolute measures and have grounds for being certain that much will be done in this direction in the nearest future. May I assure you of my deepest respect.

Source: R.P. Browder and A.F. Kerensky, The Russian Provisional Government, 1917: Documents, *II (Stanford: Stanford University Press, 1961), p. 991*

The most credible reason for Kornilov's appointment was political. In general terms, Kerensky chose him to appease the resurgent forces of the Right. More particularly, eager to entice the Kadets to enter the new coalition that he was seeking to construct, he hoped that the promotion of Kornilov would assuage them **(Munck 1987: 68–9)**. However, further doubts about Kornilov's moderation emerged immediately. The conditions that he sought to impose on the government before accepting the position of Commander-in-Chief well illustrate this point. The following ultimatum was addressed to Kerensky, as head of the Provisional Government.

Document 5.5 Kornilov's Ultimatum of 19 July

1 responsibility to my own conscience and to the people as a whole
2 no interference of any kind in my operational orders nor in my appointments to the Supreme Command
3 extension of the recently adopted measures to those parts of the rear where reserve units of the army are stationed
4 acceptance of the original demands I telegraphed to the commander-in-chief for the conference at headquarters on 16 July.

Source: J.L. Munck, The Kornilov Revolt: A Critical Examination of Sources and Research *(Aarhus: Aarhus University Press, 1987), p. 69*

The 'original demands' referred to in Document 5.5 included, among others, the restoration of the death penalty; a 'ruthless purge of the entire officers' corps';

increased powers for the officers; and a ban on all political activity within the army **(Browder and Kerensky, II, 1961: 998)**. They were overshadowed, however, by the first condition, which surprised even Denikin. Kornilov, it appeared, was seeking to remove himself from the control of the government which had appointed him. It is little wonder that an outraged Kerensky at once resolved to dismiss him. He was only persuaded against this course by the mediation of M.M. Filonenko, political commissar attached to the army, and pressure from B.V. Savinkov, Deputy War Minister. But portents of the tensions that were to bedevil the relationship between Kerensky and Kornilov were evident from the outset **(Munck 1987: 71–2)**.

Kornilov, however, remained insistent that firm action was necessary to restore discipline. On 3 August, when he travelled to Petrograd to report to the government on the military situation, he again urged that the death penalty be extended to the rear, to be applicable to civilians as well as soldiers. Kerensky admitted that he was sympathetic to Kornilov's demands, which 'set forth a whole series of measures, the greater part of which were quite acceptable, but formulated in such a way and supported by such arguments that the announcement of them would have led to quite opposite results'. His quite justifiable concern was that their adoption would have provoked the furious opposition of the socialist Ministers, and the Soviet. Accordingly, he assigned Savinkov and Filonenko the arguably impossible task of making them more palatable to 'public opinion'. Ironically, when Kornilov returned to the capital on August 10 to present this revised set of demands to the government, Savinkov's and Filonenko's interventions had rendered them even more extreme. They now proposed the extension of military discipline to the railways and war industries **(Kerensky 1972: 72, 95)**.

Kerensky was caught on the horns of a dilemma. Acceptance of these demands would rouse the ire of even the moderate socialists, the majority of whom remained firmly opposed to the reintroduction of the death penalty; the survival of the coalition would be threatened; and mass protest was all but inevitable. On the other hand, their rejection promised to estrange him from the resurgent forces of the Right. The latter's growing intransigence is reflected in the following resolution. It was adopted by the Conference of Public Figures, dominated by representatives of business and industry, the nobility, educated society and the old officers, which convened in Moscow between 8 and 10 August.

Document 5.6 Resolution of the Conference of Public Figures

The time has come openly to admit that the country . . . is on the verge of ruin. The government, if it realises its duty, must acknowledge that it has led the state on the wrong road, which must be abandoned at once for the sake of saving the country and freedom. The government must immediately and decisively sever its ties with the Utopians who have fatally influenced its actions. Let discipline be restored in the army, and power be returned to the commanding officers; let the understanding of the national interests of Russia be reborn and the trust of the Allies in her valour; let the central government, united and strong, put an end to the system of irresponsible collegiate organs in state administration; let the demands of the separate nationalities be channelled within legal and just bounds, which do not threaten the destruction of national unity; let it be left to the Constituent Assembly to determine the basic principles of the Russian state and implement the desired social reforms . . . . Only a government which recognises these national tasks as standing above party can prevent the country collapsing into ruin and with a firm hand lead it along the path of salvation. The only such government is one that decisively cuts itself free of all traces of dependence on committees, soviets and other similar organisations.

Source: Revoliutsionnoe dvizhenie v Rossii v avguste 1917g. Razgrom kornilovskogo miatezha *(Moscow: Izdatel'stvo akademii nauk SSSR, 1959), pp. 361–2*

The desire of the Right for the restoration of order and discipline, and the maintenance of the integrity of the Russian Empire challenged by increasing demands for national autonomy **(see Chapter 11)**, is clearly stated in Document 5.6. Equally striking is its impatience, evident in the last sentence, with Dual Power, which it saw as the chief source of Russia's 'ruin'. The problem, of course, was how to dismantle this system as the Soviet would not willingly surrender the power that it had claimed in March to supervise the actions of the Provisional Government. Kornilov himself appears to have grasped this nettle already. On 7 August he had ordered the Caucasian Native Division (the 'Savage Division') to be posted to the Nevel'-Novsokol'niki-Luki area, on a railway junction equidistant from Petrograd and Moscow **(Munck 1987: 85, 331)**. Kerensky's unwillingness to implement the measures proposed by Filonenko and Savinkov on 10 August prompted him to take further action. On 12 August, on his own authority, he despatched additional units to reinforce the 'Savage Division', ostensibly to strengthen the Northern Front. On being challenged by his Chief of Staff, General A.S. Lukomskii, as to the purpose of these troop movements, Kornilov revealed his true intentions.

Document 5.7 Lukomskii's Account

As you know, all our intelligence reports agree that the Bolsheviks will attempt another insurrection in Petrograd at the end of the month . . . on 28–9 August . . . . As German agents the Bolsheviks . . . will do everything to carry out a *coup* and take power into their own hands . . . I am convinced that the slugs in the Provisional Government will be swept away, or if, miraculously . . . remain in power the leaders of the Bolsheviks and the Soviet . . . will remain unpunished.

It is time to put an end to this. It is time to hang the German henchmen and spies led by Lenin, and to disperse the Soviet of workers and soldiers, yes break it up so that it can never be assembled again. You are right. I am moving the Cavalry Corps chiefly to bring it closer to Petrograd, to deal with the traitors as they deserve if a Bolshevik uprising occurs.

I wish to put General Krymov in charge of this operation. I am convinced that he will not think twice to hang all the members of the Soviet of Workers' and Soldiers' Deputies if necessary.

I have no intention to act against the Provisional Government. I hope I will succeed at the last moment to come to an agreement with it. But one must not say anything to anyone in advance for Kerensky, and more so Chernov, will not agree and will wreck the operation. If I do not succeed in reaching an agreement with Kerensky and Savinkov, then it is possible that it will be necessary to strike at the Bolsheviks without their approval. But subsequently they will be grateful to me and it will be possible to create the strong government Russia needs, free of all possible traitors.

I seek and desire nothing for myself. I only want to save Russia and I will obey unconditionally a purified and strengthened Provisional Government.

Source: A.S. Lukomskii, Vospominaniia generala A.S. Lukomskago, *volume 1 (Berlin: Otto Kirkhner, 1922), pp. 228–9*

Document 5.7 reveals Kornilov's grave doubts about the resolve of the Kerensky, and his fellow 'slugs', to take the measures that he felt necessary to save Russia from ruin and defeat. He too concluded, as the Conference of Public Figures had, that Dual Power had to be eliminated. The destruction of the Soviet, the seedbed of alleged 'German agents' and traitors, was to be carried out under the guise of defending the government from an imminent Bolshevik insurrection, one, so the evidence suggests, more in the mind of Kornilov than of the Bolsheviks themselves. The officers' unions, however, were preparing provocateurs to whip up unrest in the capital in order to justify military repression, should the Bolsheviks remain passive. More tellingly, Document 5.7 does confirm that Kornilov had set his plans in motion without the consent, or even knowledge, of the Provisional Government. But whether this action amounts to unequivocal proof of a conspiracy against the government remains a moot point, as it is clear that Kornilov still held the lingering hope of acting with, rather than against, it **(Munck 1987: 88, 101)**.

By common consent the critical turning point in the whole affair was the State Conference which convened in Moscow between 12 and 15 August. Composed along corporatist lines, with 'representatives of political, public, democratic, nation-alities, industrial and cooperative organisations, leaders of organs of the democracy, and members of the four State Dumas' present **(Browder and Kerensky, III, 1961: 1451)**, it failed to bridge the rapidly growing fissure in Russian society. On the contrary, it sharply revealed the gulf between the Soviet and the Right – and the resurgent strength of the Bolsheviks who, despite the opposition of the Moscow Soviet, successfully called an all-city strike to mark its opening. Kerensky's performance was at best highly oratorical, at worst hysterical, according to eye-witnesses such as Harold Williams **(Zohrab 1991: 153)**. That, in combination with his frantic appeals that Kornilov refrain from presenting any political demands at the Conference, eroded whatever residual faith Kornilov had in Kerensky's will to restore order within Russia **(Munck 1987: 99–100)**. He now was resolved to press on with measures to create a strong government, even without the consent of the Provisional Government. However, rapidly growing industrial unrest and the German capture of Riga on 20 August prompted Kerensky to dispatch Savinkov to the Stavka on 23 August, to inform a rather surprised Kornilov that he was now prepared to enact his proposals of 10 August. Loyal troops were to be sent to Petrograd to put down the inevitable demonstrations that would follow their enactment, though Savinkov vainly added that neither General Krymov nor the 'Savage Division' were to be included among them. A conspiracy against the government, so it seemed, had been averted, and the troop movements made earlier by Kornilov authorised, albeit *post facto*.

But before the denouement of the affair the waters were to be muddied by the intervention of V.N. L'vov, former Procurator of the Holy Synod. On 24 August he presented himself at the Stavka as a plenipotentiary from Kerensky. His mission, he claimed, was to ascertain Kornilov's response to the three strategies to strengthen the government which he alleged had been proposed by Kerensky: a dictatorship under Kerensky; an authoritarian government, in which Kornilov would be prominent; or a military dictatorship under Kornilov. On his return to Petrograd on 26 August, as less than three weeks later he told the Special Commission investigating the affair, he informed Kerensky of Kornilov's preference.

Document 5.8 V.N. L'vov's Testimony

My second meeting with Kornilov took place on the morning of 25 August . . . . First of all, Kornilov outlined the current situation: Riga has been captured, Rumania may be lost at any minute, the mood of the army is dismal . . . . Kornilov added: 'A Bolshevik rising is expected between August 27 and September 1. Their plan is to overthrow the government, install themselves in its place and conclude immediately a separate peace with Germany . . . . The government has absolutely no forces with which to stave off this danger. In Petrograd the troops are in a state of total confusion: some are for the Bolsheviks, others for the Soviet, yet others for the government, still others for no one certain. If there is a Bolshevik rising . . . the Provisional Government, without doubt, will collapse. Don't think that I am speaking for myself', Kornilov continued, 'but if the country is to be saved I see no other solution than to transfer all power, civil as well as military, into the hands of the Supreme Commander-in-Chief . . . . Who will be appointed chairman of the Provisional Government does not matter.' Then Kornilov added that he proposed that Kornilov be given the post of Minister of Justice, and Savinkov that of Minister of War. Unable to protect their lives anywhere else, he proposed that Kerensky and Savinkov come to the Stavka where he would take personal responsibility for their safety.

Source: Revoliutsionnoe dvizhenie v Rossii v avguste 1917g.: Razgrom kornilovskogo miatezha *(Moscow: Izdatel'stvo akademii nauk SSSR, 1959), pp. 427–8*

Although L'vov's claim that the proposals which he had laid before Kornilov came from Kerensky was spurious in itself, that does not invalidate his account of the meeting. As Lukomskii recalled, on the following morning Kornilov told him that he had responded positively to the idea of a military dictatorship. No doubt L'vov's report at the very least confused Kerensky, as Savinkov had only just informed him of the wholly satisfactory outcome of his negotiations with Kornilov. Kerensky may also have been alarmed at the thought of a *coup* directed against him. He sought to confirm that L'vov's report was accurate through 'conversing' directly with Kornilov by teleprinter on the evening of 26 August. In L'vov's absence Kerensky impersonated him.

Document 5.9 Conversation between Kerensky and Kornilov over Hughes Apparatus

Kerensky: Good day, General. V.N. L'vov and Kerensky at the apparatus. We beg you to confirm the statement that Kerensky is to act according to the communication made to him by V.N.

Kornilov: Good day, Alexander Feodorovich; good day, V.N. Confirming again the description I gave V.N. of the present situation of the country and the army as it appears to me. I declare again that the events of the past days and of those I see coming imperatively demand a definite decision in the shortest possible time.

Kerensky: I, V.N., ask you whether it is necessary to act on that definite
[as L'vov] decision which you asked me to communicate privately to Kerensky, as he is hesitating to give his full confidence without your personal confirmation.

Kornilov: Yes, I confirm that I asked you to convey to Aleksander Feodorovich my urgent demand that he should come to Mogilev [location of headquarters].

Kerensky: I, Alexander Feodorovich, understand your answer as confirmation of the words conveyed to me by V.N. To do that today and start from here is impossible. I hope to start tomorrow. Is it necessary for Savinkov to go?

Kornilov: I beg urgently that Boris Viktorovich shall come with you. Everything I said to V.N. refers in equal degree to Savinkov. I beg you earnestly not to put off your departure later than tomorrow. Believe me, only my recognition of the responsibility of the moment urges me to persist in my request.

Kerensky: Shall we come only in case of an outbreak, of which there are
              rumours, or in any case?
Kornilov: In any case.
Kerensky: Good day. Soon we shall see each other.
Kornilov: Good day.

*Source: H. Asher, 'The Kornilov Affair: A Reinterpretation', Russian Review,
XXIX, 2 (1970), p. 296*

The most striking feature of Document 5.9, as historians of the affair have repeatedly remarked, is its lack of precision. Kerensky failed to ask Kornilov precisely what he had communicated to L'vov. The only item of L'vov's account that Kornilov confirmed was his request that Kerensky and Savinkov flee to the Stavka. Afraid that he would be deposed, Kerensky arguably exploited the situation to remove Kornilov as Commander-in-Chief and to seek emergency powers to deal with the crisis. However, in face of Lukomskii's refusal to assume his position, Kornilov resumed his duties. On 27 August, in open defiance of the government, he ordered the advance on Petrograd to continue. Ironically, Kerensky had no choice but to call on the Soviet that he so recently had wished to curb for assistance in defending the capital. The CEC, still dominated by the Mensheviks and SRs, called upon the mass of workers and soldiers in the capital to defend the Revolution, as did even the most radical Bolsheviks who for a time found themselves allied with the moderate socialists. The railway workers halted or diverted all trains into Petrograd, while Soviet propagandists convinced the approaching troops that they had become the dupes of a right-wing conspiracy. On the other hand, splits among the officer corps and the industrialists, substantial sections of whom refused to support a military *coup*, lessened its prospects of success from the outset. Moreover, it is doubtful whether any of the pro-Kornilovite forces, with the exception of the Union of the Cossacks, could mobilise much mass support **(White 1994: 147–8)**. In the circumstances, its failure is unsurprising.

The whole affair has been, and remains, highly controversial. Three different interpretations of it are presented in Document 5.10 below: that of Kerensky himself, who alleges that it was a conspiracy against the goverment; that of Harold Williams, the New Zealand born correspondent of the *Daily Chronicle* in Russia in 1917, who implies that Kerensky reneged on his agreement with Kornilov to deploy military force to restore order in the country; and that of Sir George Buchanan, British Ambassador to Russia in 1917, who claims that it was the product of a misunderstanding between Kerensky and Kornilov, largely precipitated by the meddling of L'vov.

Document 5.10 Judgments

a) Conspiracy

There was nothing sudden in the action of the people who prepared the conspiracy of the commander-in-chief against the government which had entrusted the army into his hands in the most critical months of the War. On the contrary, the conspiracy developed slowly, systematically, with cool calculation of all the factors involved affecting its possible success or failure. Nor was the motive of conspiracy, so far as some of its backers were concerned, one of unselfish patriotism. On the contrary, the motive was extremely selfish – to be sure, not one of personal but of class selfishness. To avoid misunderstanding I want to append here one qualification: in describing the motives of criminal activity of the initiators and original leaders of the conspiracy I do not attribute these selfish class motives to General Korniloff and his close military supporters, all of whom were brave Russian patriots, who were drawn into the conspiracy after the preparatory work had been completed.

Source: A.F. Kerensky, The Catastrophe *(Millwood: Kraus Reprint, 1977), pp. 288–9*

b) Kerensky's 'Betrayal' of Kornilov

Kerensky, who had negotiated with Kornilov for the despatch of trustworthy troops to the capital for the protection of the Government and the maintenance of authority, suddenly raised a cry of panic against Kornilov, and flung himself on the Soviet for support . . . . The cavalry force that was on its way to Petrograd, in accordance with the agreement between Kerensky and Kornilov, was stopped. Kerensky dismissed Kornilov from the post of Commander-in-Chief and ordered his arrest. Kornilov was stung to open revolt, and issued a proclamation appealing for support . . . the outcry raised by Kerensky was taken up by all the socialist agitators everywhere. Attempts to secure a compromise between Kerensky and Kornilov failed, and in the end Kornilov and the other officers implicated were arrested, treated with contumely by the soldiers and imprisoned at Bykhov.

Source: I. Zohrab, 'The Socialist Revolutionary Party, Kerensky and the Kornilov Affair: From the Unpublished Papers of Harold W. Williams', New Zealand Slavonic Journal *(1991), pp. 153–4*

c) Misunderstanding

Although all my sympathies were with Korniloff, I had always done my best to discourage the idea of a military *coup d'état*, as Russia's best hope of salvation lay in a close co-operation between him and Kerensky. Korniloff, who was not a reactionary, honestly believed that Lvoff [sic] had been sent by Kerensky to ascertain his views on the political situation; and he expressed them with his usual frankness, without giving them the form of an ultimatum. The role played by Lvoff in the affair is quite impossible to explain. He misrepresented Kerensky to Korniloff and Korniloff to Kerensky; but whether he was a knave or a fool I cannot say. He was in any case an arch mischief-maker. It was only after being called on by Kerensky to resign his command that Korniloff decided to act, and in so doing he was prompted solely by patriotic motives. But while he personally would have been ready to work with Kerensky, there were men behind him who had for weeks past been plotting to overthrow the Government and who were bent on using him as their instrument and on forcing his hand.

There were so many persons in the secret of this counter-revolutionary movement that it was a secret no longer. Kerensky knew it, so that when Lvoff brought him what purported – though quite incorrectly – to be an ultimatum from Korniloff, he was already suspicious of and predisposed against him. Though Kerensky undoubtedly regarded him as a dangerous rival, who if he once got control of the army might use it against the Government, I do not believe that he purposely laid a trap for Korniloff in order to get him out of the way. But, like the latter, he had evil counsellors behind him who, for personal or party reasons, encouraged him to remove the commander-on-chief.

Source: G. Buchanan, My Mission to Russia, *II (New York: Arno Reprint, 1977), pp. 185–6*

What definitive conclusions, if any, can be drawn from the above? It is clear that Kornilov had begun to mobilise forces to crush the Soviet before Kerensky, as head of the Provisional Government, had sanctioned such action. It is arguable that Kornilov, if not his 'backers', sought to act in accord with Kerensky and the government. It is possible that Kerensky took advantage of L'vov's 'mischief' to go back on the agreement to restore order that he had arrived at with Kornilov lest he find himself removed from power **(Asher 1970: 299–300; Munck 1987: 138–42)**. No doubt the debate will continue. For the Bolsheviks, and later Soviet historiography, however, the matter was clear-cut, as the cartoon opposite (drawn retrospectively, in 1935, by the famous political satirist and poster artist, Viktor Deni) demonstrates. The whole affair was a counter-revolutionary conspiracy, with Kerensky no more than the puppet of the capitalists.

Document 5.11 An Independent Premier

[See illustration on p. 79]

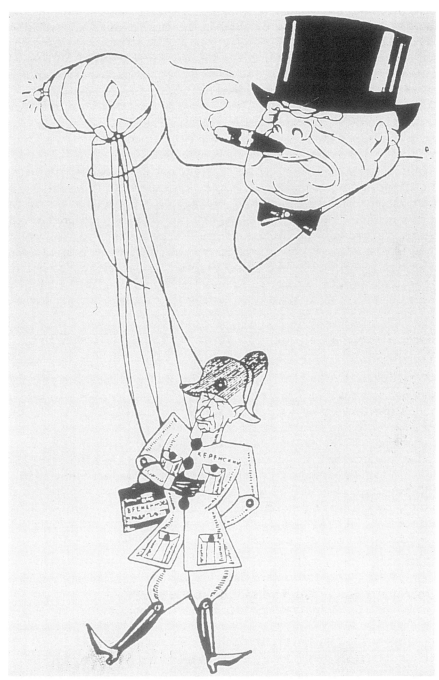

Source: A. Nenarokov, An Illustrated History of the Great October Socialist Revolution *(Moscow: Progress, 1987), p. 174*

6 | The October Revolution

The main beneficiaries of the Kornilov affair were the Bolsheviks. Their warnings against the threat of counter-revolution appeared to have been vindicated. Bolshevik majorities in the Petrograd Soviet on 31 August and the Moscow Soviet on 5 September testified to their rapidly growing support. At the very beginning of September, from his self-imposed exile in Finland, Lenin also resurrected the political strategy that he had persuaded the Party to abandon in the wake of the July Days, namely, 'All Power to the Soviets!' **(see Document 4.8)**. More curiously, he also held out the prospect of the peaceful establishment of soviet power, provided the Mensheviks and SRs steeled themselves to form a government responsible to the Soviets.

Document 6.1 On Compromises

The Russian Revolution is experiencing so abrupt and original a turn that we, as a party, may offer a voluntary compromise – true, not to our direct and main class enemy, the bourgeoisie, but to our nearest adversaries, the 'ruling' *petty-bourgeois* democratic parties, the Socialist-Revolutionaries and Mensheviks.

The compromise on our part is our return to the pre-July demand of all power to the Soviets and a government of SRs and Mensheviks responsible to the Soviets.

Now, and only now, perhaps *during only a few days* or a week or two, such a government could be set up and consolidated in a perfectly peaceful way. In all probability it could secure the peaceful *advance* of the whole Russian revolution, and provide exceptionally good chances for great strides in the world movement towards peace and the victory of socialism.

In my opinion, the Bolsheviks . . . may and should consent to this compromise only for the sake of the revolution's peaceful development – an opportunity that is *extremely* rare in history and *extremely* valuable, an opportunity that only occurs once in a while.

The compromise would amount to the following: the Bolsheviks, without making any claim to participate in the government (which is impossible for the internationalists unless a dictatorship of the proletariat and poor peasants has been realised), would refrain from demanding the immediate transfer of power to the proletariat and poor peasants and from employing revolutionary methods of fighting for this demand. A condition that is self-evident and not new to the SRs and Mensheviks would be complete freedom of propaganda and the convocation of the Constituent Assembly without further delays or even at an earlier date.

The Bolsheviks would gain the opportunity of quite freely advocating their views and of trying to win influence in the Soviets under a really complete democracy . . . . For the sake of such a possibility at such a difficult time, it would be worth compromising with the present majority in the Soviets. We have nothing to fear from real democracy, for reality is on our side, and even the course of development of trends within the SR and Menshevik parties, which are hostile to us, proves us right.

Source: V.I. Lenin, Collected Works, *25 (Moscow: Progress, 1964–5), pp. 306–8*

Nikolai Sukhanov dismissed Document 6.1 as a cynical ploy on Lenin's part. Lenin, confident of Bolshevik majorities in the Soviets, now saw 'compromise' as a viable and safe path to power, after which the Mensheviks and SRs could be dispensed with. Such a conclusion arguably underestimates Lenin's uncertainty in early September about how the Revolution would develop. When he composed this appeal he was not fully aware of the sweeping Bolshevik victories in the Petrograd and Moscow Soviets. Possibly he hoped that growing radical pressure within the moderate socialist parties would compel the Menshevik and SR leaderships at last to agree to the formation of a Soviet government. This period of 'wavering', as Robert Service has described it, proved to be short-lived. When the continued reluctance of the moderate socialists to assume power became undeniable Lenin abruptly jettisoned all attempts at conciliation. In a letter to the Central Committee begun on 12 September he insisted that the Bolshevik Party must prepare immediately to seize power.

Document 6.2 The Bolsheviks Must Assume State Power

The Bolsheviks, having obtained a majority in the Soviets of Workers' and Soldiers' Deputies of both capitals, can and *must* take state power into their own hands.

They can because the active majority of revolutionary elements in the two chief cities is large enough to carry the people with it, to overcome the opponent's resistance, to smash him, and to gain and retain power. For the Bolsheviks, by immediately proposing a democratic peace, by immediately giving the land to the peasants and by re-establishing the democratic institutions and liberties which have been mangled and shattered by Kerensky, will form a government which *nobody* will be able to overthrow. . . .

The majority of the people are *on our side* . . . . The majority gained in the Soviets of the metropolitan cities *resulted* from the people coming over *to our side*. The wavering of the Socialist-Revolutionaries and Mensheviks and the increase in the number of internationalists within their ranks prove the same thing.

The Democratic Conference represents not a majority of the revolutionary people, but *only the compromising upper strata of the petty bourgeoisie* . . . .

Why must the Bolsheviks assume power *at this very moment?*

Because the impending surrender of Petrograd will make our chances a hundred times less favourable.

Nor can we 'wait' for the Constituent Assembly, for by surrendering Petrograd Kerensky and co. *can* always *frustrate* its convocation. Our party alone, on taking power, can secure the Constituent Assembly's convocation; it will then accuse the other parties of procrastination and will be able to substantiate its accusations.

The people are tired of the waverings of the Mensheviks and Social Revolutionaries. It is only our victory in the metropolitan cities that will carry the peasants with us.

It would be naive to wait for a 'formal' majority for the Bolsheviks. No revolution ever waits for *that* . . . . It is the wretched waverings of the Democratic Conference that are bound to exhaust the patience of the workers of Petrograd and Moscow. History will not forgive us if we do not assume power now.

Source: V.I. Lenin, Collected Works, *26 (Moscow: Progress, 1964–5), pp. 19–21*

Lenin justified his call for revolution two days later, in another letter to the CC, 'Marxism and Insurrection'. He re-emphasised that now, unlike July, the Bolsheviks had majorities in both Petrograd and Moscow. Moreover, after the Kornilov revolt, both the army and the provinces had become radicalised and would not oppose a revolution in Petrograd **(Lenin, 26, 1964–5: 23–4)**. Lenin's mind was made up. The CC, however, remained unconvinced and refused to publish his calls for insurrection. While the majority of workers, peasants and soldiers may have been in favour of a Soviet government drawn from all the socialist parties, the CC was much less confident than Lenin that provincial Russia would support a Bolshevik *coup*. Rejecting Lenin's promptings it chose instead to participate in 'the wretched waverings of the Democratic Conference'.

The Democratic Conference had been summoned on the initiative of the Soviet CEC in order to determine how Russia should be governed before the Constituent Assembly convened. Dominated by representatives of the moderate socialist parties, it assembled on 14 September. The Bolshevik CC agreed that the Party should participate. Its objective was to persuade the Conference to create a government responsible to the Soviets. On 19 September the Conference voted on the critical question: whether the next Provisional Government should be a broad, rather than an all-socialist, coalition or not.

Document 6.3 The Democratic Conference and the Question of Coalition

On 19 September the matter came to the vote. As the Menshevik fraction had a week ago, the general question – 'Is a coalition necessary?' – was voted upon first. *For* a coalition – 766 votes; *against* – 688 votes; abstentions – 38.

Accordingly, coalition was carried. An amendment was put to the vote: the Kadets must be excluded from the coalition. *For* the amendment 595 votes, *Against* – 483; abstentions – 72. And so the amendment *was adopted*.

The amended resolution as a whole was put to the vote. *For* it – 180 votes; *against* – 813; abstentions – 80. There was noisy rejoicing among the Bolsheviks, confusion among the leaders, stormy arguments in different parts of the hall . . . . That night the various sections and factions held meetings . . . . Everyone felt that the heart of the matter did not lie in the vagaries of the voting, nor in the fact that the presidium had raised the question unsuccessfully . . . . The point was that the Conference did not possess a common will . . . . And while realising this, nevertheless everyone sought a form of words which could paper over the differences, unite the majority of the Conference and map some way out of the impasse.

Source: V.S. Voitinskii, 1917–i. God pobed i porazhenii *(Benson, Vt: Chalidze, 1990), pp. 266–7*

Voitinskii, himself a moderate Menshevik, was a staunch advocate of a broad coalition. At first sight, it might appear that the proponents of coalition had been victorious. Yet if there was to be a viable coalition the only non-socialist partners available were the Kadets, whom the Conference in fact had voted to exclude. Increasing numbers of Mensheviks and SRs, it appears, now were prepared to contemplate government without the Kadets. Having failed to resolve the question of coalition to anyone's satisfaction, the next day the Conference established a Provisional Council of the Republic, overwhelmingly but not exclusively socialist in composition. The new Coalition Government being formed independently by Kerensky was to be answerable for its actions to this 'Pre-Parliament'. After a period of heated debate the Bolsheviks eventually decided to boycott it.

Lenin's prognosis that the Democratic Conference would fail to take any decisive action was vindicated, though even he must have been surprised at the utter confusion into which it fell. In the circumstances it is unsurprising that his repeated and vehement calls for insurrection began to evoke a positive response within the Party. At the same time he also sought to convince it on other, more theoretical, grounds why the time was ripe for socialist revolution in Russia.

Document 6.4 Lenin's Defence of the Viability of Socialist Revolution in Russia

The chief difficulty facing the proletarian revolution is the establishment on a country-wide scale of the most precise and most conscientious accounting and control, of *workers' control* of the production and distribution of goods.

Without the Soviets, this task would be impracticable, at least in Russia. The Soviets *indicate* to the proletariat the organisational work which *can* solve this historically important problem.

This brings us to another aspect of the question of the state apparatus. In addition to the chiefly 'oppressive' apparatus – the standing army, the police and the bureaucracy – the modern state possesses an apparatus which has extremely close connections with the banks and syndicates, an apparatus which performs an enormous amount of accounting and registration work, if it may be expressed in this way. This apparatus must not . . . be smashed. It must be wrested from the control of the capitalists; the capitalists and the wires they pull must be *cut off, lopped off, chopped away from* this apparatus: it must be *subordinated* to the proletarian Soviets; it must be expanded, made more comprehensive and nation-wide. And this *can* be done by utilising the achievements already made by large-scale capitalism (in the same way as the proletarian revolution can, in general, reach its goal only by utilising these achievements).

Capitalism has created an accounting *apparatus* in the shape of the banks, syndicates, postal service, consumers' societies, and office employees' unions. *Without big banks socialism would be impossible.*

The big banks *are* the 'state apparatus' which we *need* to bring about socialism, and which we *take ready-made* from capitalism; our task here is merely to *lop off* what *capitalistically mutilates* this excellent apparatus, to make it *even bigger*, even more democratic, even more comprehensive. Quantity will be transformed into quality. A single State Bank, the biggest of the big, with branches in every rural district, in every factory, will constitute as much as nine-tenths of the *socialist* apparatus. This will be country-wide *book-keeping*, country-wide *accounting* of the production and distribution of goods, this will be, so to speak, something in the nature of the *skeleton* of socialist society.

Source: V.I. Lenin, Collected Works, *26 (Moscow: Progress, 1964–5), pp. 104–6*

The argument that Lenin is putting forward in Document 6.4 is, at first sight, difficult to fathom. Speaking in a language familiar to Marxists, he in fact was belatedly responding to the criticisms levelled against him when he first promulgated his *April Theses* **(Document 4.3)**. Emphasising the rapid growth of the large banks and syndicates during the war (he referred to the coal, metal and sugar industries), Lenin now insisted that capitalism had developed to sufficiently high levels within Russia to permit socialist revolution. It had created the centralised administrative structures which, according to Marxist theory, the construction of a planned socialist economy demanded.

Having explained to his own satisfaction at least why the economic and political preconditions for socialist revolution had matured, his task now was to persuade his comrades to act. Conscious that the tide was flowing in his direction after the shambles of the Democratic Conference and buoyed by the conversion of leading Party organisations in Petrograd and Moscow to his point of view he returned, still in heavy disguise, to the capital on 7 October. He attended the historic meeting of the Central Committee on 10 October which passed, against the dissenting voices of Kamenev and Zinoviev, a resolution in favour of insurrection.

Document 6.5 On an Armed Uprising

The CC recognises that both the international situation of the Russian Revolution (the mutiny in the German navy, an extreme sign of the growth throughout Europe of world socialist revolution, together with the threat of peace among the imperialists aimed at smothering the Revolution in Russia), and the military situation (the decision unquestionably made by the Russian bourgeoise and Kerensky and Co. to surrender Petrograd to the Germans) and the acquisition by the proletarian party of a majority in the Soviets – all this taken together with the peasant revolt and the shift in popular confidence towards our party (the Moscow elections) and, finally, the obvious preparations for a second Kornilov affair (the withdrawal of troops from Petrograd, the transfer of cossacks to Petrograd, the surrounding of Minsk by cossacks, etc.) – all this places an armed rising on the agenda.

Recognising therefore that an armed rising is inevitable and that the time for it has matured, the Central Committee orders all party organisations to follow this path and to discuss and resolve all practical questions (the Congress of Soviets of the northern region, the withdrawal of troops from Petrograd, the reaction of our people in Moscow and Minsk, etc.) from this point of view.

Source: Revoliutsionnoe dvizhenie v Rossii nakanune Oktiabr'skogo vooruzhennogo vosstaniia (1–24 oktiab'ria 1917g.) *(Moscow: Izdatel'stvo akademii nauk SSSR, 1962), p. 67*

A subsequent meeting of the CC on 16 October, with Lenin again present, reaffirmed the decision taken on 10 October.

Document 6.6 On the Armed Insurrection

The meeting fully welcomes and wholly supports the CC resolution. It calls on all organisations and all workers and soldiers to make thorough and most intensive preparations for an armed insurrection and to support the Centre created for this end and expresses its full confidence that the CC and the Soviet will indicate at the proper time the favourable moment and the appropriate methods of attack.

Source: Revoliutsionnoe dvizhenie v Rossii nakanune Oktiabr'skogo vooruzhennogo vosstaniia (1–24 oktiab'ria 1917g.) *(Moscow: Izdatel'stvo akademii nauk SSSR, 1962), p. 94*

Documents 6.5 and 6.6 reveal that Lenin, as he had in April, again had succeeded in 're-arming' the Party, on this occasion in favour of insurrection. But Lenin's victory was not unqualified. Both resolutions were hesitant and vague, failing to specify either a date for the projected insurrection or the precise methods by which it was to be carried out. Their hesitancy reflected continuing doubts among even radical party activists whether adequate preparations had been made to ensure that the workers and soldiers in Petrograd would participate in an immediate rising. Reports from many districts of the capital heard at the session of the Petersburg Committee on 15 October and at the 16 October meeting of the CC confirmed these doubts. Provincial Russia too, it was argued, remained unprepared for a *coup* against the Provisional Government **(Rabinowitch 1976: 211–21)**. Moreover, splits within the Party hierarchy also deterred the Bolsheviks from striking against the Provisional Government at once. Leon Trotsky spoke for those who preferred to delay any move against the government until the Second Congress of Soviets convened on 20 October (in fact, it was postponed until 25 October). Anticipating that it would have a Bolshevik majority he reckoned that it would legitimate whatever actions had to be taken to transfer power to a Bolshevik-dominated Soviet government. On the right of the Party, voices of moderation cautioned against insurrection. They feared that it would fail and open the door to counter-revolution. The most famous moderates, or 'strike-breakers' as Lenin sarcastically dubbed them, were Lev Kamenev and Grigorii Zinoviev. They were far from being the cowardly mavericks or traitors to the Revolution as subsequent Soviet historiography was to depict them. In fact, they expressed the reservations of numerous party organisations, including the powerful Moscow City Committee, and, according to I. Zhukov, a member of the Petersburg Committee, of a majority of rank-and-file members in the capital **(Gusev 1993: 143)**.

Document 6.7 Kamenev's and Zinoviev's Opposition to Insurrection

We are deeply convinced that to proclaim an armed insurrection now is to put at risk not only the fate of our party but also the fate of the Russian and the international revolution.

As a result of the massive growth in our party's influence in the towns and especially in the army, a position has been reached at the present moment that it is becoming ever more impossible for the bourgeoisie to block the Constituent Assembly.

Our party's chances in the elections to the Constituent Assembly are excellent . . . . The influence of Bolshevism is growing. Whole strata of the working population are only beginning to be captured by it. With the right tactics, we can get a third of the seats in the Constituent Assembly, or even more. The position of the petty-bourgeois parties . . . will not be exactly the same as it is now. Above all, their slogan 'for land, for freedom, wait for the Constituent Assembly' no longer is appropriate, while the intensification of need and hunger and the peasant movement will put ever greater pressure on them and force them to seek an alliance with the proletarian party against the landowners and capitalists represented by the Kadet Party.

The Constituent Assembly too can only rely on the Soviets in its revolutionary work. The Constituent Assembly plus the Soviets – here is that mixed type of state institution that we are going towards. Based on this, our Party's policy gets a tremendous chance of real victory.

In Russia the majority of workers and a considerable part of the soldiers are for us. But all the rest are questionable . . . [and] the majority of peasants will vote for the SRs . . . . The bulk of the soldiers support us not behind the slogan of war but for the slogan of peace. This factor is extremely important . . . . If we, having seized power now on our own, find it necessary (as a result of the whole world situation) to conduct a revolutionary war, the bulk of the soldiers will rapidly desert us.

And now we come to the second assertion, that the majority of the international proletariat as it were now supports us. This, unfortunately, is not the case. The mutiny in the German fleet is a symptom of enormous significance. The portents of a serious movement exist in Italy. But it remains a very long way from this to any active support of a proletarian revolution in Russia which declares war against the entire bourgeois world. To overestimate our strength is extremely dangerous.

What are our prospects in the near future? . . . we can and must confine ourselves now to a defensive position. The Provisional Government is often powerless to carry out its counter-revolutionary intentions . . . . The soldiers and workers have sufficient strength to prevent such moves . . . . The Provisional Government lacks the power to fix the Constituent Assembly elections . . . . In the Constituent Assembly, we will be so strong as an opposition party that, with universal suffrage in the country, our opponents will be forced to make concessions to us at every step. Or we will construct a ruling bloc together with the Left SRs, the non-party peasants and others which will basically have to carry out our programme. That is our opinion.

But anyone who wants to do more than just talk about a rising is also obliged to evaluate its chances of success soberly . . . . The strength of the opposition is greater than it seems. Petrograd is the deciding factor and in Petrograd the enemies of the Proletarian Party have amassed considerable forces: 5 000 military cadets, excellently armed, organised, keen . . . and able to fight, then the headquarters staff, the shock troops, the cossacks, a considerable section of the garrison, and a very significant amount of artillery deployed in a fan around Piter.

The strength of the Proletarian Party, of course, is very considerable. But the decisive question is whether the mood exists among the workers and soldiers of the capital that they themselves see salvation only in a street battle . . . . This mood does not exist. The advocates of action themselves declare that the mood among the mass of workers and soldiers in no way is reminiscent of attitudes before 3 July.

The Party of the Proletariat will grow . . . . And there is only one means whereby its success can be disrupted: just by taking the initiative for a rising in the present circumstances and by that putting the proletariat at the mercy of all the forces of a united counter-revolution, supported by *petty-bourgeois* democracy.

Source: *K.V. Gusev, 'V zashchite "shtreikbrekherov revoliutsii"'*, Otechestvennaia istoriia *(2), 1993, pp. 145–8*

Contrary to Lenin's allegation, the full text of this letter was not published in *Novaia zhizn'* (*New Life*), the paper of the Social Democrat Internationalists. However, a brief statement by Kamenev, expressing his and Zinoviev's opposition to insurrection, did appear in it on 18 October. Many of their doubts were borne out. The international revolution, the imminence of which Lenin had introduced in support of insurrection in Russia, proved to be chimerical. The elections to the Constituent Assembly confirmed that the Bolsheviks remained a minority in the countryside – and, as we shall see in Chapter 7, the Assembly itself was dissolved by force. After an armistice with Germany was signed on 14 November the soldiers, as Kamenev and Zinoviev had predicted, simply refused to fight any war, revolutionary or not – and Soviet Russia was left with no choice but to sign the Draconian peace of Brest–Litovsk. However, their fears that a rising would face stiff opposition were exaggerated, at least in Petrograd, if not Moscow. Most of the old officer corps refused to assist a regime headed by Kerensky, the 'betrayer' of Kornilov **(see Document 5.10b)**. Moreover, General Alekseiev's offer to organise those ready to resist any Bolshevik assault on the government (curiously, he too believed 5000 of the 15000 officers present in the capital would have done so) was ignored **(Pipes 1992: 489)**. The satirical cartoon opposite **(see Chapter 4)** depicts the growing isolation of Kerensky. The caption reads: 'You sit alone and look with despair as the fire burns pitifully low.'

Document 6.8 Kerensky's Isolation

[See illustration on p. 89]

Kamenev's and Zinoviev's preferred strategy was virtually identical to that proposed by Lenin in early September in his *On Compromises* **(see Document 6.1)**. In other words, they sought the peaceful formation of an all-socialist government in which the Bolsheviks ultimately would emerge as the dominant force. Ironically, such a strategy may well have been viable then as the patience of increasing numbers of Mensheviks and SRs had become exhausted by the

Source: N. Mitrofanov, Dni velikogo shturma. Povest'–Khronika o sobytiiakh pervykh dnei Oktiabr'skoi revoliutsii *(Moscow: Sovetskaia Rossiia, 1987), no page number*

procrastination of Kerensky and the Provisional Government on the issues of peace, land and the Constituent Assembly **(see Chapter 14)**. Fedor Dan, a leading Menshevik and for long an advocate of coalition government, recalled the final – vain – efforts of the Mensheviks and SRs to prod the government into decisive action on the very eve of the October Revolution.

Document 6.9 The Last Days of the Provisional Government

The fundamental sense of my resolution, which sharply criticised the Bolsheviks, was that if they were to be resisted successfully firm measures regarding peace, the transfer of *pomeshchik* lands into the hands of the peasants and the speedy summoning of the Constituent Assembly were necessary. Such measures alone would pull the rug from under the feet of the Bolsheviks who were exploiting for their own ends the mood of the disintegrating, mainly peasant, army and would give the government sufficient strength to oppose all attempts to overthrow it by force. In our faction . . . this resolution was adopted with little difficulty. Even the Menshevik-Internationalists (Martov's group), at that time a separate faction, adopted it . . . it met very strong opposition among the SRs, where a rather large wing was prepared to truckle to Kerensky. However, another section of the SRs, led by A.R. Gots, stubbornly fought for the same point of view that was contained in our resolution.

As a result of this struggle within the Council [of the Republic] . . . the resolution was adopted by a small majority. I will note here in passing that one of the first acts of the Bolsheviks after they had seized the telegraphs was to issue an order that this resolution was neither to be transmitted nor published: they obviously considered it would harm the success of their action if the population were to be informed that the Council of the Republic had adopted such a resolution.

As soon as the resolution had been adopted the question arose: 'What was to be done next?' since it was clear that every minute was precious and that there was no time to be lost. I had the idea to proceed at once to the current session of the Provisional Government and demand in the name of the majority of the Council of Republic that posters should be printed immediately and that same night pasted across the entire city. They were to declare that the Provisional Government: 1) would demand from its allies that they immediately propose an armistice to all warring countries and begin negotiations for a general peace; 2) would order by telegraph the transfer of all *pomeshchik* lands, pending the final resolution of the agrarian question, into the control of the local land committees; 3) would hasten the convocation of the Constituent Assembly.

We demanded that Kerensky report to the government which was still in session on the resolution of the Council of the Republic . . . and on our wish to be admitted to the session and heard. Kerensky turned sharply and went into the neighbouring hall where the government was in session. After several minutes he returned and coldly declared that the government had taken into consideration our refusal to offer it unconditional support, that it did not need advice from outside and that it would act alone and itself deal with the rising. We immediately replied that by such action the government not only condemned itself and the Revolution but also deprived us and the parties that we represented of any possibility of making common cause with it and offering it actual support.

Source: F. Dan, K istorii poslednikh dnei Vremennogo Pravitel'stva', Letopis' revoliutsii (Berlin: Izdatel'stvo Z.I. Grzhebina, 1923), 1, pp. 172–5

The moving force behind this newly formed Left bloc was not simply Dan, but Julius Martov, the leader of the Menshevik-Internationalists, who since July had been urging the formation of an all-socialist government **(see Document 14.2)**. Its immediate objectives were to avert a Bolshevik rising by appropriating its most effective policies (slogans in favour of peace and land division had won the Bolsheviks the increasing sympathy of the soldiers and peasants) and imposing them on the government. Equally, if such policies were carried out, the moderate Bolsheviks, such as Kamenev and Zinoviev and the many others sceptical of an insurrection, might be encouraged to resist Lenin's schemes more vigorously. But this new-found resolution among the moderate socialists to stem the rising tide of radicalism came too late. The chain of events that sparked off the October Revolution already had been set in motion **(Brovkin 1987: 10)**.

As we have seen, the Bolsheviks had not drawn up a precise blueprint for the seizure of power. In fact, the insurrection was precipitated by Kerensky's decision forcibly to close down the Bolshevik press during the night of 23–4 October. In response, the recently formed Military Revolutionary Committee of the Petrograd Soviet, purportedly organised to defend the capital from counter-revolution and now effectively in control of all the troops in the city, mobilised its forces to re-open it. Thereafter, the Bolsheviks exploited their control of the MRC to deploy forces to occupy key points within the city. The stations, the telegraph office and the telephone exchange were seized, allegedly to secure them against incipient counter-revolution. The insurrection had begun. However, no immediate action was taken to depose the government. This inaction prompted Lenin to risk emerging from his haven in the Vyborg district to return to Bolshevik headquarters in the Smolny Institute. He appeared about midnight. His arrival witnessed a subsequent escalation in Bolshevik activity.

Document 6.10 Lenin's Role in the Insurrection

. . . the most significant moment of the October Revolution is one of the least documented, for reasons that can be only guessed. The memoirists are unusually vague and contradictory about Lenin's arrival at Smolny and the impact it had on the course of events. Obviously it must have electrified the entire Soviet headquarters. There is reason to believe that Lenin, by direct command or perhaps by his mere presence, had a decisive effect in changing the orientation of his lieutenants from the defensive to the offensive.

If the operations of the MRC during the night are carefully followed, it is apparent that a marked change in tone and direction occurred after midnight. A new spirit of bold and systematic attack appeared, exemplified in orders to military units to seize outright the public institutions that were not yet under the control of the MRC. Up to this point the moves of the MRC had all been peaceful or defensive . . . . Lenin, apparently, provided the catalyst to turn the soviets' cautious defenders into the aggressive heroes of the insurrection.

One memoirist, Lomov, comes close to the probable truth . . . . Before Lenin's arrival, he wrote, 'Neither we nor Kerensky risk taking the path of a final engagement. We wait, fearing that our forces are still not sufficiently encouraged and organised. Kerensky is afraid to take the initiative in his own hands. . . .

'Thus things go on . . . . Suddenly Comrade Lenin appears. He is still in his wig, completely unrecognizable. Everything decisively changes. His point of view triumphs, and from this time we go over to a determined offensive.'

Source: R.V. Daniels, Red October: The Bolshevik Revolution of 1917 *(London: Secker & Warburg, 1967), pp. 162–3*

Lenin was unrecognisable as he still maintained the disguise which he had assumed after the July Days when, in fear for his life, he fled Petrograd, ultimately to seek sanctuary in Finland **(see Chapter 4)**. The photograph opposite reveals how he appeared, clean-shaven and in a wig.

Document 6.11 Lenin in Disguise

[See illustration on p. 93]

Unrecognisable or not, Lenin's critical contribution to the October Revolution is generally acknowledged **(see Chapter 1)**. He was primarily responsible for persuading, or browbeating, the CC to accept insurrection as a necessary part of Bolshevik strategy. However, Document 6.8 may exaggerate his personal impact on the events of 25 October themselves. No doubt his presence coincided with, perhaps even caused, an intensification in Bolshevik activity. Yet his insistence that the largely defenceless Provisional Government be overthrown before the Second Congress of Soviets convened, as Robert Service has argued, advanced its fall by no more than a few hours **(Service 1991: 262)**. Despite his promptings, military inefficiency and the desire to avoid unnecessary bloodshed delayed its

Source: Vospominanii o Vladimire Il'iche Lenine, *volume 2 (Moskva: Izdatel'stvo politicheskoi literatury, 1969), facing p. 305*

surrender until 2 a.m. on 26 October, after the Second Congress of Soviets had opened late the previous day. The same evening Lenin addressed the Congress. In proclaiming his famous decrees, promising peace, and land to the peasants, he sought to secure the support of the majority of the population behind the new, Bolshevik-dominated government.

The seizure of power in Petrograd, if protracted, was remarkably bloodless. Sadly, October in the second capital, Moscow, it was a more protracted and grim affair, with more than 1,000 killed in a week of bitter streetfighting. Many Bolsheviks argued that it was the indecision of many of the Moscow party leaders that was responsible for this sorry state of affairs. At a meeting of the Moscow *Oblast'* Bureau on 9 November Vera Iakovleva, of the radical Left, blamed the right-wing 'conciliators' within the Party.

Document 6.12 October in Moscow: Bolshevik Explanations

October 26 and 27 saw the mobilisation of our forces and those of the newly formed Committee of Public Safety. These days witnessed the eruption of a constant and bitter struggle between the Party Centre and the Bolshevik section of the Military Revolutionary Committee. The Party Centre urged decisive action while the MRC aspired to delay this decision, hoping that it could be avoided. One must add, however, that at the key moments the Party Centre split, with part of it going over to the side of the waverers. For example, during the evening of 26 October Riabtsev proposed to the MRC that it enter negotiations to find a means to stop what was going on. A joint session of the Party Centre and the Bolshevik section of the MRC was called. Two points of view immediately were revealed: 1) since a civil war has begun it is too late to go back . . . in such circumstances a breathing-space . . . will be advantageous not for us but for our enemies who will use it to summon and organise their forces . . . 2) our forces are small; we do not know upon whom we can rely; we need a breathing-space to organise our forces; we must negotiate with Riabtsev.

Despite the resolute struggle of the representatives of the *Oblast'* Bureau, a majority of nine against five voted to negotiate with Riabtsev. This was a decisive, in a certain sense historical, vote as it determined the protracted character of the October conflict . . . . Immediately after Riabtsev was informed that the MRC had agreed to negotiate the Kadets attempted to attack the Arsenal and take the post and telegraph offices. Negotiations had led to nothing other than what was to be expected . . . . By the evening of October 27 . . . Riabtsev already had twenty-four hours in which to organise and at 11 p.m. telephoned an ultimatum: the MRC must be dissolved, an investigation into the causes of the Civil War will be organised and those organisations and individuals who initiated it will be brought to trial; if the ultimatum is not accepted Riabtsev will begin military operations . . . .

Comrade Nogin . . . strongly urged that negotiations be renewed and even tried to conceal the demand about the dissolution of the MRC. This time the ultimatum was rejected. Military actions began.

Source: Triumfal'noe shestvie sovetskoi vlasti, *volume 1 (Moscow: Akademiia nauk SSSR, 1963), pp. 313–14*

Many leading Bolsheviks in Moscow, such as Viktor Nogin and other 'moderates' who dominated the City Committee, hoped that negotiations would lead to a peaceful and bloodless transfer of power to the Soviet. In consequence, they failed to neutralise all potential centres of resistance, so giving the opposition the time and opportunity to organise its forces. Other reasons also help explain the lengthy and bitter character of the insurrection in Moscow. First, the officer corps in Moscow was more willing to resist a Bolshevik 'coup'. Second, the Muscovite bourgeoisie was considerably more cohesive and confident than its Petrograd counterpart and thus more prepared and willing to fight **(Grunt 1976: 266, 306–11)**. However, reinforcements from other towns in the Moscow region (where soviet power already had been established) and from Petrograd helped the Bolsheviks to eventually crush the opposition.

Fortunately, the events in Moscow proved to be exceptional. In many cities of Russia the Bolsheviks had become the dominant force before 25 October. They used their power to ensure a peaceful and generally bloodless transfer of power to the soviets. The Volga town of Saratov, itself the subject of a detailed study by Donald Raleigh, was a typical example. Here on the night of 26 October the Soviet pronounced the transfer of power to itself.

Document 6.13 October in Saratov

Antonov: Comrades! You hear what they are saying . . . these leaders . . . these socialists. At a terrible hour for us . . . at the hour of the greatest events for Russia, perhaps the whole world . . . . At the hour when our brothers, our comrades – the workers of Petrograd – are breaking the tables of the past . . . when with arms in their hands they are rising against the centuries-old enemy – the oppressor, against the bourgeoisie . . . . When at the same time as news of the rising reached us so did news that Kaledin's troops were storming our bulwark – red Tsaritsyn – these gentlemen found nothing better to do than threaten us with Kerensky, threaten us with a bloodbath (uproar, cries, stormy indignation against the Mensheviks and SRs). They found nothing better than to demand from us, the ambassadors of the workers and peasants, an infamous and shameful silence, an infamous and shameful refusal to support the comrades who have risen (cries: 'shame', 'scoundrels' – stormy indignation). Moreover, with naked cynicism they demanded we condemn and . . . damn it! . . . support Kerensky, the butcher of the soldiers (cries: 'never', 'traitors', 'murderers' – stormy indignation). Really, you, socialists . . . you whom we recently called comrades. How do you dare to insult this distinguished meeting of representatives of the working class! How did you dare to think only that the Saratov workers are traitors, that fear would lead them to refuse to help the insurgents in Petrograd (cries: 'they judge by their own standards', 'down with them!')! You are lying! You want to deceive the bulk of workers and peasants by your lies! This will not succeed! Workers . . . soldiers . . . Who of you opposes the slogan of the rising, 'All Power to the Soviets'? Who? (From the entire ranks of the huge meeting no more than ten hands are raised. . . .) Who supports the Soviet? Who supports the rising? (a thousand-fold forest of hands. The results of the vote are greeted with a thunderous 'Hurrah' and a storm of applause) . . . . Here is the Soviet's answer to you. . . . Long live the revolutionary proletariat of Petrograd. Long live the Saratov worker and peasant, dressed by Kerensky in a soldier's greatcoat! (Stormy applause).

Source: Saratovskii sovet rabochikh deputatov (1917–1918): Sbornik dokumentov *(Moscow, Leningrad: Gosudarstv. sotsial'no-ekonomicheskoe izdatel'stvo 1931), pp. 217–18*

As Raleigh has pointed out, this largely spontaneous proclamation of soviet power, prompted by reports of the insurrection in Petrograd, was implemented with the minimum of resistance. There was sporadic fighting on 27 October, but few casualties. Unlike Moscow, the bourgeoisie was weak in Saratov. The vast majority of the soldiers also supported the establishment of soviet power, while most workers had become disillusioned with the moderate policies of the Mensheviks and SRs. October in Saratov was no conspiracy **(Raleigh 1986: 266–87, 322)**. Rather, it reflected the growing popular belief that the Bolsheviks' programme offered the best solution to the problems of the war and economic disintegration **(see Document 6.14b)**.

Compared to the confusion still surrounding the February Revolution, the history of the October Revolution is comparatively straightforward. It remains, however, one of the most contentious questions of twentieth-century history, as the following, contradictory judgements reveal.

Document 6.14 Judgements

a) . . . according to Malaparte, the characteristic quality of modern revolutions is precisely the bloodless, almost silent seizure of strategic points by small detachments of shock troops. The assault is carried out with such surgical precision that the public at large has no inkling of what is happening.

This description fits the October *coup* in Russia (which Malaparte had studied and used as one of his models). In October, the Bolsheviks gave up on massive armed demonstrations and street skirmishes, which they had employed, on Lenin's insistence, in April and July, because the crowds had proven difficult to control and provoked a backlash. They relied instead on small, disciplined units of soldiers and workers under the command of their Military Organisation, disguised as the Military Revolutionary Committee. to occupy Petrograd's principal communications and transport centers, utilities and printing plants – the nerve centers of the modern metropolis. Merely by severing the telephone lines connecting the government with its Military Staff they made it impossible to organize a counterattack. The entire operation was carried out so smoothly and efficiently that even as it was in progress the cafes and restaurants along with the opera, theaters and cinemas were open for business and thronged with crowds in search of amusement.

Source: R. Pipes, The Russian Revolution, 1899–1919 (London: Harvill, 1990), pp. 485–6

b) The central question of why the Bolsheviks won the struggle for power in Petrograd in 1917 permits no simple answer. To be sure, from the perspective of more than half a century, it is clear that the fundamental weakness of the Kadets and moderate socialists during the revolutionary period and the concomitant vitality and influence of the radical left at that time can be traced to the peculiarities of Russia's political, social and economic development during the nineteenth century and earlier. The world war also inevitably had a good deal to do with the way the 1917 revolution in Petrograd turned out. Had it not been for the Provisional Government's commitment to pursue war to victory, a policy which in 1917 enjoyed no broad support, it surely would have been better able to cope with the myriad problems that inevitably attended the collapse of the old order and, in particular, to satisfy popular demands for immediate fundamental reform.

As it was, a major source of the Bolsheviks' growing strength and authority in 1917 was the magnetic attraction of the Party's platform as embodied in the slogans 'Peace, Land and Bread' and 'All Power to the Soviets'. The Bolsheviks conducted an extraordinarily energetic and resourceful campaign for the support of the Petrograd factory workers and soldiers and Kronstadt sailors. Among these groups, the slogan 'All Power to the Soviets' signified the creation of a democratic, exclusively socialist government representing all parties and groups in the Soviet and committed to a program of immediate peace, meaningful internal reform, and the early convocation of a Constituent Assembly. In the late spring and summer of 1917, a number of factors served to increase support for the professed goals of the Bolsheviks, especially for transfer of power to the soviets. Economic conditions steadily worsened. Garrison soldiers became directly threatened by shipment to the front. Popular expectations of early peace and reform under the Provisional Government dwindled. Concomitantly, all other major political groups lost credibility because of their association with the government and their insistence on patience and sacrifice in the interest of the war effort. In the wake of the Kornilov affair, among the lower strata of the Petrograd population the desire for an end to coalition government with the Kadets became very nearly universal.

That in the space of eight months the Bolsheviks reached a position from which they were able to assume power was due as well to the special effort which the Party devoted to winning the support of military troops in the rear and at the front; only the Bolsheviks seem to have perceived the necessary crucial significance of the armed forces in the struggle for power.

Source: *A. Rabinowitch,* The Bolsheviks Come to Power *(New York: Norton, 1976), pp. 310–1*

The implication of Pipes's judgement is that the October Revolution was no more than a well-planned military *coup*, carried out without the knowledge, and against the wishes, of the people. In other words, it was illegitimate. Rabinowitch disputes Pipes's conclusion that October was simply a *coup* foisted on an unwitting and unsuspecting majority by a tiny and unrepresentative minority. He correctly stresses the growth in support for the Bolsheviks during 1917 as its policies increasingly appeared to satisfy popular demands. By October Bolshevik majorities could be found in the soviets in the north, the Urals, the Volga **(see Document 6.12)** and Siberia, as well as in the capitals. His observation, however, that the majority of those who supported, or accepted, the Bolshevik insurrection did so in anticipation of the creation of a democratic, all-socialist government is well founded. Their hopes were to be dashed, as the following Chapter, tracing the origins of the Bolshevik dictatorship, will reveal.

The origins of the Bolshevik dictatorship

The Bolshevik insurrection dealt a fatal blow to the formation of a democratic, all-socialist government that increasing numbers of Mensheviks and SRs (and not a few Bolsheviks, such as Kamenev) had come to support. They walked out of the Second Congress of Soviets in protest against the Bolsheviks' unilateral action (while Trotsky sneeringly consigned them to the rubbish heap of history). Yet, as Geoffrey Swain has recently argued, a Bolshevik dictatorship was not quite the foregone conclusion that it appears in retrospect. The main protagonist in attempting to salvage an all-socialist government was the Vikzhel, the All-Russian Executive Committee of the Union of Railway Workers.

Document 7.1 Vikzhel Appeal for an All-socialist Government, 29 October 1917

To All, All, All!

The country is without an organised government, and a bitter struggle for power is in progress. Each of the contending parties is trying to create a government by means of force, and brother is killing brother. At the very time when the foreign foe threatens the freedom of the people, democracy settles internal quarrels with blood and iron. The Provisional Government with Kerensky at its head has proved itself too weak to retain the reins of power. The government of the Soviet of People's Commissars, formed at Petrograd by one party only, cannot expect to be recognised or supported by the country as a whole. It is, therefore, necessary to form a government that will have the confidence of democracy as a whole and have enough prestige to retain power until the meeting of the Constituent Assembly. Such a government can be formed only by the common consent of democracy but never by force. Civil war never has and never can create a government that has the backing of the whole country. A people that is opposed to the death penalty as a means of justice, and is rejecting war as a method of settling international disputes, cannot accept civil war as a means to settle internal quarrels. Every civil war leads straight to counter-revolution and is advantageous only to the enemy of the people. In order to guard the liberty of the country and to save the Revolution, the Central Committee of the All-Russian Union of Railwaymen has, from the very beginning of this civil strife, assumed a strictly neutral attitude and has declared that the only way to obtain internal peace is by forming a homogeneous ministry, made up of the socialist parties, from the Bolsheviks to the Popular Socialists inclusive. Our stand has been accepted and approved by many public organisations and parties in Petrograd and Moscow. The Central Executive Committee has repeatedly declared and declares once more that it will place the whole railway service at the service of those who accept its platform. The Central Executive Committee makes clear its determined position to all citizens, workers, soldiers, and peasants and categorically demands that the civil war be ended and that a homogeneous revolutionary-socialist government be formed. The Railwaymen's Union gives notice that it will make use of every means at its disposal, even to complete stoppage of all train movements, to carry out its decision. Train services will be suspended at midnight today, 29–30 October, if by that time the fighting in Petrograd and Moscow has not ceased. All railwaymen's organisations are to take the necessary steps to strike and to appoint strike committees. The Railwaymen's Union denounces as enemies of democracy and as traitors to the country all those who continue to settle internal quarrels by means of force.

Source: R.A. Wade (ed.), Documents of Soviet History, Volume 1: The Triumph of Bolshevism 1917–1919 *(Gulf Breeze: Academic International, 1991), p. 22*

The objectives of the Vikzhel are clearly stated in Document 7.1: to prevent a civil war within the ranks of the democratic camp by the creation of an all-socialist government, including the Bolsheviks. The majority of workers, and soldiers, also favoured such a solution to the question of power. Moreover, important factions, including the Menshevik-Internationalists, the Left SRs and the moderate Bolsheviks, also supported this strategy. Even those Mensheviks and SRs who had abandoned the Congress of Soviets were prevailed upon to agree, albeit insisting intransigently that neither Lenin nor Trotsky be included in the new government. While the conditions imposed by the Right Mensheviks and SRs contributed to the failure of the negotiations initiated by Vikzhel to produce a democratic socialist government **(Burganov 1993: 36)** the major stumbling block was Lenin. His unwillingness to participate in a broad coalition was strengthened by the Bolsheviks' victory on 29 October, at Pulkovo, on the outskirts of Petrograd, over the forces sent by General Krasnov to restore the Kerensky government. In early November he persuaded the CC to reject the policy of conciliation urged by Kamenev, David Riazanov and Aleksei Rykov. At the same time he heartily condoned the arbitrary actions of the MRC which continued to arrest opponents of the Bolsheviks, as well as keep those newspapers critical of the Bolshevik insurrection closed. In these circumstances no agreement was possible **(Swain 1991: 223–8)**.

However, Lenin was also faced with another political quandary: What was to be done regarding the forthcoming elections to the long-promised yet oft-delayed Constituent Assembly? – elections which he himself had repeatedly championed before October **(see Documents 6.1, 6.2)**. No doubt he would have preferred to dispense with them. Shortly after the October Revolution he unequivocally argued that '[t]here must be no government in Russian other than the *Soviet Government*' **(Lenin, 26, 1964: 303)**. Yet the elections were allowed to proceed, despite Bolshevik forebodings that they would fail to secure a majority. Democratic scruples had little to do with this decision. Rather, the majority of Bolsheviks reckoned that their cancellation, or even postponement, as Lenin desired, would be counter-productive, providing their opponents with the opportunity to attack them as blatantly undemocratic **(Zhuravlev and Simonov 1992: 4)**.

In the second half of November the elections duly took place. They were conducted relatively fairly, although recently published archival material has confirmed that democratic procedures were not always slavishly adhered to.

Document 7.2 Irregularities in the Elections to the Constituent Assembly

There were many cases when ballot papers for the mainly anti-soviet parties were distributed. In a series of *uezdy* lists were issued to Kadets or those who promised to vote for the Kadets. In Kursk *guberniia*, for example, lists were issued only to the literate, while the illiterate received only Kadet lists. Voting papers for the Bolsheviks were issued in limited quantities. There were cases of the forgery and destruction of the latter . . . . There were many instances when entire plants and villages were excluded from the elections, for example, in Ufa *guberniia*. In Tambov *guberniia* (Morshanskii *uezd*) Bolshevik campaigning was forbidden . . . in the village of Sokura, Saratov *guberniia*, educated society arranged a meeting and set up the ballot boxes. The superintendent of the voting station and the *kulaki* insisted that everyone vote for list number 12 (the SRs). They took the voting papers and against the will of the peasants deposited them in the ballot box. The peasants were outraged and cried that they must vote for list number 10 (the Bolsheviks), since this was the best party, but the *kulaki* shouted that they would whip whoever supported the Bolsheviks, as they had in 1905. There were many cases of the *kulaki* beating those peasants who dared to vote for the [Bolshevik] list.

Source: S. Vakunova (ed.), "Zato teper' svoboda . . . " Pis'ma krest'ian i gorodskikh obyvatelei v Uchreditel'noe sobranie i obzor khoda izbiratel'noi kampanii 1917g.', Neizvestnaia Rossiia: XX vek, 1992 (II), p. 192

Similar reports of discriminatory practices directed against the Bolsheviks came in from all parts of the country. The Bolsheviks themselves were not blameless. As Oliver Radkey has pointed out, pro-Bolshevik soldiers intimidated the electorate in Saratov, Odessa, Riazan', Kostroma and, presumably, elsewhere. He concluded, however, that whatever irregularities did take place, in the main the elections were fair and free. In particular, the Bolsheviks did not seek to control the elections, even in the large cities and towns, where they had the power to do so (they patently lacked the organisational 'muscle' to do so in the countryside) **(Radkey 1950: 50)**. The results below, based on the most recent study of the elections, confirm this conclusion.

Document 7.3 Results of the Elections to the Constituent Assembly

A)

	Total votes	%
SRs	19 070 637	40.4
Bolsheviks	10 947 862	23.2
Mensheviks	1 380 649	2.9
Popular socialists	374 518	0.8
Other socialists*	6 704 681	14.2
Kadets	2 172 187	4.6
Right parties	279 227	0.6
Landowners	191 109	0.4
Trade and industry	36 941	0.1
Cooperators	28 913	0.1
Religous parties	301 514	0.6
National parties	3 648 943	7.7
Cossacks	1 024 268	2.2
Others	1 006 172	2.2
Total	47 167 621	100.0

B)

	In the rear (civilians, non-front line soldiers)		At the front (soldiers on active service)	
	Total votes	%	Total votes	%
SRs	17 287 287	40.4	1 783 350	40.7
Bolsheviks	9 220 543	21.6	1 727 319	39.5
Mensheviks	1 240 309	2.9	140 340	3.2
Popular socialists	363 521	0.8	10 997	0.3
Other socialists*	6 178 821	14.4	525 860	12.0
Kadets	2 098 588	4.9	73 599	1.7
Right parties	279 227	0.6		
Landowners	191 109	0.4		
Trade and industry	36 941	0.1		

Cooperators	28,913	0.1		
Religous parties	301,514	0.6		
National parties	3,607,855	8.4	41,088	0.8
Cossacks	1,024,268	2.2		
Others	930,411	2.3	75,761	1.7
Total	42,789,307	100.0	4,378,314	100.0

* Neo-Populist (i.e., SR) or Social Democratic national parties, and also single lists of socialist parties.

C)

Population	Bolshevik	SRs	Mensheviks	Other socialists	Kadets	Others
Urban	33.6	16.0	6.4	8.0	20.3	15.7
Rural	19.3	45.6	2.2	17.0	1.8	14.1

Source: L.G. Protasov, 'Vserossiiskoe Uchreditel'noe Sobranie i demokraticheskaia al'ternativa', Otechestvennaia istoriia, 1993, 5, pp. 13, 15

Notwithstanding the flaws in the organisation and conduct of the elections, the turn-out was impressive. Protasov estimates that over 47 million of the 80 million eligible voters participated. Moscow and Petrograd (but not the provincial towns) and much of the countryside witnessed heavy polling, with 70 per cent or more of the electorate voting. As the tables of Document 7.3 demonstrate, the Bolsheviks performed best in the industrial regions, and in the army (especially in those units on the Northern and Western Fronts, the Baltic fleet and the garrison towns). The Kadets also did well in urban Russia, coming first or second in the capitals and many provincial towns, but made no impression in the countryside. For the Mensheviks, the elections were an unmitigated disaster and suggest that their vacillations during 1917 had cost them much of their working-class constituency. The national parties also were more successful than the tables indicate as the 'other socialists' were composed almost exclusively of parties of the national minorities (**Miller 1993: 22**). But the clear victors unsurprisngly appeared to be the SRs, the self-professed party of the peasantry, with over 40 per cent of the vote and a majority of seats in the Assembly itself. Of the 765 elected deputies there were 396 SRs, including about 40 Left SRs; 179 Bolsheviks; 24 Mensheviks; 14 Kadets; 68 nationalists; 16 Cossacks; and numerous other small groups **(Protasov 1993: 14)**. Bolshevik fears about the outcome of the elections seem to have been justified. On the eve of the first (and only) session of the Constituent Assembly they responded by publishing the following Declaration:

Document 7.4 Declaration of the Rights of the Working and Exploited People

The Constituent Assembly resolves:

I   1 Russia is hereby proclaimed a Republic of Soviets . . . . All power, centrally and locally, is vested in these soviets.

2 The Russian Soviet Republic is established on the principle of a free union of free nations, as a federation of soviet national republics.

II   . . . the Constituent Assembly further resolves:

1 Private ownership of land is hereby abolished. All land together with all buildings, farm implements and other appurtenances of agricultural production, is proclaimed the property of the entire working people.

2 The soviet laws on workers' control and on the Supreme Economic Council are hereby confirmed for the purpose of guaranteeing the power of the working people over the exploiters and as a first step towards the complete conversion of the factories, mines, railways . . . into the property of the workers' and peasants' state.

3 The conversion of all banks into the property of the workers' and peasants' state is hereby confirmed. . . .

4 . . . universal labour conscription is hereby instituted.

5 . . . to eliminate all possibility of the restoration of the power of the exploiters, the arming of the working people, the creation of a socialist Red Army . . . and the complete disarming of the propertied classes are hereby decreed.

III 1 . . . the Constituent Assembly whole-heartedly endorses the policy pursued by soviet power of denouncing secret treaties, organising most extensive fraternisation . . . and achieving at all costs, by revolutionary means, a democratic peace . . . without annexations and indemnities and on the basis of free self-determination of nations.

2 . . . the Constituent Assembly welcomes the policy of the Council of People's Commissars in proclaiming the complete independence of Finland . . . and . . . self-determination for Armenia.

3 The Constituent Assembly regards the Soviet law on the cancellation of the loans contracted by the governments of the tsar, the landowners and the bourgeoisie as a first blow struck at interational banking, finance capital.

IV   Having been elected on the basis of party lists drawn up prior to the October Revolution, when the people were not yet in a position to rise en masse against the exploiters . . . the Constituent Assembly considers it would be fundamentally wrong, even formally, to put itself in opposition to soviet power . . . . Power must be vested wholly and entirely in the working people and their authorised representatives – the Soviets of Workers', Soldiers' and Peasants' Deputies. Supporting Soviet power and the decrees of the Council of People's Commissars, the Constituent

Assembly considers that its own task is confined to establishing the fundamental principles of the socialist reconstruction of society.

. . . the Constituent Assembly confines its own task to setting up the fundamental principles of a federation of Soviet Republics of Russia, while leaving it to the workers and peasants of each nation to decide independently at their own authoritative Congress of Soviets whether they wish to participate in the federal government and in other federal Soviet institutions, and on what terms.

Source: V.I. Lenin, Collected Works, *26 (Moscow: Progress, 1964–5), pp. 423–5*

Drafted largely by Lenin, this Declaration was tantamount to an ultimatum. Essentially, the Bolsheviks demanded of the Constituent Assembly what Lenin had enunciated since mid-November, 'that it unreservedly recognises Soviet power'. It was also to approve the major legislation already enacted by the Bolsheviks: regarding the division of land amongst the peasants; the institution of workers' control; the transformation of Russia into a federal Republic **(see Document 7.7 below)**; as well as the negotiations for peace with Germany. Thereafter it would become redundant. However, the majority of delegates present when the Assembly convened in the Tauride Palace on 5 January refused to be browbeaten. Viktor Chernov was elected President of the Assembly, not Maria Spiridonova, a leading Left SR and the Bolsheviks' favoured candidate. With Chernov presiding the Assembly proceeded to debate and pass three main laws: the first transferring the land to the peasants; the second advocating the negotiation of a general and democratic peace; and the third transforming Russia into a democratic, federal republic. After ten months of vacillation the SRs at last had steeled themselves to act decisively, but it was too little, too late. On the morning of 6 January the Bolshevik guard, largely Baltic fleet sailors, brought its proceedings to an abrupt end. The Bolsheviks defended the dissolution of the Assembly in the following manner.

Document 7.5 Decree on the Dissolution of the Constituent Assembly

The Russian Revolution created the Soviets as the only organisation of all the exploited working classes in a position to direct the struggle of these classes for their complete political and economic liberation. During the period of the Revolution the Soviets increased and multiplied. Perceiving the illusion of an understanding with the *bourgeoisie* and the deceptive parliamentary organisations of the democratic *bourgeoisie*, they arived at the solution that the liberation of the oppressed classes was an impossibility without a complete rupture of every kind of understanding. Therefore the Revolution of October arose, giving all authority to the Soviets.

The Constituent Assembly, elected on the old register, appeared as an expression of the old *regime* when the authority belonged to the *bourgeoisie*.

Then the people who voted for the Revolutionary Socialists were unable to distinguish between the Revolutionary Socialists of the Right, partisans of the *bourgeoisie*, and the Revolutionary Socialists of the Left, the partisans of Socialism. Therefore, this Constituent Assembly was expected to become the chief authority of the *bourgeois* republic, setting itself against the October Revolution and the authority of the Soviets.

The authorities installed by the October Revolution, giving authority to the Soviets, and through them the working classes, came to the conclusion that the old *bourgeois* parliamentarianism has seen its day, that it is unable to cope with the tasks before Socialism, and that only the institutions of the classes, such as the Soviets, are in a position to overcome the opposition of the rich classes and to create a new socialist State. Every refusal to recognise the authority of the Republican Soviets and every attempt to put back into the hands of the Constituent Assembly and the *bourgeoisie* the liberty that has been won would be a step backwards and towards the bankruptcy of the workmen's and peasants' revolution.

The Constituent Assembly which opened on 18 [5] January gave a majority, for known reasons, to the Revolutionary Socialists of the Right, the Party of Kerensky, Tchernoff, and Avksentieff. It is comprehensible that this faction has refused to debate the just and clear programme of the Central Executive Committee and to recognise the declaration of the rights of the exploited working classes, as well as the October Revolution and the authority of the Soviets.

Thus the Constituent Assembly broke with the Republican Soviet of Russia. The departure of the Bolshevists and the Revolutionary Socialists of the Left, who have a considerable majority in the Soviets, was thereupon inevitable.

The Revolutionary Socialists of the Right are fighting openly against the authority of the Soviets and directly supporting the opposition of the exploitation of Labour. It is clear that only this remaining faction might play a part that would lead to *bourgeois* counter-revolution for the deposition of the Soviets.

The Central Executive Committee, therefore, orders the Constituent Assembly to be dissolved.

Source: The Times, *22 January 1918*

Document 7.5, essentially based on a decree drafted by Lenin, was officially released to the press on 7 [20] January 1918. It appears to be simply a cynical attempt by the Bolsheviks to justify their actions. However, there is more consistency to it than first meets the eye. While the Bolsheviks had advocated the speedy convocation of the Constituent Assembly during 1917, they also had repeatedly argued, Lenin in particular, that soviet power was superior to 'bourgeois parliamentarianism' **(see Document 4.3)**. Moreover, the Left SRs, junior partners of the Bolsheviks in government since mid-November, had only coalesced into a separate party after the elections to the Assembly had taken place. According to Marcel Liebman, they had won a majority in the elections to the Soviet of Peasant Deputies in December 1917 yet had only 40 seats in the Assembly. Their underrepresentation arguably was the result of the manipulation of lists of party candidates by the Right (and Centre) SRs to ensure their own supporters were elected **(Radkey 1950: 72)**. The Left SRs thus had insufficient weight to ensure that the Assembly approve the Bolshevik resolution that it transfer all power to the soviets, a resolution that they wholeheartedly endorsed. But whatever defences can be mounted to justify the Bolsheviks' action they remain culpable for the dissolution of the Constituent Assembly. Yet culpability was not theirs alone. In Oliver Radkey's opinion, the Provisional Government, together with the Menshevik and SR leaderships, must shoulder a substantial portion of the blame. As with the Kadets, they feared that a democratically elected Assembly would not support war to a victorious conclusion. Acordingly, they repeatedly postponed the elections to the Assembly, until it had become redundant **(Radkey 1990: 91–6)**. The best testimony to its redundancy was the absence of mass opposition to its dispersal, in Petrograd, Moscow and even the SR heartlands in rural Russia. The following letter suggests why this was the case. It was written by an ordinary (yet unnamed) soldier on 6 January 1918, and addressed to the members of the Assembly, and has only recently been published after the collapse of the Soviet Union.

Document 7.6 A Soldier's Opinion of the Constituent Assembly

Comrades! Having read of the events surrounding the opening of the Constituent Assembly on January 5 I see that you, representatives of the people, have gathered together to pursue party squabbles, not to work to reconstruct the new republican system. There has been enough uproar; there has been enough fraternal blood shed – what is needed is the construction of a new, peaceful, radiant life; it is necessary to end the war at any price; it is necessary to conclude a democratic peace, with honour for all peoples. The uproar you make is not necessary – what is needed is productive work to give back life to the starved peasants, soldiers and workers. All our energies must be devoted to sowing the fields, to supplying the toiling peasantry with all necessary agricultural equipment, which alone makes it possible to ward off the growing, universal famine. Hunger exists; the suffering people are dying from hunger and cold. Russia must be led onto the path of construction, not of destruction.

  All you who have gathered there, as far as I can see, do not represent the true toilers. You are people who crave great sensations and are lovers of scandal and self-aggrandisement. I tell you (my vote sent you there) that there is a limit to everything. Listen to the voice of the people – it wants peace, it wants rest after this damned war. I who have served in the army three and a half years in peacetime and the same time in war tell you that you must give us, who have suffered in mind and body, peace. Before I donned the damned army greatcoat I bore on my hands thousands of bloody callouses; I was left half dead on the snowy mountains of the Carpathians – I want peace, while you, our representatives, in order to pursue your party squabbles, want to take the remaining half of my life and leave to the whims of fate my wife and children. You have played too long on our [blue] veins as on the strings of a harp. They need peace, not a painful death from hunger. There has been enough death.

Be warned, our patience will wear out and we will kill and drive you all out and we will say that we will govern ourselves without any parties. There will be one party of labour and justice; there will be neither Rights nor Lefts. My voice is the voice of the suffering people. There are a legion of us, just like me.

Source: S. Vakunova (ed.), '"Zato teper'svoboda . . . " Pis'ma kvest'ian i gorodskikh obyvatelei v Uchreditel'noe sobranie i obzor khoda izbiratel'noi kampanii 1917g.', Neizvestnaia Rossiia, *XX, II, (1992), pp. 189–90*

Document 7.6 arguably reflects the gulf between the basic concerns of ordinary Russians and the aspirations of their political representatives, drawn largely from educated society **(see Chapter 1)**. There was no patience for democratic politics, and its associated conflicts and debates, unsurprising in a society with little experience of the procedures of representative government. It also clearly shows what the majority expected the Revolution to bring: peace, land and a better material life. Soviet power itself had already promised to satisfy these expectations. An armistice existed and peace, though neither democratic nor honourable, was imminent. The Decree on Land of 26 October had effectively given the land to the peasants. The fact that the Constituent Assembly had little concrete to offer helps to explain the muted response to its dissolution **(Protasov 1993: 13–15)**.

Having dispersed the Constituent Assembly it was now incumbent upon the Bolsheviks to elaborate the principles upon which the soviet state would be constructed, as the Third Congress of Soviets in January 1918 recognised. Yet for three months the task of framing a new constitution hung in abeyance, as the crisis provoked by the Draconian peace terms proposed by the Germans at Brest–Litovsk dominated Soviet politics. Eventually, on 5 April, a constitutional commission convened. Iakov Sverdlov, the Secretary of the Bolshevik Party, presided, with representatives from the Bolsheviks, Left SRs, and SR-Maximalists present. It deliberated for three months. The main bone of contention was the insistence of Lenin, mindful of gaining the support of the non-Russian minorities, that the new constitution should be federal in form, with the right to national autonomy, even self-determination, entrenched within it **(see Chapter 11)**. Ultimately, in face of bitter opposition from many Bolsheviks and Left SRs, Lenin, ably assisted by Stalin, got his way. The Constitution was introduced on 19 July

(Service 1995: 20–3). Its first section was the 'Declaration of the Rights of the Working and Exploited People' **(see Document 7.4)**. The remainder of it is a rather lengthy and verbose document, and only its salient sections are reproduced below.

Document 7.7 Constitution of the Russian Socialist Federal Soviet Republic

9 The fundamental aim of the Constitution . . . is to establish a dictatorship of the city and village proletariat and the poorest peasantry in the form of a powerful All-Russian Soviet Government which has the purpose of crushing completely the bourgeoisie, of ending the exploitation of man by man, and of establishing socialism, under which there will be no division into classes and no state authority. . . .

11 Soviets of regions which have distinctive customs and national characteristics may unite in autonomous regional units, at the head of which . . . stand the regional congresses of soviets and their executive organs. These autonomous regional unions enter the Russian Socialist Federated Republic on a federal basis.

12 Sovereign power . . . is vested in the All-Russian Congress of Soviets and, in the interim between congresses, in the All-Russian Central Executive Committee.

23 To safeguard the interests of the working class as a whole, the Russian Socialist Federated Soviet Republic deprives individuals and groups of the rights which they may use to the detriment of the socialist Revolution.

24 The All-Russian Congress of Soviets is the supreme authority in the Russian Socialist Federated Soviet Republic.

25 The All-Russian Congress of Soviets consists of representatives of city soviets on the basis of one deputy for every 25,000 electors, and of representatives of *guberniia* congresses of soviets on the basis of one deputy for every 125,000 inhabitants.

31 The All-Russian Executive Committee is the supreme legislative, executive, and regulative organ of the Russian Socialist Federated Soviet Republic . . . .

37 The Soviet of People's Commissars has the general direction of affairs of the Russian Socialist Federated Soviet Republic.

56 Within the limits of its jurisdiction the congress of soviets (*oblast'*, *guberniia*, *uezd*, and *volost'*) is the supreme authority throughout the given territory.

61 The *oblast'*, *guberniia*, *uezd*, and *volost'* organs of the Soviet Government, as well as the soviets of deputies, have the following functions:

a) The enforcement of all orders of the higher organs of the Soviet Government. . . .

c) The settlement of all questions which have a purely local character. . . .

62 The congresses of soviets and their executive committees have the right to exercise control over the acts of the local soviets (i.e., the *oblast'* congress exercises control over all soviets of the *oblast'*, the *guberniia* over all soviets of the *guberniia*, except city soviets which are not included in the *uezd* congresses of soviets, etc.). The *oblast'* and *guberniia* congresses of soviets and their executive committees have in addition the right to repeal decisions of the soviets in their areas. . . .

Source: J. Bunyan, Intervention, Civil War, and Communism in Russia, April–December 1918: Documents and Materials *(New York: Octagon, 1976), pp.510–20*

Richard Pipes has described this Constitution as 'short and confused'. Confused it certainly was, failing precisely to delineate the different functions of the Congress of Soviets, the All-Russian CEC and the Sovnarkom (Soviet of People's Commissars) (articles 24, 31, 37). Moreover, the 'supreme authority' apparently granted to the local soviets (article 56) was severely constrained by articles 61 and 62 which in effect limited the autonomous powers of lower-level soviets. It also denied universal suffrage. Those who were to be deprived of rights (article 23) included businessmen, financiers, the clergy, former policemen as well as criminals and the insane (article 65). Furthermore, article 25 sought to ensure greater representation to the workers, presumably to counter the weight of the peasant majority. Ironically, the federal principle that Lenin had fought to include was rarely mentioned. Apart from article 11, only articles 22 (prohibiting discrimination on the grounds of nationality) and 49e (vaguely recognising the right of national self-determination) made any reference to it. It also made no mention of the real source of power in the country, the Bolshevik Party **(Pipes 1992a: 516; Service 1995: 23–5)**. By the time the Constitution was promulgated it had assumed dictatorial power after ejecting all its rivals from the soviets. The first to suffer were the Mensheviks and SRs who had returned to the CEC after the Fourth Congress of Soviets in March to oppose Bolshevik policies from within. They were expelled from the CEC on 14 June.

Document 7.8 Expulsion of the Mensheviks and SRs from the Central Executive Committee

Taking into consideration:
1) Soviet power is facing an extremely difficult period, resisting simultaneously an attack by international imperialism on all fronts and by its allies within the Russian republic, who do not refrain from using any methods, from the most barefaced slander to conspiracies and armed uprising, in their struggle with the Workers' and Peasants' Government;
2) The presence in soviet organisations of representatives of parties which clearly aspire to discredit and overthrow the authority of the soviets is completely inadmissible;

3) Documents published earlier and also those made public at the present session clearly reveal that the representatives of the SRs (Right and Centre) and of the Mensheviks, right up to the most responsible leaders, have been proven guilty of organising armed risings against the workers and peasants in alliance with undoubted counter-revolutionaries: on the Don with Kaledin and Kornilov; in the Urals with Dutov; in Siberia with Semenov, Horvat and Kolchak; and, finally, most recently with the Czechoslovaks and the Black Hundreds who have joined them.

The All-Russian CEC resolves to exclude from its membership representatives of the parties of the SRs (Right and Centre) and of the Mensheviks, and also to propose to all Soviets . . . to remove representatives of these factions from their ranks.

Source: Protokoly zasedanii Vserossiiskago Tsentral'nago Ispolnitel'nago Komiteta 4-go sozyva: Stenograficheskii otchet *(Moscow: Gosudarstvennoe izdatel'stvo, 1920), p. 439*

The reasons given in Document 7.8 for the expulsion of the Mensheviks and SRs conceal the Bolsheviks' true motivation. Admittedly, small Allied forces had landed in the north, at Murmansk, and the Japanese in Vladivostok; and the SRs, with the aid of the Czech legions, had established the Committee of Members of the Constituent Assembly (Komuch) in Samara and begun to organise an army to depose soviet power **(see Chapter 8)**. But both intervention and civil war were in their embryonic stages and there is little evidence that the SRs and Mensheviks had allied with the White Generals (though the Komuch did seek to enlist the services of old tsarist officers). Vladimir Brovkin suggests that other, more threatening, developments underlay the Bolsheviks' decision. In the cities, disillusion caused by unemployment and food shortages, and by the Bolsheviks' brutal and authoritarian treatment of workers' protest, was growing rapidly. It had two major consequences. First, the Mensheviks were gaining majorities in many, newly re-elected urban soviets. Second, organisations independent of the soviets, most notably the assemblies of factory workers, opposed to Bolshevik rule were springing up in many towns and cities **(see Document 10.7)**. In the countryside, the SRs also were staging a political comeback, one likely to be reinforced by peasant opposition to the recently introduced policy of grain requisitioning **(see Document 9.9)**. Fearing that it would be unable to dominate the forthcoming Fifth All-Russian Congress of Soviets the Bolshevik leadership, after some heated debate, plumped for pre-emptive action – and expelled its SR and Menshevik opponents from the CEC. In so doing it also satisfied its provincial organisations where pressure to purge the soviets of all non-Bolshevik elements had been mounting during the spring. A great step towards the creation of a one-party dictatorship had been taken **(Brovkin 1987: 220–32)**. The culmination came in July. On 6 July two leading Left SRs, Nikolai Andreev and Iakov Bliumkin, assassinated Count Wilhelm von Mirbach, the German Ambassador in Moscow. Left SR thinking is explained in the following resolution of 24 June, signed by Maria Spiridonova.

Document 7.9 The Left SRs' Reasons for the Assassination of Mirbach

At its session of June the CC of the PLS-R Internationalists, having discussed the current political state of the Republic, found that in the interests of the Russian and international revolution it is vital in the immediate future to put an end to the so-called breathing-space created by the ratification of the Brest Treaty by the Bolshevik government. For these ends the CC considers it to be possible and expedient to organise a series of terrorist acts against prominent representatives of German imperialism. At the same time the CC resolved to mobilise its reliable military forces to achieve this end and to take every measure to ensure that the toiling peasantry and working class participate in a rising and actively support the Party in its action . . . . As far as concerns the method by which we shall implement our current line of conduct, then it was resolved that terror should be implemented when Moscow gives the signal. Such a signal may be a terrorist act or it may occur in another form. . . .

Source: Izvestiia TsK KPSS, *1989 (5), 162–3*

Document 7.9 (a reprint of material first published in 1920 in *Krasnaia kniga V.Ch.K. – The Red Book of the Cheka*) reveals that the purpose behind the Left SRs' assassination of Mirbach was to provoke a renewed war with Germany. It would force the Bolsheviks to abandon the Treaty of Brest–Litovsk which the Left SRs regarded as transforming Russia into little more than a German colony. The resolution goes on to state that they did not seek to overthrow the Bolshevik Government, but simply to change its policy (on grain requisitioning as well as the Brest peace), as Fel'shtinskii has reaffirmed **(Fel'shtinskii 1985: 150–1)**. It also casts doubt on more 'conspiratorial' interpretations of the assassination which suggest that it was engineered by the Bolsheviks to provide them with a pretext to purge the Left SRs. That, of course, was what did occur. Their 'rising' was put down by the Latvian units at the Bolsheviks' disposal in Moscow and their plans came to naught. Many were arrested (though few executed) and the remainder were expelled from the CEC and the local soviet **(Pipes 1992a: 636–45)**. The dictatorship was complete.

Underpinning this dictatorship was the new secret police. The All-Russian Extraordinary Commission, the Cheka, was established on 20 December 1917, largely on Lenin's initiative. Its task essentially was to uncover and suppress 'all acts of counter-revolution and sabotage'. Within three years it had grown to be 250,000 strong. The mentality of the Bolshevik Chekisty is revealed in the following resolution adopted by them on 12 June 1918.

Document 7.10 The Strategy of the Cheka

In view of the threatening and exceptional circumstances of the time the following resolutions are submitted:

1 To employ secret agents.
2 To withdraw from circulation the prominent and active leaders of the Monarchist-Kadets, Right SRs and Mensheviks [abstention].
3 To register and have shadowed the generals and officers, to put under surveillance the Red Army, the officer staff, clubs, circles, schools, etc.
4 To execute prominent and clearly exposed counter-revolutionaries, speculators, robbers and bribe-takers [5 abstentions].
5 In the provinces to adopt strict and decisive measures to suppress the distribution of the bourgeois, conciliationist and gutter press.
6 To propose to the CC to recall comrade Uritskii from his post in the Petrograd Extraordinary Commission and replace him with a more steadfast and decisive comrade who will be able firmly and unbendingly to implement a policy of merciless suppression and struggle with hostile elments who are destroying soviet power and the Revolution [2 opposed, 6 abstentions].

Source: G.A. Bordiugova (ed.), 'Pravda dlia sluzhebnogo pol'zovaniia. Iz dokumentov lichnogo fonda F. Dzerzhinskogo', Neizvestnaia Rossiia. XX vek, 1992 (I), p. 30

The wishes of the Cheka were soon to be realised. On 30 August the attempted assassination of Lenin and the murder of Moisei Uritskii, still chairman of the Petrograd Cheka, precipitated the unleashing of a policy of Red Terror. The powers of the secret police grew rapidly, unchecked by the Party leadership which, with few exceptions such as Lev Kamenev, increasingly came to support a policy of arbitrary terror against all opposition. Its rise to become perhaps the most powerful institution within the new soviet state (some would argue that it *was* the state) proved to be irresistible, with fatal consequences for the Party itself 20 years later.

8 | The Civil War

Recent studies of the Civil War stress its sheer complexity, a complexity that defies both simple narration and analysis. Debates continue about when it first started. Recently, Evan Mawdsley persuasively argued that it 'began with the October Revolution' **(Mawdsley 1987: 3)**. Its initial phase, he continues, lasted through the winter of 1917–18. First, the Bolsheviks easily rebuffed the feeble Cossack forces sent by General Petr Krasnov to restore the Kerensky government in Petrograd in late October. Then, in the early months of 1918, they quelled the resistance of the various Cossack hosts, notably the Orenburg Cossacks led by Ataman Dutov in the Urals and the Don Cossacks of General Aleksei Kaledin. Finally, in the spring, the embryonic Volunteer Army (composed of nationalist army officers) that had formed in the south of Russia, in the Don region, was defeated and its commander, Lavr Kornilov, killed **(Mawdsley 1987: 16–22)**. It is little wonder that on 23 April Lenin declared 'with confidence that in the main the civil war is at an end'.

Sadly, Lenin's confidence was misplaced. In mid-May a conflict emerged in the Urals between the Soviet authorities and the Czechoslovak legions seeking to leave Russia for the Western front, via Siberia and Vladivostok. Typically heavy-handed Bolshevik responses, including threats to disarm, even shoot, the Czechoslovaks caused the latter to rise against soviet power. This rebellion, in the opinion of Vladimir Brovkin (and many historians before him), marked the real beginning of the Civil War. In particular, it provided the SRs with the military backing that enabled them effectively to challenge the Bolsheviks. Brovkin also emphasises that it is no longer tenable to view the Civil War simply as a struggle between the Reds (the Bolsheviks) and the Whites (the nationalist officers, supported by the industrialists and old landowners). Rather there were three quite distinct civil wars. In the second half of 1918, the so-called era of democratic counter-revolution, the conflict was essentially one between the Bolsheviks and the SRs. The period from the autumn of 1918 until General Petr Wrangel's defeat in the autumn of 1920 was dominated by the struggle between the Reds and Whites (the conventional image of the Civil War). With the final defeat of the Whites in the autumn of 1920 the focus shifted dramatically to the Green movement (widespread, if uncoordinated, insurrections of disgruntled peasants) which emerged as the main challenge to Bolshevik power **(Brovkin 1994: 403–5)**. The first two phases of the Civil War will be dealt with in this chapter, with discussion of the Green movement deferred until we examine the general crisis that confonted Bolshevik rule in the winter of 1920–21 **(see Chapter 15)**.

The first serious challenge to the Bolsheviks came from the Committee of Members of the Constituent Assembly (Komuch). It was set up by the Right SRs in Samara on 8 June 1918, with the aid of the insurgent Czechoslovak legions. It soon controlled the Volga provinces of Kazan', Samara and Simbirsk, and parts of Saratov, as well as the Urals' province of Ufa. It sought to extend its power across Siberia, too. Its main objectives were to restore the Constituent Assembly and tear up the Brest–Litovsk treaty, although it abhorred the terror tactics deployed by the Left SRs to provoke a renewed war with Germany **(see Chapter 7)**. It issued a detailed programme on 25 July.

Document 8.1 The Komuch Programme

The Soviet regime is overthrown and Bolshevism suffered complete defeat on all the territory which is now subordinated to the Committee of Members of the All-Russian Constituent Assembly. Nevertheless there are still not a few people who dream of a return of the Soviet regime. These persons, together with the dregs of the population, energetically stir up the workers and peasants against the new government, exploiting their inadequate knowledge and capacity for organisation. These agitators suggest to them that the workers will again be under the power of capital and that the peasants will be deprived of the land and subjected to the landlords.

The Committee, regarding such agitation as clearly provocative, states that there is absolutely no basis for it and, in order to put an end to such malicious inventions, makes the following general declaration:

1 The land has once for all passed into the possession of the people and the Committee will not permit any attempts to return it to the landlords.
2 The existing laws and decisions about the protection of labour preserve their force until they are revised in legislative order.
3 The Department of Labour . . . is strictly instructed to watch out vigilantly for the execution of these laws and decisions and the judicial and examining authorities are instructed immediately to investigate and settle cases of the violation of labour laws.
4 Workers and peasants are requested to defend their interests only by legal means, in order to avoid anarchy and chaos.
5 Dismissal of workers and stoppage of the work of undertakings, if not justified by the conditions of production, or if undertaken by the employers in concert as a means of struggle with the workers or with the Government, are forbidden under pain of severest liability to punishment.
6 Enterprises may only be shut down with the permission of the state organisations which are supervising economic life.
7 The department of Labour is commissioned to create appropriate organisations for the protection of labour in provincial and county-seat towns.

8 The rights of trade unions, as defined by law, preserve their force until the legal provisions are revised. Representatives of the workers and of the employers must be invited to participate in the preparation for a re-examination of the laws about the protection of labour.

9 Collective agreements must preserve their validity until they are set aside by an agreement of the parties or until laws affecting these agreements are revised.

Having in mind, at the same time, the interests of industry and of the economic life of the country . . . and desiring to cooperate with those better representatives of the commercial and industrial classes who honestly desire to promote the reestablishment of normal economic life, the Committee . . . also considers it a duty to declare for general knowledge:

1 The employers possess the right to demand from the workers intensive and efficient labour during all the working time which is prescribed by law and contract and to dismiss those workers who do not submit to these demands. . . .

2 The employers possess the right to dismiss superfluous workers, observing the laws and rulings which have been established in this connection.

President of the Committee, Volsky
Members of the Committee: N. Shmelev, I Nesterov, P. Belozerov,
I. Brushvit, P. Klimushin and V. Abramov.

Source: W.H. Chamberlin, The Russian Revolution, 1917–1921, *volume II (Princeton: Princeton University Press 1987), pp. 470–1*

Document 8.1 reveals that the Komuch accepted much of the economic and social transformation that had been wrought during 1917. It attempted to secure the support of the peasants by reassuring them that the fruits of the Revolution, the land, would not be taken from them (section 1). The forced requisitioning of grain that had been introduced by the Bolsheviks **(see Document 9.9)** and fixed grain prices were also to be abolished. Similarly, for the workers there was to be no return to the harsh, uncouth and arbitrary industrial regime of the autocracy. Laws to protect labour from excessive exploitation and guaranteeing the rights of trade unions were reaffirmed while the workers were to be protected from arbitrary lockouts on the part of the employers (sections 2, 3, 5, 6 and 8). Such policies, however, did not inspire the peasants and workers to volunteer en masse for the Komuch army. At the same time, they alienated the educated and propertied classes **(Mawdsley 1987: 64–5)**. Despite this failure of mass mobilisation, the combined forces of Czechoslovaks and Komuch, the so-called People's Army, still succeeded in capturing Kazan' on 6–7 August. As Leon Trotsky remarked, only Nizhnii Novogorod lay between them and Moscow **(Trotsky 1974: 413)**. However, the Bolsheviks rallied and recaptured Kazan' on 10 September. In a speech given in Kazan' itself on 12 September Trotsky remarked on one of the causes of the victory of the Red Army.

Document 8.2 Trotsky's Explanation of Victory at Kazan'

The latest communique [from Lenin] bears witness to the fact that our Red forces are victoriously advancing or repelling our enemies' attacks not only here but everywhere on all sectors of the front, while a month ago we were weak – if not weak as regards enthusiasm and readiness to die, of which qualities workers conscious of their cause have always ample store, our organisation was a somewhat weak one in comparison with the organisation of our enemies, who could bring their officers' battalions into operation.

Source: J. Meijer (ed.), The Trotsky Papers, 1917–1922, *Volume 1: 1917–1919 (The Hague: Mouton, 1971), pp. 129–31*

The poor organisation of the Red Army that Trotsky referred to in Document 8.2 in large part had been caused by the system of dual authority that existed within it. In particular, suspicion of many of its officers, recruited from the former Imperial Army, had caused the Bolsheviks to appoint politically reliable commissars, with no military qualifications, to supervise their actions. In the opinion of Trotsky himself, and others, such as Aleksandr Egorov, the chief military commissar, the latter had been prone to meddle in purely military affairs, technically in the hands of the old officers, the so-called military specialists (*spetsy*), with disastrous consequences. The fall of Kazan' prompted Trotsky to demand that such intervention cease. Political commissars remained, to ensure that the old officers did not use their power in ways harmful to the Revolution, but in questions of military strategy and tactics they were subordinated to the *spetsy*. The restoration of what can be termed 'one-man management' in the army proved to be an important factor in the eventual success of the Red Army in the Civil War **(Mawdsley 1987: 276)**, although Trotsky's championing of the old officers was to bring him into conflict with the Left of the Party **(see Chapter 12)**.

Another major source of Bolshevik victory had been its ability to reinforce its eastern front so that the Red Army, as Trotsky also conceded, had a 'substantial superiority' over its enemies. The introduction of mass conscription on 29 May no doubt played its part in achieving this superiority. Also vital was the successful negotiation of a new trade treaty with Germany in early August (it was formally signed on 27 August) which enabled the Bolsheviks to transfer 30,000 troops to the Volga, secure in the knowledge that the Germans would not take advantage of the situation to advance further into Russia **(Swain 1996: 251–2)**. On the other hand, few additional forces came to assist the Komuch to retain Kazan', despite numerous anti-Bolshevik risings in the Urals and the dispatch of Allied forces to Archangel in early August.

In retrospect, the fall of Kazan' to the Bolsheviks can be seen as a critical turning-point in the fortunes of the democratic counter-revolution. Samara itself fell to the Red Army on 24 September. In the meantime, on 8 September the Komuch had met with representatives of the more conservative Siberian regional government, and various other less-important local organisations, at a conference held in the Urals' town of Ufa. The outcome of this conference was the creation of a Russian Provisional Government, headed by a five-man Directory: N.D. Avksentiev (SR), General V.G. Boldyrev (SR), V.A. Vinogradov (Kadet), P.V. Volgogodskii (Kadet) and V.M. Zenzinov (SR). However, this return to the coalition politics of 1917 proved to be short-lived. On 18 November the Directory was overthrown in a military *coup*. With the support of the Kadets and the industrialists, as well as the Cossacks, the old officers erected a dictatorship under Admiral Alexander Kolchak **(White 1994: 195–6)**. The Civil War now had been transformed into one primarily between the Reds and the Whites, with another White army, the Volunteer Army under Denikin, also firmly established in the south, in the Kuban, in the autumn of 1918. Many Mensheviks, and some SRs, now abandoned their opposition and rallied, reluctantly, behind the beleaguered Bolshevik regime **(see Chapter 14)**.

In December Kolchak's armies began their advance from Siberia. By the end of April 1919 they were approaching the Volga. However, they were to advance no further and were rapidly forced back into Siberia, where they all but disintegrated. Mawdsley attributes Kolchak's defeat essentially to military factors: the superior resources (human and material) of the Bolsheviks; the poor quality of Kolchak's forces, both officers and rank and file; and the difficulties in supplying his armies with the equipment provided in abundance by the British, but landed thousands of miles away in Vladivostok, at the far end of the trans-Siberian railway **(Mawdsley 1987: 144–54)**. Moreover, Denikin's decision in the spring of 1919 to deploy the bulk of the Volunteer Army to defend the Donbass, rather than ordering it north to establish a common front with Kolchak's forces, compounded the inferiority of the latter **(Pipes 1995: 80–1)**. In a speech to his supporters on 4 November 1919, Kolchak himself claimed that sheer lack of numbers was at the root of his retreat.

Document 8.3 Kolchak Explains why his Armies were Defeated

[T]he essence of the problem was this: the enemy was able to reinforce his ranks with new forces more quickly than we could.

How can this have happened?

Our units which were formed from men called up in the area behind the front, from Bolshevik-minded elements, crossed over to the Red side; this experience bred distrust of the new reinforcements among both commanders and veterans. We sent reinforcements, but detachment commanders refused to dilute their units with these reinforcements.

We had to reinforce with great selectiveness, while the enemy freely used local manpower which was favourable to him.

Source: Cited in E. Mawdsley, The Russian Civil War *(London: Allen & Unwin, 1987), p. 155*

There is no reason to doubt Kolchak's conclusion that his armies found themselves outnumbered by the Red Army. This was to be a common problem facing all the White armies, and overall Bolshevik superiority in men and materials was a critical factor in their victory. However, Document 8.3 does not explain why Kolchak found it so difficult to mobilise sufficient reliable troops. This failure was analysed by General R. Gajda, the commander of the Czechoslovak legions, who had continued to serve Kolchak after his own men had left Russia. He began rather conventionally by confirming that logistical problems had undermined the progress of Kolchak's forces, in particular, the fact that they had advanced too far beyond the capacities of their supply lines. However, he quickly proceeded to highlight other shortcomings which he deemed to be equally, if not more, important in explaining their defeat.

Document 8.4 Gajda's Report to Kolchak, September 1919

One of the reasons for the collapse of the Western Army was the policy and propaganda of its staff, in spreading an anti-democratic spirit and inflaming racial hatreds through anti-Semitic exhortations, its relations with the Bashkirs. Both were so unsuccessful that they resulted in risings in the immediate rear of the army.

At the same time as difficulties were occurring on the front, internal complications are not diminishing but continue without cessation . . . we have to do with something of a more solid nature than occasional flare-ups.

First of all, one is struck by the wide extent of these disturbances and risings . . . and by their occurrence in districts where there is hardly any reason for Bolshevism.

Nearer the front things are noticeably quieter, but even there have been recorded the risings of Tiumen (conscripts & workmen), Kustunai (peasants, colonists, and conscripts). It is characteristic that most of the risings have the appearance of town movements but start and spread principally in the villages and country. The rebel detachments are beginning to assume fairly large proportions . . . . The extent to which their efforts sometimes reach may be judged from the following. For two weeks the Amur Railway did not function, being occupied by the rebels . . . . The bands frequently possess intelligent organisers (in some cases even officers) . . . they apparently meet with no active opposition and more frequently are helped by the local population.

In general all disturbances and risings are explained by the activities of Bolshevik agitators, who collect around them former Red Guards . . . . But . . . an explanation is necessary as to how these agitators were able to obtain influence among the agricultural population, which not so long ago enthusiastically welcomed their overthrowal. Secondly, in many cases the motive for rising can be shown to have nothing whatever to do with the Bolsheviks

. . . statements [were] heard on station Kaishet by those who captured it from the 'Reds' such as 'we are not Bolsheviks, we are the peasants' union, we are fighting against Kolchak, whips and taxes'.

Thirdly, in places, the 'intelligent' agriculturists were observed to take part (generally those who had suffered severely from Bolsheviks).

All this leads us to think that we have to do with phenomena of a different order to the imagined risings incited by Bolshevik agents, and must seek deeper and wider spread roots which are developing in Siberian territory.

The overthrowal of Bolshevik power was received everywhere with enthusiasm by the most varied elements of the population . . . . In the course of two or three months, in most towns, the picture changes . . . in private discussions where general opinion flows, the subject of the high cost of living 'which reminds one of the Bolsheviks' or the excessively tiresome length of war [are heard] . . . . Not infrequent are symptoms of general discontent with the system of government . . . . Speculation, gambling, the selfish profiting by the efforts to which the war drives the country. Patriotic feeling, instead of being a constant stimulus to self-sacrifice, is weakening.

The coincidence of our failures on the front, interior disturbances and general dissatisfaction, forces the conclusion that there are reasons for these symptoms, and that these reasons must be sought for in the methods of government of the country . . . a number of serious deficiences can be observed in this respect.

1) In opposition to the general declaration of the government, actual local practice presents a picture of arbitrary acts quite out of conformity with the ideas of law and culture . . . the practice of corporal punishment . . . many cases of shooting without trial or investigation left unpunished . . . . Numerous cases of arrests, deportation and lengthy imprisonment without trial, of persons wholly unconnected with Bolshevism.

. . . in local matters of internal government, the law is replaced by 'prikazi', which alter with the changes of commandants and heads of the garrisons . . . very often the contents of these orders are far from being suitable for their task or to the dignity of authority.

In some places pure Bolshevik methods are employed (e.g., the shooting of hostages by Rozanoff in Krasnoiarsk).

It is not felt that a democratic course is being followed. . . .

The results of the discussions on the legislative body gave the impression that the authorities had no desire to meet the democrats half way. . . .

The declaration of the government about land is full of obscurities, which can create doubt among the peasant classes . . . nothing is said of the decision of the land question in its entirety by the Constituent Assembly [see Chapter 7].

Behind all these defects is hidden the general and real blemish of the government's course. It is occupied almost entirely with town questions. The country, which is suffering more severely from the effects of arbitrary acts, does not feel that the authorities are troubling about it . . . . The peasantry . . . have much more weight than all the town population together.

No authority can carry out its task unless the peasantry considers it as 'its' authority.

. . . we must pay attention to the fact that the Bolsheviks, under the pressure of defeat, are beginning to change the course of their policy . . . at the March [1919] conference of the Bolsheviks [the Eighth Party Congress], it was decided to stop the repressive measures with the intelligent peasantry and poorer bourgeoisie. The 'stake on the peasantry' has been announced.

It is imperative now, before it is too late, to get rid of the mentioned defects in government, and then, tracing out a clear and democratic course of state policy, follow it with unwavering strictness.

The government must declare that its final aim is the calling of the Constituent Assembly, on the basis of universal, equal, direct and secret electoral rights.

Source: Public Record Office, FO538/2/14421, Results of the Spring Offensive

Gajda's report is an extremely important source. It was composed in the late summer of 1919, before the eventual outcome of the Civil War between the Reds and Whites was known, and by an active participant, although as a Czech one arguably rather more detached from the passions of Russian politics than most other participants. Its significance is that it highlights the political failure of the White leadership to win the confidence of the majority of the people, a failure that more partisan observers subsequently came to argue was a critical cause of the Whites' defeat. As Paul Miliukov, the Kadet leader, remarked, 'in a civil war everything depends on the state of mind of the population living under the competing systems of government'. Once the character of its 'leading elements' (nationalist officers, landowners and industrialists) was taken into account, he continued, it should have been no surprise that the reactionary policies of the Whites lost them the battle for the hearts and minds of the people. Even Denikin, who had succeeded Kornilov as leader of the Volunteer Army, agreed with the essence of Miliukov's analysis **(Denikin 1930: 299–301; Miliukov 1922: 172–3)**.

The detailed picture that Gajda paints of Kolchak's regime is a sad, if credible, one. Initially, it was seen as one promising liberation from Bolshevik tyranny and depredations and, as such, was greeted with considerable sympathy. This sympathy rapidly dissolved in response to its inability, even unwillingness, to offer any prospects of fair and democratic administration and economic and social reform. The authoritarian, even terroristic, methods of Bolshevik rule had been replaced by equally arbitrary (and corrupt) ones which, as Gajda unequivocally pointed out, had provoked widespread opposition among all strata of society. More critically, perhaps, the regime's refusal to give any assurances to the peasants that the land that they finally had won as a result of the Revolution was secure in their hands irrevocably cost it the support of the vast majority of the Russian population. The Bolsheviks, at least, did not threaten this fundamental gain, though grain requisitioning, and their often half-hearted attempts to promote collective agriculture, continued to provoke general peasant resentment (their attempts to conciliate the peasants after the Eighth Party Congress of March 1919 referred to by Gajda did little to appease them). Such failings were not confined to Siberia, but were typical of the various White movements. Most importantly, the regime of Denikin and the Volunteer Army in the south increasingly became identified with lawlessness and wanton brutality, the appropriation (or plain looting) of peasant property, and the return of the landlords **(Mawdsley 1987: 207–11)**. Recently published extracts from private letters compiled by the local departments of the office of the Military Censor during 1919 testify to rapidly growing disillusion amongst those caught up in the advance of Denikin's forces.

Document 8.5 Popular Opinions of the Volunteer Army

Denikin occupied Kamyshin . . . life, they say, is ugly. Tatars, Circassians, Koreans, all this band treat the peasants very badly. Everything is being destroyed (Astrakhan province, Plesetskoe, 17 August, 1919).

When the Whites advanced they slaughtered all the cattle and it is impossible to say anything to anyone. They removed the good shoes from our feet and took away all our clothing. The Reds did not treat us so badly. They did not slaughter our cattle and bought everything that they needed (Volynskaia province, Dedovyn, 15 August, 1919).

Denikin's bands behave with terrible brutality towards the inhabitants left behind in their rear, and especially towards the workers and peasants. First of all, they are beaten unmercifully with ramrods or parts of their bodies are cut off, for example: ears, nose, eyes are put out or a cross is engraved on their back or chest (Kursk, 14 August, 1919).

Source: I Davidyn, V. Kozlova (eds), 'Chastny pis'ma epokhi grazhdanskoi voiny Po materialam voennoi tsenzury', Neizvestnaia Rossia. XX vek, II, 1992, p. 239

Another political failure of the Whites that Gajda alluded to **(in Document 8.4)** was their Great Russian nationalism, even chauvinism. Anti-Semitism was pandemic, less so in Siberia where there were few Jews. In 1919, however, as Denikin's Volunteer Army advanced through the Ukraine to threaten Moscow itself, an orgy of pogroms was instituted against the Jews, as many of the other letters collected by the military censor confirm. The main culprits may have been 'irregular' forces of Ukrainians and Cossacks attached to the Volunteer Army, as Pipes suggests, but that should not absolve from responsibility the White leadership which proved to be incapable of preventing such atrocities **(Pipes 1995: 104–11)**. Even more damaging was the refusal of the White generals to contemplate offering any measure of autonomy to the various national minorities of the former Empire. Denikin's appeal to the Ukrainian people in August 1919 illustrates their desire to resurrect the old Russian state.

Document 8.6 To the Population of Little Russia, August 1919

By the valour and blood of the armies one Russian region after another is being freed from the yoke of the madmen and traitors who have given the deceived people slavery instead of happiness and freedom.

Regiments are approaching ancient Kiev, 'the mother of Russian cities', resolute in their desire to return to the Russian people their lost unity, that unity without which the great Russian people, weakened and splintered, losing their younger generations in fratricidal struggles, would not have the strength to preserve their independence – that unity without which would be unthinkable a full and normal economic life in which the north and south, the east and west of a vast power take to one another in free exchange the wealth of every area, every region – that unity, without which would not have been created the mighty Russian language, which was woven in equal share by the centuries-long efforts of Kiev, Moscow and Petrograd.

Desiring to weaken the Russian state before declaring war on it, the Germans strove, long before 1914, to destroy the unity of the Russian tribe, which had been forged by hard struggle.

With this goal in mind they supported and encouraged in South Russia a movement with the declared aim of separating from Russia her nine southern provinces under the name of the 'Ukrainian state'. The aspiration to tear from Russia the Little Russian branch of the Russian people has not been abandoned even now. The former henchmen of the Germans, Petliura and his cronies, having begun the dismemberment of Russia, continue even now to complete their evil business of creating an independent 'Ukrainian state' and of struggling against the renascence of a United Russia.

Source:A.I. Denikin, Ocherki russkoi smuty, *volume V (Berlin: Mednyi Vsadnik, 1930), pp. 142f*

While hastening to concede that the Ukrainians would enjoy a degree of self-administration (the details were not spelled out) and use of their own language in local affairs, the main thrust of Denikin's message was clear: the restoration of a united (and centralised) Russian state largely within its former frontiers. The vast majority of White officers aspired to the same end. Their reluctance to offer significant concessions to the various non-Russian peoples on occasion was to have a fatal impact on their prospects. Having grudgingly accepted that Polish independence was a *fait accompli*, their intent to limit its territorial scope (to the confines of the tiny kingdom of Congress Poland, set up by the Congress of Vienna in 1815) alienated Josef Pilsudski, leader of the new Polish state. His response was to strike a deal with the Bolsheviks during 1919. In return for acquiescence to his territorial demands, Pilsudski promised the Bolsheviks that Poland would remain neutral as they fought against Denikin's Volunteer Army in the south. As a year earlier in their struggle with the Komuch, the Bolsheviks, secure in the knowledge that the Poles would not attack, again were able to redeploy substantial forces from their Western front to reinforce the army facing Denikin. Moreover, relations between Denikin and the Cossacks, especially the Kuban Cossacks, were strained by the former's emphasis on a 'Russia one and indivisible' and the latter's aspiration for a considerable degree of autonomy **(Mawdsley 1987: 208–9)**. Similarly, Kolchak's refusal to recognise Finland's independence frustrated the attempts of General N.N. Iudenich to win the support of General Karl Mannerheim and his Finnish divisions, which was vital to the success of the planned assault on Petrograd in the autumn of 1919 **(Pipes 1995: 88-94)**.

The threats posed to the Bolsheviks in 1919 impelled them to mount a massive propaganda campaign to discredit the Whites and mobilise mass support for the defence of the Revolution. Political posters played perhaps the most prominent part in this campaign. The poster reproduced as Document 8.7, first composed by Dmitrii Moor in 1919, reveals what the workers can expect should the enemy (Death, bearing the Tsar on its arm) win. The caption reads: 'The Enemy is at the gates! He brings slavery, hunger and death! Destroy the dark and foul creatures! All to defence! Forward!' The lack of evidence, however, makes it impossible to estimate precisely what impact such posters had on the population.

Document 8.7 Bolshevik Political Poster of the Civil War

[See illustration on p. 125]

A combination of Bolshevik superiority and the political failures of the Volunteer Army checked Denikin's advance towards Moscow in October 1919. In the winter of 1919–20 the remnants of the Volunteer Army was driven back to the North Caucasus, and thence out of Russia. A minority succeeded in fleeing to the Crimea where it regrouped in the spring of 1920, now under the command of Wrangel. More sensitive to the political nature of the Civil War, he strove to articulate a broad programme of reform designed to mobilise and retain popular support in territories occupied by his forces. The flaws in his proposed reforms were highlighted by Paul Miliukov.

Document 8.8 Miliukov's Critique of Wrangel's Reform Programme

In a few weeks Wrangel succeeded in raising the spirit of the army and in restoring its confidence. However, the secret of his success was soon brought out in strong relief. It was the spirit of caste with which the army was now imbued, and the solidarity of crime and lawlessness had taken the place of military discipline. The prevailing influence rested in a group of

Source: S. White, The Bolshevik Poster *(New Haven: Yale University Press, 1988), p. 44*

young officers, to whom everything was permitted. They tolerated only such superiors as shut their eyes to their debauched conduct and simply refused to recognise such nominations as did not please them. A civilian was to them a nonentity. As a matter of fact no civil administration existed. The only courts of justice that existed, the military courts, were completely disregarded if the culprit belonged to the privileged caste, and they were forced to sanction hangings and shootings, if the privileged ones condescended to put their victims before the tribunals. It was only natural that when this army went on an offensive, looting and robbing of the population at once became universal . . . . The population soon began to ignore the mobilizations: certain cantons . . . instead of 1,000 gave six to ten men. Gen. Wrangel ordered that the property of the relatives of the deserters be confiscated, and the 'punitive expeditions' were thus practically free to loot the whole population.

Now, there was another idea which had become axiomatic: the land was to be left with the peasants . . . . But, here again, he was unable to carry out a really democratic solution . . . the agrarian regulations of May 25, 1920, were full of loopholes and tricks to restore whatever possible from the landed estates to the gentry. The size of plots, the way of remunerating the former owners was to be the 'Land Councils' in the townships, and the influence of the squires on the decisions of these 'Land Councils' can be measured by the great size of the estates restored to the former possessors. Under the peculiar conditions of land ownership in the Crimea, the reform did not provoke open resistance. But outside of the Crimea word soon spread that General Wrangel was an enemy of the peasants, and the name 'Krivoshayin' [Krivoshein, the former Tsarist Minister of Agriculture and a supporter of Wrangel] was enough to persuade them that this was true. The peasants boycotted Wrangel's agrarian regulations and waited for some new power to come to their rescue.

A third point whereat Wrangel earnestly wished to improve upon Denikin was the question of autonomy or federation. The very use of the word 'federation' had been strictly forbidden under Denikin. It was now made use of by Wrangel's advisers. But, again, the choice of advisers and executors was dictated by Wrangel's political connections. To improve the relations with the nationalities and with the Cossack territories a man was chosen who was as much suspected of favoring centralism, as Krovoshayin [sic] was of landlordism. It was Mr. P.B. Struve, the well-known protagonist of Russian – and even of 'Great-Russian' nationalism. So far as the Cossacks were concerned, the result was the sham agreement with the 'State formations of the Don, Kuban, Terek and Astrakhan territories' of August 4, 1920, which the atamans were ordered to sign in twenty-four hours, in order to 'demonstrate their union with Wrangel before Europe.' . . . An agreement with the Ukraine was as essential for Wrangel's military schemes as that with the Cossacks. On September 23 Gen. Wrangel consented to receive a delegation from one of the moderate Ukrainian federalist groups ('the Ukrainian National Committee in Paris'). The official statement sent out by Mr. Struve after that interview was as follows: 'Prompted by the desire to unite all the anti-Bolshevik forces, Gen. Wrangel is ready to support the development of national democratic forces *on the same lines* as proclaimed by the agreement with the Cossack regions. Gen. Wrangel does not admit the possibility of allying himself with any separatist movement.' Even for the 'federalists' such a statement was hardly satisfactory . . . . As a matter of fact, nothing came of the negotiations.

A formula was found by partisans of Wrangel's policy which very well emphasizes its political meaning. It was the 'left (i.e., liberal) policy carried out by the right (e.g., conservative) hands.' . . . Gen. Wrangel's policy . . . was a clumsy attempt to cheat the world with liberal catchwords for the benefit of a small group who were over-confident that they alone knew the real Russia, the Russia of illiterate peasants ruled by benevolent squires, with methods of patriarchal compulsion.

Source: P.N. Miliukov, Russia Today and Tomorrow *(New York: Macmillan, 1922), pp. 177-81*

As a leading representative of Russian liberalism, Miliukov's critique of the un-progressive policies of Wrangel (and by implication of the other White generals) is unsurprising. He fails to point out that many of his fellow Kadets had whole-heartedly supported them during the Civil War. They too had sought to maintain 'Russia, one and indivisible' and opposed the economic and social reforms required to win mass support (ironically, as Miliukov himself had done in 1917). He had only belatedly come to accept the necessity of such support if the Bolsheviks were to be defeated **(Rosenberg 1974: 471)**. Yet his emphasis on the equivocal character of Wrangel's reforms is quite credible as they failed to mobilise the peasants, the Cossacks or the minorities in any significant numbers. It remains doubtful, however, whether anything that Wrangel could have done would have made any difference to his fate. Lacking any foreign support (Britain categorically refused any assistance) the limited success of his offensives in the summer of 1920 were largely the product of the Red Army's involvement in an ill-conceived war to 'export' socialist revolution to Poland. When this ended in Soviet defeat, with an armistice signed on 18 October, the vastly superior forces of the Red Army were transferred to the south, where they inflicted a crushing defeat on the remnants of the Volunteer Army. The Civil War was over, so it seemed, with the Bolsheviks as victors. But victory brought its unintended consequences. Finally free from the fear of a restoration of the old order, the Green movement escalated. In the winter of 1920–1 the Bolsheviks found themselves confronted by massive and widespread peasant insurrections (and strikes in urban Russia) which threatened their very survival. The nature of this threat, and how the Bolsheviks overcame it, will be recounted in Chapter 15.

The issues of the Revolution

Agriculture and the peasants | 9

1917 witnessed a profound transformation in the Russian countryside. The old landlords were engulfed by a tidal wave of peasant revolution which left the peasants, for a time, masters of their domains **(Figes 1989: 355–6)**. The question of the underlying sources of this revolution, however, remains much more complex. It is no longer possible to attribute it simply to the growing impoverishment of the peasant mass. Recent studies suggest that despite an agrarian productivity that remained low in comparison to West Europe, peasant standards of living generally had been rising before 1914 **(Channon 1992a: 117; Perrie 1992: 19)**. Yet substantial pockets of rural poverty did exist, most noticeably in the Black Earth region (embracing much of the Central Agricultural and Middle Volga regions) and the Ukraine. The majority of peasants, moreover, continued to believe that a free and equal redistribution of all land not in their hands (especially that of the gentry and the 'separators', those peasants who had taken advantage of the Stolypin reforms of 1906–11 to set up their own farms independent of the old village commune) would resolve all their problems. The aspirations of the peasants were set out in their famous 'Model Mandate'. Drawn up and published by the SRs in the *Izvestiia* of the All-Russian Congress of Peasant Deputies in August it was based on the 242 sets of instructions given by local peasant communities to their delegates to the First All-Russian Congress of Soviets of Peasant Deputies which convened in Petrograd on 4 May. It began by expressing support for a democratically elected Constituent Assembly which was to transform Russia into a federal republic, one in which civil liberties were to be inviolable. It also accepted that the state should preserve its monopoly on the distribution of grain which was to be implemented by democratically elected, local food committees. The price of grain, and of other items of mass consumption, was to be fixed. It also outlined the peasants' vision of land reform.

Document 9.1 Peasant Mandate on the Land

The land question in its entirety can be resolved only by the national Constituent Assembly. The most just settlement of the land question must be the following:

1 The right to private ownership of the land is to be abolished forever; land may not be sold, purchased, leased, mortgaged or otherwise alienated. All

land, state, crown . . . monastery, church . . . private, public, peasant, etc., is to be confiscated without compensation, to be converted into the property of the whole people, and to pass into the use of all those who cultivate it.

2 All mineral wealth . . . and also all forests and waters which are of importance to the state pass into the exclusive use of the state. All small rivers, lakes, woods, etc., pass into the use of the communes, on the condition that they are administered by local organs of self-government.

3 Estates which are cultivated by highly developed techniques – orchards, plantations . . . nurseries, hothouses, etc. – are not to be divided up, but are to be converted into model farms and assigned to the exclusive use of the state or to the communes, depending on the size and importance of such estates.

4 Stud farms, government and private pedigree stock and poultry farms, etc., are to be confiscated, converted into the property of the whole people, and pass into the exclusive use either of the state or the commune, depending on their size and significance. The question of compensation is to be examined by the Constituent Assembly.

5 All livestock and equipment of the confiscated estates pass into the exclusive use of the state or commune . . . without compensation. The confiscation of equipment does not extend to small peasants.

6 The right to use the land is granted to all citizens of the Russian state (regardless of sex) who wish to cultivate it by their own labour, with the help of their families, or in an association, but only so long as they are able to cultivate it. The employment of hired labour is not permitted . . . . There must be complete freedom in the methods employed to work the land, by household, individually, communally or cooperatively, as will be decided in each separate village or settlement.

7 Land tenure must be equal, i.e., the land is to be distributed among the working people according to labour or consumption criteria, taking into consideration local conditions.

8 All the land . . . becomes part of the national land fund. The distribution of it among the toilers is to be administered by local and central organs of government, beginning with democratically organised village and city communes . . . and ending with central regional government institutions. The land is to be subject to periodical redistribution, depending on the growth of population . . . . The land of members who leave the commune shall revert to the land fund.

Source: A.V. Shestakov (ed.), Sovety krest'ianikh deputatov i drugie krest'ianskie organizatsii , 1 (Mart – Noiabr' 1917g.) *(Moscow: Izdatel'stvo Kommunisticheskoi akademii, 1929), pp. 152–3*

Document 9.1 illustrates the basic belief of the Russian peasants that land should belong only to those who actually worked it – hence their desire for the abolition of all private property in land, without compensation. Once expropriated, all the land, with the exception (in theory) of the more advanced and productive model estates, was to be divided amongst the peasants equally. Periodic redistribution, by altering the amount of land held by a peasant family as the number of members within it rose or fell, would ensure that the principle of equality would be preserved. Finally, despite the freedom ostensibly granted to individual farmers in point 7, the Mandate repeatedly revealed the peasants' commitment to maintain their traditional communal pattern of life, which the Stolypin reforms had threatened to destroy. In the interim, until the Constituent Assembly convened and determined the final shape of land reform, a number of positive measures were to be taken. In particular, the sale of land was to be forbidden, to prevent, for example, existing owners selling it to foreigners which would preclude its future redistribution **(see Document 9.2)**. The laws enacted by Stolypin permitting peasants to leave the commune and take their land with them as private property were to be repealed immediately. Locally elected land committees were to be given the authority to ensure, among other things, that uncultivated land was worked; that the fruits of the land were properly harvested and not wasted; that the necessary stocks and equipment were fairly distributed among the peasants; that wages and rents were fixed equitably; and, finally, that there were no arbitrary attempts to seize the land. In the spring of 1917, it might be argued, peasant Russia was displaying a considerable degree of patience and restraint. These demands were largely incorporated in the resolutions of the Congress. As Graeme Gill has pointed out, however, it went beyond the peasant instructions in seeking to make the land committees responsible for the administration of all the land until the Constituent Assembly met, a policy also favoured by Viktor Chernov, the new (SR) Minister of Agriculture in the First Coalition **(Gill 1979: 123)**.

The problem was that the peasants' restraint was not rewarded. The Provisional Government, with the support of the Soviet, procrastinated on the land question, as we saw in Chapter 4. Its first pronouncement on the agrarian question on 19 March failed to state that all land would be redistributed amongst the peasantry. It declared that land reform required careful preparation and could only be carried out by the the Constituent Assembly. The First Coalition was a little more forthcoming, committing itself to 'the transfer of land to the toilers'. In practice, it did little and also assigned its final resolution to the Constituent Assembly, which it too repeatedly deferred **(see Document 4.7)**. Peasant impatience at government inaction quickly grew. It emerged too at the Congress of Peasant Deputies. B. Gurevich, an SR, recalled how this impatience was, apparently, overcome.

Document 9.2 Peasant Desires for Immediate Land Reform

In truth, the advocacy of land seizures on the part of the Bolsheviks among the peasant deputies did not meet with success, but then . . . the question arose about the immediate introduction of agrarian reform, without waiting for the convocation of the Constituent Assembly. It rose initially, as I recall, in a rather peculiar and naive form, in the manner of a resolution that the

Congress should decree land socialisation itself. This idea was received sympathetically in view of the fact that many of the delegates did not especially clearly understand, first, the difference between the declaration of some principle and the introduction of a law in accord with it, and, second, the difference between a resolution of the Congress, which expresses an opinion, and a decree of the government, which has the force of law. The majority of the deputies who supported the idea of the immediate socialisation of the land, so to speak 'by telegraph', apparently had not the slightest intention to encroach upon any of the prerogatives of the government or to place it in a difficult situation. The talk turned simply to the most rapid realisation of this idea which was attractive to the peasants. They had nothing against the fact were the government itself, and not the Congress, to pass the decree on socialisation. However, when it was explained to the peasants that socialisation demands an exceptionally complex and lengthy period of preparatory work to calculate the exact quantity of the land available, to determine how much of it was arable and the fertility of the soil, and also to work out a plan for its redistribution, then our deputies became lost in thought. The idea of carrying out at once an all-embracing black repartition was abandoned and it did not take much effort to convince the Congress that the fundamental land law and all measures for its implementation must be sanctioned by the Constituent Assembly.

In the local land committees which were empowered to prepare the ground for reform and collect the necessary data in their districts the representatives of the local peasant congresses and soviets played an important role. In such a way the business of land reform was almost wholly in their own hands. There was also complete trust in the Ministry of Agriculture. Therefore, it seemed to us that the peasants at the Congress were satisfied by a statement of the principles underlying the future reform, by the despatch of their delegates into the Land Committees and by the regulation of land relations in the interests of the toilers.

However, it soon emerged that we had misjudged both the attitude of the Congress and also of all the peasantry in the localities. In fact, the peasants had nothing against a thoughtful and careful preparation of land reform and an organised redistribution of it in the future, but this in no way meant that they simply were prepared passively to wait for future blessings. While the prohibition on the old notaries to ratify the sale or mortgaging of landed property protected the peasantry (and equally the state) from attempts by the *pomeshchiki* to secure, if not their estates themselves, then their equivalent value, by transferring their rights to foreigners, this alone still could not eliminate the suspicion of the wary peasantry. The peasants already anticipated the delights of possession of the long-cherished *pomeshchik* land and all its valuable assets and feared that the 'masters', pending the reform, would after all find the means to render their estates valueless by creaming off from them whatever was possible. Therefore, while still not pressing for the immediate redistribution of *pomeshchik* land, the peasants energetically sought to alienate it from the *pomeshchiki*, to convert it into state property or, as it were, the legal declaration of this. In other words, there was still no talk of socialisation, but only of a preliminary nationalisation of the land.

Source: B. Gurevich, 'Vserossiiskii Krest'ianskii S"ezd i pervaia koalitsiia', Letopis' revoliutsii, 1 *(Berlin: Izdatel'stvo Z.I. Grzhebina, 1923), pp. 191–2*

Gurevich's account accurately reflects the attitudes of the Congress, dominated by SR intellectuals (mainly of the moderate Right of the Party) rather than peasants themselves. The SR intelligentsia supported the principles contained within the 'Model Mandate' but at the same time had its reasons for delaying their implementation. Charitably, its position can be defended on the grounds that it genuinely believed that only a carefully planned and organised redistribution of the land would be just, ensuring that all the peasants, not just the rich, gained from it. Less charitably, it also feared that immediate land division would be disruptive of Russia's war effort, tempting peasant soldiers to desert from the frontline, and also worsen the already critical food supply situation. Ironically, it found itself in the same camp as the Kadets, who also opposed land reform lest it jeopardise the successful prosecution of the war, although the increasing influence of the provincial gentry at the grassroots of the Party also led them to defend 'vested agrarian interests' **(Atkinson 1983: 138–9; Rosenberg 1974: 127–9)**. As we shall see, the Bolsheviks alone were prepared to approve the peasants' increasingly strident calls for action.

However, Gurevich's forebodings about the rising impatience of the peasants were also borne out. It was fuelled by a deepening sense that the February Revolution had not resulted in any tangible improvements in their lives. Apart from little being done in practice to promote land redistribution and the fact that the landlords remained able to sell their land freely, the Provisonal Government had taken few steps to replace the authority of the old landlords and bureaucrats in the countryside. In March and April it had even shown that it was prepared to resort to force to maintain order in rural Russia **(Gill 1978: 67)**. Rapidly growing peasant disillusion with the inaction of the Provisional Government (and with the SRs, themselves part of this government after the First Coalition was established on 5 May) was reflected, arguably quite typically, at the peasant assembly in Samara that convened on 20 May. One of the rank-and-file peasant delegates, Egorov, expressed their dissatisfaction clearly.

Document 9.3 The Growth of Peasant Radicalism

Igaev [leader of the Popular Socialist party in Samara] speaks of judicial rights. I am no judge and don't know the law. When I was a boy my father told me that I was a peasant. I believe that land means freedom. It is wrong to pay the landowners for the land. Will we be any better off if we wait for the

Constituent Assembly to resolve the land question? In the past the government decided the land question for us, but their efforts led us only into bondage. Now the government says there must first be order. We are always being told 'later, later, not now, not until the Constituent Assembly' . . . . The land question must be resolved now, and we should not put our trust blindly in the political parties.

Source: O. Figes, Peasant Russia, Civil War: The Volga Countryside in Revolution (1917–1921), *(Oxford, 1989), pp. 41–2*

Document 9.3 illustrates the mounting preparedness of the peasants to resolve the land question on their terms and in their own way. Moreover, the attitude to political parties expressed in it in fact reflected a heightened peasant distrust of all outsiders, especially intellectuals. This distrust became increasingly manifest during 1917 as the peasants ignored the formal organs of administration set up in the countryside by the Provisonal Government (and external agitators too). They asserted their own hegemony by electing their fellows to staff the various committees at the *volost'* and village level where, in practice, traditional, if reinvigorated and democratised, communal village assemblies wielded real power **(Figes 1989: 33–40)**.

As the Provisional Government continued to drag its heels on the issue of land reform, its other policies also raised peasant hackles. In particular, during the summer the peasants came to oppose the state monopoly in grain that they had earlier welcomed. The urgency of supplying both the army and towns with food had prompted the Provisional Government to enact a law on 25 March to create provincial, and lower-level, food committees. Their task was to requisition all surplus grain, above norms that they themselves established. In return, the price of grain was raised by 60 per cent. However, this policy soon ran into difficulties. First, the goods required by the peasants remained in short supply as industry continued to produce mainly for the war. The prices of the goods that were available rose rapidly, soon far outstripping the decreed rise in grain prices and removing any incentives for the peasants to give up their grain **(Atkinson 1983: 119–20)**. In response, the peasants resisted all efforts to requisition their grain, especially violently in areas of the Black Earth region that had suffered drought in the summer. The Provisional Government, lacking effective power in the countryside, proved to be unable to extract the grain required to feed the army and the towns. The belated attempt to appease the peasants, by grudgingly doubling the price of grain on 27 August, achieved little, bar fuelling inflationary pressure that hit not only the urban workers but also those poorer peasants who were unable to produce sufficient food to meet their family needs the whole year round **(Gill 1979: 87–8)**.

Peasant discontent became transformed to direct action during the spring and summer. The tables shown in Documents 9.4 and 9.5 provide a picture of the escalation, focus and geographic pattern of peasant actions in 1917.

Document 9.4 The Peasant Movement, March–October 1917 (number of incidents)

Period	1917(a)	1971(b)	1975(c)	1977(d)
March	16	183	190	257
April	193	445	508	879
May	253	580	682	1232
June	562	836	1036	1809
July	1100	900	1358	1860
August	665	569	856	1461
September	599	693	1033	1690
October	729	1210	1635	2176
Total	4117	5416	7298	11364

Source: D. Atkinson, The End of the Russian Land Commune, *1905–1930 (Stanford: Stanford University Press, 1983), p. 163*

Dorothy Atkinson compiled the table above from a): reports filed by the police in 1917; b) N.A. Kravchuk's study in 1971; c) V.I. Kostrikin's study in 1975; and d) Kostrikin's later study in 1977. The absolute number of incidents recorded has risen for two reasons. First, in 1917 itself the police arguably tended to minimise the extent of peasant unrest in their particular regions. Second, later research in local archives, combined with a culling of the local press, has led Soviet historians to arrive at ever-increasing estimates of the levels of peasant action in 1917 **(Figes 1989: 47)**. However, the data presented must be treated with some caution, as historians have no agreed definition of what an incident was, for example, whether it involved a single estate in a district, or all the villages within it. In other words, the raw numbers themselves do not tell the whole story of the peasant revolution in 1917 and may even be misleading. As Maureen Perrie has reminded us, other, admittedly also incomplete, evidence suggests that only 15 per cent of private land had been seized between March and October, so 'indicating ... that the main attack on private landownership came after rather than before the October Decree on Land' **(Perrie 1992: 13)**. Yet the table of Document 9.4 does illustrate the ebb and flow of the peasant movement in 1917, which can only be understood if we consider it in relation to the demands of working the land, the so-called agrarian cycle. A relatively peaceful March was followed by an escalation of peasant actions in the spring, which rose sharply in June and July after the fields had been sown. The relative lull in August has been variously explained, by reference either to demands of the agrarian cycle (the harvest had to be gathered then and the winter sowing completed) or to increased government repression, or a combination of both. Once the crop had been harvested the peasants were able to recommence their actions, which again rose sharply **(Figes 1989: 48; Gill 1978: 76–8)**.

However, the table of Document 9.4 fails to indicate the shifting focus of peasant actions between March and October, a phenomenon also largely determined by the agrarian cycle. Let us consider the following.

Document 9.5 Typology of Peasant Actions, by Percentage Weight per Month

Action	March	April	May	June	July	Aug.	Sept.	Oct.
Open land seizure	2.6	24.9	34.3	37.0	34.5	35.8	23.6	18.2
Destruction	51.3	8.0	6.7	3.6	4.3	10.0	19.7	23.4
Personal violence	7.7	12.7	10.6	9.1	7.1	11.2	12.3	7.5
Crop seizure	7.7	1.9	2.6	7.8	23.7	22.2	11.9	11.3
Seizure of timber	25.6	20.2	19.9	17.9	10.9	11.0	26.7	32.6
Seizure of inventory	–	4.7	8.6	10.1	9.6	6.0	3.9	5.1
Establish rental rates	2.5	5.6	3.8	1.0	0.8	0.7	0.2	0.2
Remove labour	2.6	22.1	13.4	13.5	9.1	3.2	1.6	0.2

Source: G. Gill, Peasants and Government in the Russian Revolution *(Macmillan, 1979), p. 189*

Document 9.5 suggests that it would be incorrect to equate peasant actions simply with the appropriation of land. Again, the pattern of their actions was influenced by the agrarian cycle. For example, the high level of timber seizure and, relatively speaking, of crops in March was the product of the peasants' need after a particularly cold winter to replenish their stocks of firewood, of materials to repair their dwellings, and of food. The renewed focus on timber in September and October can be explained by the desire to store up fuel for the forthcoming winter, while the marked decline in crop seizure (in comparison to July and August) reflects the fact that much of the peasantry had laid in sufficient supplies during the harvest (that crop seizures remained significantly above the April to June levels was the product of regional differences that composite tables fail to indicate, in this case, the poor harvests following the drought in the Central Agricultural Region). Moreover, in March and April arable land was the main target of the peasants, as their attention then was on sowing their summer crops. They only turned to the meadows in May, to acquire the pasture land on which to graze their cattle. Land seizure remained high in August and even September, the period of winter sowing **(Gill 1978: 76–8)**. However, our picture of peasant revolution between March and October still remains incomplete. The final table indicates the geographical intensity of peasant actions, by regions.

Document 9.6 Peasant Unrest Provided by Each Region (in percentage terms)

Region	%	Region	%
Central Agricultural	21.8	Lakes	6.2
Middle Volga	16.6	Lower Volga	4.9
Little Russia and the Southwest	14.3	Urals	4.1
Byelorussia and Lithuania	13.9	Baltic	3.0
Central Industrial	7.3	Northern	0.5

Source: G. Gill, Peasants and Government in the Russian Revolution *(London: Macmillan, 1979). p. 191*

In general, unrest was greatest in those regions (the Central Agricultural, the Middle Volga and Little Russia) where relatively high proportions of the land were in the hands of non-peasants, and where population pressure and peasant 'land hunger' was most severe. There the peasants were compelled to rent additional land from the landowners, which offended their deeply rooted belief that only he (or she) who worked the land should possess it **(see Document 9.1)**. Moroever, in the Black Earth region, where the village commune remained strong, traditional communal sentiments exacerbated the scale and destructiveness of peasant unrest. In addition, the catastrophic harvest in this region, caused by drought until the end of June and heavy rains in July, ruined much of the harvest and produced a food crisis, which intensified peasant despair and precipitated a particularly violent assault on the landowners, and the 'separators'. Those regions close to the front, Little Russia and the south-west and Byelorussia and Lithuania, subject to severe pressures to supply the army with food and thrown into ferment as increasing numbers of soldiers deserted to ensure their stake in land redistribution, also suffered high levels of unrest. In all regions, except Byelorussia and the Lakes, where lumbering was a major industry and timber was the focus of peasant aspirations, peasant actions were chiefly targeted on land seizure. The seizure of timber and crops, while widespread, were still of less concern to the peasants than the land itself **(Gill 1979: 157–68)**.

The only party to respond effectively to this mounting peasant unrest was the Bolshevik Party. Lenin again was the driving-force behind the revision of Bolshevik agrarian policy in the summer of 1917. Sensitive to the aspirations expressed in the peasant mandate **(see Document 9.1)** in the summer of 1917 he persuaded an often reluctant party to abandon the policy of nationalisation of the land that he himself had exposed in his *April Theses* **(see Document 4.3)**. He self-professedly embraced the agrarian programme of the SRs, land socialisation. He now was prepared to accept the equalised distribution of land among the peasants, which hitherto he had categorically resisted, and downplayed, in public at least, any emphasis on the virtues of collective agriculture. His report to, and the Decree on Land adopted by, the Second Congress of Soviets on 26 October reflected his new thinking.

Document 9.7 Lenin's Report and the Decree on Land

. . . the Revolution has proved and demonstrated how important it is that the land question should be put clearly. The outbreak of the armed uprising, the second, October, Revolution clearly proves that the land must be handed over to the peasants . . . . The government of the workers' and peasants' revolution must first of all settle the land question – the question which can pacify and satisfy the overwhelming mass of poor peasants. I shall read to you the points of a decree which your Soviet Government must issue. In one of the points of this decree the Mandate to the Land Committees, compiled on the basis of the 242 mandates from local Soviets of Peasants' Deputies, is incorporated.

DECREE ON LAND

1 *Pomeshchik* landownership is abolished immediately without any compensation.

2 The *pomeshchik* estates, as well as all crown, monastery and church lands, with all their livestock, equipment, buildings and possessions, are to be placed at the disposal of the *volost'* committees and *uezd* soviets of peasants' deputies pending the convocation of the Constituent Assembly.

3 Any damage to confiscated property, which henceforth belongs to the whole people, is proclaimed a serious crime, to be punished by the revolutionary courts. The *uezd* soviets . . . shall take all necessary measures to assure the observance of the strictest order during the confiscation of the *pomeshchik* estates, to determine the size of estates, and the particular estates subject to confiscation, to draw up a precise inventory of all property confiscated and to protect in the strictest revolutionary way all the farms transferred to the people, with all their buildings, equipment, cattle, reserves, etc.

4 The following peasant Mandate, compiled . . . from the 242 local peasant mandates . . . must serve everywhere to guide the implementation of the great land reforms, pending a final decision on the latter by the Constituent Assembly.

5 The land of ordinary peasants and ordinary Cossacks shall not be confiscated.

[Lenin reads Document 9.1 above]

The entire contents of this Mandate . . . is proclaimed a provisional law which, pending the convocation of the Constituent Assembly, is to be carried into effect as far as possible immediately. . . .

* * *

Voices are being raised here that the decree itself and the Mandate were drawn up by the Social Revolutionaries. So be it! It is a matter of complete indifference who drew them up! As a democratic government, we cannot ignore the decision of the masses of the people, even though we might disagree with it . . . . The old government . . . wanted to resolve the land problem with the help of the old, unreformed tsarist bureaucracy. But instead of resolving the problem, the bureaucracy only fought the peasants. The peasants have learned something during the eight months of our revolution; they want to decide all the land problems themselves . . . . We trust that the peasants themselves, better than us, will be able to solve the problem correctly. Whether they do it in our spirit or in the spirit of SR programme is beside the point. The point is that the peasants should be firmly assured that there are no more landowners in the countryside, that they themselves decide all questions and that they themselves arrange their own lives.

Source: T.A. Remizova (ed.), Agrarnaia politika sovetskoi vlasti (1917–1918 gg.) Dokumenty i materialy *(Moscow: Izd. akad. nauk SSSR, 1954), pp. 113–15*

Little further need be said on the essence of Document 9.7, embodying as it did the peasant demands discussed in relation to Document 9.1. However, it also highlights Lenin's own pragmatism (some would argue, opportunism). By bowing to the desires of the peasantry he sought to secure its support – or, in John Keep's opinion, at the very least 'neutralise' its opposition – to the seizure of power by the Bolsheviks **(Keep 1976: 391)**. There is little doubt that he succeeded, for a time. The Land Socialisation Law of 19 February 1918, despite fleeting references in support of the economic superiority of collective agriculture and the creation of 'model farms', incorporated the basic principles of the Decree and sanctioned the 'distribution of the land among the toilers . . . on an equal basis'. The peasantry at last had secured the land which it had long sought. Its victory proved to be some-what Phyrric. On average, each peasant received less than one *dessiatina* (2.7 acres) of land and often lacked the resources to work it efficiently. Land socialisa-tion also brought a series of unintended, and unwelcome, consequences for the Bolsheviks, as Lev Kritsman recalled in his seminal (and still untranslated into English) *magnum opus, The Heroic Period of the Russian Revolution.*

Document 9.8 The Impact of Land Socialisation

The Land Socialisation Law, which put into practice all the demands of the peasantry in the agrarian question, together with the withdrawal from the imperialist war, served as the foundation of the political union of the proletariat and peasantry, which secured the support of the latter in the proletariat's conquest and consolidation of power. But while creating the first, and vital, precondition for proletarian revolution – the transfer of power into the hands of the proletariat, at the same time it placed considerable limits on it; in agriculture large-scale estates were not socialised, but destroyed, parcelled out – instead of the proletarian expropriation of capital a petty-bourgeois (peasant) expropriation took place. This not only heightened . . . the economic incompleteness of the proletarian revolution but also reduced its social basis very perceptibly. Millions of agricultural workers disappeared, transformed in the main into petty proprietors. Finally, the agrarian base for industry and the towns generally was reduced, because the most socialised, in market terms, most commercial, part of agriculture – capitalist agriculture – was transformed into small-scale agriculture, producing more for its own needs; the loss in marketable output at least amounted to one-sixth of all agrarian production put on the market.

Source: L. Kritsman, Geroicheskii period russkoi revoliutsii *(Moscow: Gosudarstvennoe izdatel'stvo, 1924), pp. 44–5*

Kritsman's pessimistic evaluation was not simply the product of hindsight. In early 1918 the Left Communists had warned Lenin of the economically destructive potential of land division. By destroying the productive large estates, it would lower agrarian productivity, critically reduce the surplus that hitherto had gone to feed the towns and simply exacerbate the food crisis. Their fears were well founded. If anything, Kritsman's calculation of the impact of land socialisation erred on the generous side. According to Silvana Malle, it destroyed the estates which had produced an estimated 70 per cent of all marketed grain before the war **(Malle 1985: 324)**. Implicit in Kritsman's analysis was another, political, concern which the Left Communists repeatedly brought to Lenin's attention **(see Chapter 13)**. 'Black repartition', they argued, would eliminate the only reliable allies of the proletariat in the countryside, the landless labourers (*batraki*). It would transform them into petty proprietors and swell the ranks of the middle peasants. Satisfied with gaining the land, they would tenaciously defend their plots and pose immense obstacles to the introduction of collective socialist agriculture in the future. Lenin's response, that land division was not fundamentally inimical to the eventual transition to socialism, provided power remained 'in the hands of a workers' and peasants' government, if workers' control has been introduced, the banks nationalised, a . . . supreme economic body set to direct [regulate] the *entire* economic life of the country', proved to be remarkably sanguine **(Lenin, 26, 1964–5: 335)**.

This gloomy prognosis soon proved to be remarkably prescient. Land division, combined with the loss of the 'bread basket' of Russia, the Ukraine, as a result of the Brest–Litovsk Treaty **(see Chapter 13)**, did make it increasingly difficult to supply urban Russia and the peasants. As the fear of famine in the towns and cities loomed ever larger in the spring of 1918, the Bolsheviks resorted to increasingly coercive measures to compel the peasants to surrender food in sufficient quantities. On 9 May, even before the Czech rebellion erupted and the Komuch was established **(see Chapter 8)**, the Bolshevik government, with Lenin's enthusiastic support, established a 'food dictatorship'.

Document 9.9 The Food Dictatorship

The disastrous breakdown in the country's food supply . . . continues to spread and become more intense. While the consuming provinces are starving, there are . . . large reserves of grain . . . in the producing provinces. This grain is in the hands of the *kulaks* and the rich, in the hands of the village bourgeoisie. Well fed and provided for . . . the village bourgeoisie remains stubbornly deaf and indifferent to the cries of the starving workers and poor peasants. It does not bring its grain to the collection points, calculating on forcing the government to ever newer increases in grain prices and at the same time sells grain . . . at incredible prices to speculators and bagmen.

This stubbornness of the greedy village *kulaks* and rich must be put to an end. The practice of food supply in preceding years has shown that the abolition of fixed prices on grain and of the grain monopoly, while it would make it easier for a handful of our capitalists to gorge themselves, would make grain totally inaccessible for millions of workers and would inevitably condemn them to death from hunger. The answer to the violence of the owners of grain against the starving poor must be violence against the bourgeoisie. Not one pood of grain must remain in the hands of its holders, excluding the amount necessary to sow their fields and feed their families until the new harvest.

And this must be implemented immediately, especially after the occupation of the Ukraine by the Germans, when we are forced to satisfy ourselves with grain resources which are barely sufficient for sowing and a sharply reduced food supply.

Having considered the situation which has been created . . . the All-Russian Central Executive Committee resolved:

1 Affirming the permanent character of the grain monopoly and of fixed prices, and also of the need for merciless struggle with grain speculators and bagmen, to compel every owner of grain to declare for delivery within a week after the announcement of this decision in every *volost'* all his surplus, above the quantity required for sowing the fields and for personal consumption, according to the established norms.

2 To call on all working and landless peasants to unite immediately for a merciless war against the *kulaki*.

3 To declare all who possess surplus grain and do not take it to the delivery points, and also those who waste grain reserves by making home-brewed alcohol, enemies of the people . . . the guilty should be condemned to imprisonment for at least ten years, banished forever from their commune and all their property confiscated. Beyond that, the brewers of alcohol should be condemned to forced labour.

4 In the event that someone is discovered with undeclared surplus grain

. . . the grain is taken away from him without compensation. The value of the undeclared surplus . . . is paid half to the person who reveals the hidden surpluses and half to the village community.

Source: I.M. Volkov (ed.), Sbornik dokumentov i materialov po istorii SSSR sovetskogo perioda (1917–1958 gg.), *(Moscow: Izdatel'stvo moskovaskogo universiteta, 1966), pp. 80–1*

Document 9.9 concluded by granting virtually dictatorial powers to the Commissariat of Food (Narkomprod) to implement these measures, including the use of armed force against those who resisted the requisitioning of their surpluses. Underlying this strategy was the Bolsheviks' conviction that, despite the swingeing losses imposed by the Brest peace, sufficient grain (but 'only just enough', according to Lenin) remained to feed the people. The cause of the food crisis was the selfishness of the rich peasants, who refused to surrender their grain surpluses. The only solution was, in the final analysis, to use coercion to force them to give them up. To this end food detachments were sent to the countryside, and on 11 June committees of poor peasants (*kombedy*) were created, to assist the detachments in uncovering and sequestrating the surpluses held by the *kulaki*. At the same time, more attention was to be paid to establishing collective forms of agriculture. The 'honeymoon' between the Bolsheviks and the peasantry was at an end. In early July Lenin himself candidly conceded at the Fifth All-Russian Congress of Soviets that it might have been a mistake to have enacted the Land Socialisation law.

Unsurprisingly, this assault on the peasants provoked widespread opposition. At the very least, grain was concealed and there also were numerous instances of localised peasant rebellions across the entire country. The attempt to foment class war in the countryside, by turning the poor against the rich peasants, also failed. The peasantry proved to be far less stratified than Lenin had calculated and, with communal solidarity much strengthened during 1917, remarkably resistant to Bolshevik attempts to divide it into rich and poor. By the end of 1918 the Bolsheviks retreated in face of peasant intransigence. The *kombedy* were dissolved on 2 December and the promotion of collective agriculture considerably moderated. But the food dictatorship remained in effect, as the Narkomprod had no choice but to persist with requisitioning if the Red Army and the cities were to be fed **(Patenaude 1995: 554–5)**. It created great animosity between urban and rural Russia and sundered the alliance between the workers and peasants symbolised in the poster produced in 1918 by Aleksandr Apsit to celebrate the first anniversary of the October Revolution.

Document 9.10 The Year of Proletarian Dictatorship, October 1917–October 1918

[See illustration on p. 145]

Source: N. Barburina, The Soviet Political Poster, 1917–1980
(Harmondsworth: Penguin, 1985), p. 12

Requisitioning, for which the peasants received little in return, proved to be a continuing source of friction. The following, recently published material, extracts from letters compiled by the local departments of the office of the Military Censor across the country, reveals the depth of peasant opposition towards this policy.

Document 9.11 Peasant Resentment at Requisitioning

We are told: 'I am requisiting [food] from you.' It would be better if they said: 'I am robbing you' (Kaluga province, Plokhino, 4 June 1919). . . .

'What most of all provokes resentment among the people is the fact that their spare horses are taken from them . . . they begin to rail at soviet power' (Vitebsk province, Surazh, 11 June 1919).

'Matters are going very badly for us. The collection of grain . . . proceeds poorly. In the *volost'* to which we were sent there have been five requisitions. There is no grain. The peasants are very hostile. Agitation is of no use (Simbirsk province, Sengileevskaia *volost'*, 3 August 1919).

'Our grain has been taken away, leaving us with only one pood per head per month. Everything has been taken from us: eggs, butter, veal, yokes, sledges . . . cattle and hay, leaving only sixty poods per horse' (Viatka province, Riabinovskaia *volost'*, 10 August 1919).

'All our houses have been destroyed, our grain has been picked clean and it is impossible to say a word. This is what we have come to and it is impossible to complain anywhere. The bourgeoisie have established themselves in the executive committee and they work together' (Vologda province, Chungaly, 28 November 1919).

'We have suffered enough. Give us peace soon. Our bread, potatoes, hay, cows, pigs, sheep, horses, sheepskin coats, overcoats and shoes have been taken – everything has been taken, and we don't even get salt in return' (Gomel' province, Gory, 28 July 1919).

Source: I. Davidyn and V. Kozlova (eds), 'Chastnye pis'ma epokhi grazhdanskoi voiny. Po materialam voennoi tsenzury,' Neizvestnaia Ross XX, II, (1992), pp. 213–16

Document 9.11 reveals the extent of requisitioning (though a vast black market in food survived, supplying up to 50 per cent of urban Russia's requirements). The peasants were stripped not just of their grain, but of their produce generally, livestock and often their other possessions. The process too was often ruthless, even arbitrary, viz, the repeated requisitioning in Sengileevskaia *volost'*. It is also credible that in many villages opportunists ('the bourgeoisie' referred to in Document 9.11) controlled the food detachments and frequently abused their power to feather their own nests **(see the examples presented in the Appendix of Figes**

1989). Peasant opposition towards the Bolshevik government consequently grew. However, mass elemental rebellions against the Bolsheviks did not erupt until the final defeat of the Whites secured the peasants against the possible return of the old landlords, as we shall see in Chapter 15.

10

Industry and the workers

As we saw in Chapters 2 and 3 **(especially Documents 2.4, 2.7 and 3.7)**, a combination of economic grievances – accelerating inflation, long hours of work in frequently appalling conditions, and growing food shortages – opposition to the war, and the often brutal repression of any protests, eventually provoked the workers to rise against the autocracy, first in Petrograd, then in the other cities of the Empire. However, as was the case with the peasantry, initial hopes that the February Revolution would usher in a new, more harmonious and economically secure future, for both industrialists and workers, rapidly faded. Disillusion and bitter conflict increasingly enveloped the factories and plants. The development of this conflict has been the subject of extensive research which has added considerably to our understanding of dynamics of the Revolution in urban Russia, especially in Petrograd and Moscow (few Western studies of the provincial towns exist). Yet there is no consensus on precisely what the dynamics of the urban revolution were. At one extreme, John Keep, while conceding that the material grounds for working-class dissatisfaction did grow during 1917, still emphasises the role of Bolshevik chicanery in mobilising the legitimate concerns of the workers for their own political ends. On the other hand, as we saw in Chapter 1, the studies of the recent school of social historians has concluded that the workers were not simply the pawns of the Bolsheviks. Rather their radicalisation in 1917 was in large part caused by a perceptibly worsening disintegration of industry, to which they elaborated their own economic and political solutions. Those who shaped these solutions, moreover, appear to have been drawn from the most skilled, most literate, most urbanised strata of the working class, not the displaced, recently recruited elements, arguably more vulnerable to Bolshevik manipulation and demagogy **(Perrie 1987: 433–45)**.

After the collapse of the autocracy workers across Russia immediately began to demand better pay, with wages to be calculated on a daily basis, instead of piece work; improved conditions of work and hygiene; polite forms of address on the part of management; the end to personal searches, expecially demeaning to women workers; and, in particular, the introduction of the eight-hour day **(Sirianni 1982: 21)**. Despite opposition from the industrialists and the majority of the Provisional Government (and, as we saw in Chapter 4, many moderate socialist leaders who feared it would provoke a dangerous split with the bourgeoisie), the intransigence of the workers led, on 10 March 1917, to a settlement of this question, at least in

Petrograd. Negotiations between the Petrograd Soviet and the Petrograd Society of Factory and Plant Owners led to the following agreement.

Document 10.1 Agreement on the Eight-hour Day in Petrograd

An agreement has been reached between the Petrograd Soviet . . . and the Petrograd Society of Factory and Plant Owners on the introduction of an eight-hour day in factories and plants and on the creation of factory committees and conciliation chambers.

I   The eight-hour working day
1 Pending the publication of a law standardising the working day, the eight-hour working day . . . applying to all shifts, is introduced in all factories and plants.
2 On Saturdays the working day is to be only seven hours.
3 The reduction of working hours must not affect the workers' wages.
4 Overtime is permitted, only with the consent of factory committees.
II   Factory committees
1 Factory committees (councils of elders), elected from the workers of a given enterprise on the basis of universal, equal and etc. suffrage, are to be established in all factories and plants.
2 The tasks of these committees are: a) to represent the workers in a given enterprise in their relations with government or public institutions; b) to put forward opinions on questions concerning the economic and social life of workers in a given enterprise; c) to resolve problems arising from the internal problems among the very workers in a given enterprise; d) to represent workers before the managers, and owners, in questions regarding labour-management relations.
III   Conciliation chambers
1 Conciliation chambers are to be set up in all plants and factories, in order to settle all misunderstandings arising from labour–management relations.
2 Conciliation chambers are to be composed of an equal number of elected representatives from the workers and management of an enterprise.
IV   The removal of foremen and other members of management without the approval of a conciliation chamber, and their subsequent removal (by physical force) are prohibited.

Source: Revoliutsionnoe dvizhenie v Rossii posle sverzheniia samoderzhaviia *(Moscow: Izdatel'stvo akademii nauk SSSR, 1957), pp. 242–3*

Elsewhere, for example in Moscow, the mines of the Donbass, and the Urals, the employers were far from as conciliatory as their Petrograd counterparts. But even there the eight-hour day was imposed from below by the workers themselves, without the owners' consent. What is also significant about Document 10.1 was the recognition accorded to factory committees, which were formally legalised across the Empire by a statute of the Provisional Government issued on 23 April. Their initial purpose was not to institute a system of workers' control, or even management, as occurred later in 1917. Their object was more modest, to check the arbitrary, often oppressive, treatment of workers by management that had typified factory life before the Revolution. Point IV also requires further explanation. It was designed to limit the spontaneous acts of retribution taken by workers in the early days after the Revolution. On many occasions they had dealt with particularly abusive foremen and managers with varying degrees of violence, for example, forcibly removing them from the factories by 'wheeling them' out in barrows **(Mandel 1983: 97–102)**.

The gains made by the workers ushered in a brief 'honeymoon period' in industrial relations, lasting until late April. Then a new wave of strikes arose. It steadily mounted across the country until early July, when it temporarily ebbed in the wake of the July Days. While the beginnings of this phase of worker unrest coincided with the political crisis provoked by Miliukov's note **(see Document 4.4)**, and the subsequent formation of the First Coalition, its roots were largely economic. First, the wage rises granted in early March had been eroded as prices, especially for food, continued to rise rapidly. Second, shortages of materials and fuel were leading to short-time working, in some cases to the closure of factories. With their very livelihood threatened, some workers did not simply strike, but also took steps to intervene in the running of the factories. Some factory committees began more actively to supervise the actions of management, on occasion to remove apparently inefficient foremen and managers, and also to seek supplies of fuel and material. Such actions arguably were designed more to maintain production, and thus wages, rather than consciously usurp the managerial prerogatives of the owners. However, many workers had grown increasingly suspicious, not without some justification, that some capitalists sought to exploit supply problems facing industry by restoring discipline over the workers by the threat of unemployment and 'the bony hand of hunger' **(see Document 10.4)**. The First All-Russian Congress of Representatives of Industry and Trade, which met in Petrograd in June, revealed the increasing doubts harboured by the owners about the concessions they had made in March **(Mandel 1983: 149–54; Rosenberg and Koenker 1987: 309–14)**. Bitterly opposed to any form of intervention by the workers in the management of their enterprises they attributed the decline in industrial production to 'growing anarchy'. In particular, they insisted that high wages (especially 'the change from piecework to daily wages') and the eight-hour day were primarily responsible for the recent, sharp reduction in productivity. Should the situation remain unaltered, they concluded, then there was no alternative but factory closure and unemployment **(Browder and Kerensky, 2, 1961: 671)**. It was in these circumstances, of accelerating industrial decline and increasingly open conflict between capital and labour, that the First Conference of Petrograd Factory Committees met on 30 May. It passed the following resolution, proposed by the Bolsheviks, that envisaged a more active form of control of industry by the workers.

Document 10.2 The Resolution of the First Conference of Petrograd Factory Committees on Workers' Control, 3 June 1917

1 The total disintegration of all economic life in Russia has reached such a level that a catastrophe of unprecedented scale, which will halt production in a whole series of important industries, undermine agriculture, disrupt the railways, and deprive the millions-strong urban working class of food, is inevitable. What is more, the destruction has already begun, having gripped a number of sectors of the economy. A successful struggle against this destruction is possible only with utmost exertion of the efforts of the people and the adoption of a series of immediate revolutionary measures both at the local and state level.

2 It is impossible to seek salvation by bureaucratic means, i.e., by the creation of institutions dominated by capitalists and officials, with the profits of the capitalists preserved, with the preservation of their authority over production, under the rule of finance capital.

3 The salvation of the country from catastrophe demands that the workers and peasants be fully convinced, not by words but by deeds, that government agencies, at the local and central level, will not baulk at handing over to the people the bulk of the profits, income and wealth of the great magnates in banking, finance, commerce and industry.

4 The path to salvation . . . lies only in the establishment of real workers' control over the production and distribution of products. Such control demands: first, that the workers' organisations [trade unions, soviets . . .], plant committees, be guaranteed a majority of no less than two-thirds in all central institutions carrying out this work and that the owners, and their qualified personnel, who have not fled their businesses be conscripted to participate [in running industry]; second, that factory and plant committees, as well as trade unions, be granted the right, to participate in this control at the enterprise level and have compulsory access to all its commercial and financial data.

5 Workers' control, on the same principles, must be extended to all banks.
. . .

6 Workers' control, already accepted by the capitalists in a number of cases where conflict has arisen, must be immediately developed, by means of a series of carefully considered, yet promptly implemented, measures into a complete system of regulation over the production and distribution of goods by the workers. . . .

10 The systematic and successful introduction of these measures is possible only if all state power is transferred into the hands of the soviets.

Source: Revoliutsionnoe dvizhenie v Rossii v mae-iiune 1917g: Iiunskaia demonstratsiia *(Moscow: Izdatel'stvo akademii nauk SSSR, 1959), pp. 290–1*

Without denying the rise of Bolshevik influence within the factory committees, the measures urged in Document 10.2 were not foisted on the factory committees. Their membership was not composed of simpletons, easily manipulated by the Bolsheviks, as Richard Pipes has recently restated **(Pipes 1992a: 408)**. Admittedly, the Bolsheviks, initially their militant supporters at the shop floor, had gone beyond advocating merely state control of production by the soviets **(see Document 10.3)** in favour of workers' control over management in the factories and plants. This pressure had driven Lenin in the same direction and it was on his resolution of 25 May on how to cope with economic disorganisation **(Lenin, 24, 1964–5: 513–5)** that the above resolution was clearly modelled. The committees embraced it as they perceived it to be a rational step to provide them with some economic security. In establishing workers' control they sought (in vain, it was to prove) to halt the growth of industrial chaos, for example, by procuring fuel and monitoring material supplies and redistributing them to factories in need **(Smith 1983: 146–8)**. Point 10, too, is indicative of the committees' rapid loss of patience with the system of Dual Power. By early June they had come, in effect, also to support the Bolsheviks' political strategy, namely, the transfer of power to the soviets as the precondition to any improvement in their economic situation.

This response to the deepening crisis, however, was to bring the factory committees into collision with the trade unions, which had also blossomed after February. It has been estimated that by June 1917, 967 unions, with almost 1,500,000 members, existed **(Browder and Kerensky, 2, 1961: 747–8)**. Their differences came to light at the Third All-Russian Conference of Trade Unions which convened in Petrograd on 20 June. Mainly composed, according to Diane Koenker, of union leaders, rather than the rank and file, the objectives of the unions were clearly outlined in the following resolution presented by the Mensheviks, N.A. Garvi and N. Astrov.

Document 10.3 Mutual Relations between the Unions and the Factory-plant Committees

1 The anarchy of production that reigns supreme in capitalist society, intensified to a catastrophic degree by the imperialist war and the management of the tsarist regime, demands the immediate intervention of the state in the economic life of the country, to be realised by means of the planned regulation and control of production.
2 The trade unions must take the most active part in both the central and local organs set up with this aim in view.
3 In the business of control over production a role of exceptional importance falls to the plant committees. The trade unions, as fighting organisations which pursue the aims of protecting the rights and interests of hired labour under capitalist production in any shape or form, even if it is subject to state control and regulation, cannot assume administrative-managerial responsibilities in production.

4 The trade unions must energetically assist the creation and consolidation of factory-plant committees, while aspiring to transform them into the their local cells, which carry out the general policy of the trade unions. In fulfilling the functions of representing and defending the interests of the workers of a given enterprise, the factory-plant committees are the primary instance of control to ensure both the laws for the protection of labour and the collective agreements negotiated by the unions are observed.

5 Elections to the plant committees must be carried out under the direction of the trade unions and according to their lists. All members of the plant committee . . . must be drawn into the union.

6 In turn, the plant committees must conduct agitation to incorporate into the union all workers in their enterprises.

7 The plant committees must surrender direction over conflicts that arise to the trade union, for this purpose placing all their apparatus at the disposal of the union for the organised conduct and liquidation of the conflict.

8 In view of the exceptional significance which the regulation of the labour market has for the struggle with economic ruin and approaching unemployment, the factory-plant committees must regularly provide the bureau of labour attached to the trade unions with exact information about all vacancies, and equally watch over the timely and correct communication of all vacancies to the municipal labour exchange by plant managements.

8 Only a proper separation of the functions of the trade unions and the factory-plant committees and their close cooperation make it possible to achieve total agreement, planned action and unity in the conduct of the economic struggle of the proletariat and of their fruitful participation in the business of control and regulation by the state of the economic life of the country.

Source: D. Koenker (ed.), Tret'ya vserossiiskaya Konferentsiya Professional'nykh Soyuzov 3–11 Iyulya (20–28 Iyunya st. st.) 1917 goda. Stenograficheskii Otchet *(New York: Kraus 1982 – reprint of 1927 original), pp. 452–3*

The more moderate stance adopted by the trade unions is attributable to the fact that they were dominated by the Mensheviks. While arguing that state regulation was a vital element in preventing further industrial decline (point 1), nevertheless they did not believe that such regulation was tantamount to socialism. On the contrary, it was quite consistent with the continuation of capitalism (point 3). Under capitalism, it was not the function of the unions, or the factory committees, to participate in the management of industry in any way (just as, theoretically, socialists should not participate in any government ensuing from a bourgeois-democratic revolution, as we saw in Chapter 3). The task of the unions, and committees, then, was not workers' control but remained solely that of defending the rights of workers against capitalist exploitation (point 4). Moreover, perceiving the committees to be rivals for authority within the working class, the union leaders sought to incorporate them as nothing more than 'their local cells' within broad industrial unions (points 4, 5, 7). Despite conciliatory words on both sides, harmonious relations between the unions and the committees were not achieved. The ever-accelerating industrial decline and an employers' offensive against labour in the summer and autumn of 1917 drove the committees rapidly to the left. They came to endorse more firmly than ever the transfer of power to the soviets, while the union leadership continued to support coalition government until late September.

The intent of the employers, encouraged by the defeat inflicted on the Bolsheviks in early July **(see Chapter 4)**, to seek to reverse the gains made by the workers since February was clearly signalled by P.P. Riabushinskii, the leader of the Moscow industrialists, in early August. *Izvestiia*, the offical paper of the Soviet, reported the speech that he delivered to a conference of financiers and industrialists on 4 August.

Document 10.4 The Capitalist Counter-offensive

A conference of financiers and industrialists [was held] at which the capitalist bourgeoisie, through the lips of Mister Riabushinskii, expressed in an unusually clear manner their total crude self-interest, their total and cynical class egotism, their total indifference to the fate of Russia and the Revolution. 'We wish to be masters, and if the people does not wish this, let the bony hand of hunger teach it' – this is the meaning, in brief, of the speeches of Mr. Riabushinskii, applauded by the Kadet paper, *Rech'*.

Source: Izvestiia soveta rabochikh i soldatskikh deputatov, *8 August 1917*

The resistance of the capitalists was not confined to Moscow, but embraced Petrograd, the Ukraine, the Urals and the other industrial regions of the country. Words were matched by deeds. Demands for higher wages to keep pace with inflation were rejected, and increasing numbers of factories and plants were closed. It remains impossible to calculate how many of these closures were deliberate acts of the owners and how many in fact were the product of supply shortages. In a few cases, the factory committees responded by taking over the enterprise and trying to manage it itself, for example, the Brenner engineering works in Petrograd **(Ferro 1980: 149–53)**. This was a sensible enough strategy. The workers, now reinforced by all accounts by even the unskilled, and women, workers who had not participated much in protests before July, could ill afford to resist the employers' offensive by mass strikes, or by expulsion of supervisory staff from the factories and plants. Such actions would jeopardise the maintenance of production to which their very existence was linked. Food speculators, however, became a target of the workers' wrath **(Rosenberg and Koenker 1987: 315–21)**. The workers became increasingly embittered with the Provisional Government, especially when the Menshevik Minister of Labour, M.I. Skobelev, in late August forbade the committees to encroach on the managerial prerogatives of the owners, particularly in the area of the hiring and firing of labour. Radicalised even further by the Kornilov affair **(see Chapter 5)**, growing hunger and unemployment, they saw the only answer to their problems in politics, not in futile strikes that in the final analysis solved little. More and more of them, including rank-and-file trade unionists, swung behind the Bolshevik solution, namely, the transfer of power to the soviets.

The October Revolution enshrined the major gains that the workers had made since February. A decree legalising the the eight-hour day was enacted on 29 October, the principle of daily pay was acknowledged, and unemployment and sickness insurance was introduced on 11 and 22 of December respectively **(Carr, 2, 1966: 109)**. Moreover, workers' control in industry was ratified by decree on 14 November.

Document 10.5 Decree on Workers' Control [14 November 1917]

1 . . . workers' control over the production, purchase and sale of products and raw materials, and of their storage, and also over the finances of the enterprise is introduced in all industrial, commercial, agricultural, cooperative and other enterprises which employ hired labour or put out work to it to be done at home.

2 Workers' control is to be exercised by all workers of a given enterprise through elected organs, such as factory and plant committees, councils of elders, etc., into which representatives of office workers and technical personnel may also enter.

3 In every large city, *gubernii* or industrial region a local soviet of workers' control is to be created . . . [and] is composed of representatives of the trade unions, the factory and plant committees and workers' cooperatives.

4 Pending the Congress of Soviets of Workers' Control an All-Russian Soviet of Workers' Control will be established in Petrograd.

5 Commissions of specialist inspectors (technicians, bookkeepers, etc.) are to be attached to the higher bodies of workers' control. They are sent out either on the initiative of these bodies or at the request of lower organs . . . to inspect the financial and technical operations of an enterprise.

6 Organs of workers' control have the right to supervise production, set minimum production norms for an enterprise and act to determine production costs.

8 The decisions of organs of workers' control are binding on the owners of enterprises and can be overruled only by the decree of superior organs of workers' control.

12 The All-Russian Soviet of Workers' Control elaborates the general plans of workers' control, issues instructions and binding decrees, regulates relations between district councils of workers' control and acts as the supreme authority for all matters related to workers' control.

13 The All-Russian Soviet of Workers' Control co-ordinates the activity of organs of workers' control with all other institutions engaged in the organisation of the economy.

Regulations about the relations between the All-Russian Soviet of Workers' Control and the other institutions . . . will be issued specially.

Source: Sbornik dokumentov i materialov po istorii SSSR sovetskogo perioda (1917–1958 gg.) *(Moscow: Izdatel'stvo mosk. universiteta, 1966), pp. 55–6*

The thinking behind Document 10.5 requires some explanation. In the absence of any plan to transfer the major industries of the country into the possession of the state (full-scale nationalisation only occurred on 28 June 1918) a system of workers' control was necessary to ensure that the old owners ran their enterprises efficiently and did not sabotage production. At the same time it would provide the workers with the opportunity to learn how to manage industry, as Bolshevik ideology demanded **(White 1994: 187)**. To this end the various organs of workers' control at the enterprise level were granted extensive powers over its operation (point 6). To prevent these organs acting in the narrow interests of their enterprise they were subordinated to the All-Russian Council of Workers' Control (ARCWC), though quite how this was to be achieved in practice was left rather vague (point 12). Moreover, the actual functions of the ARCWC *vis-à-vis* the 'other institutions engaged in the organisation of the economy' (point 13) remained unspecified. The failure to define with any precision how workers' control was to operate soon led to renewed conflict between the factory committees and the trade unions. On 7 December the Central Council of Factory Committees (CCFC) issued its instructions on workers' control. Responsibility for its implementation was the prerogative of the factory committees. Their actions at the enterprise level were to be guided by directives of the Supreme Council of the National Economy (Vesenkha), established on 1 December 1917 (and itself given the general, ill-defined, task of coordinating the actions of all other economic organs in the country). Managerial power was to be severely curtailed, though no exact statement of what remaining management rights were was forthcoming. What the CCFC was proposing, as Steve Smith has concluded, was not simply workers' control but, in effect, workers' self-management. This proved to be a step too radical for the All-Russian Congress of Trades Unions, which included only five delegates from the factory committees themselves. It put forward its own, rather different, proposals. It was essentially a trade union charter, supported by both Bolshevik and Menshevik unionists. It envisaged that control in the factories should be exercised by commissions which in turn were subordinate to the unions, organised by branch of industry. Moreover, it emphasised that the their task should be limited to control, with management still responsible for the actual running of the enterprises **(Smith 1983: 211–14)**.

The battle, apparently, had been won by the unions. On 14 January 1918, the final day of the First All-Russian Congress of Trades Unions, the committees were formally transformed into the local branches of the unions. Ironically, the unions soon found themselves in the position of implementing the committees' policies. A combination of supply shortages and sabotage of production by the capitalists compelled them to intervene more and more in the actual management of many enterprises in the attempt to keep them running. A wave of 'nationalisations from below' swept across much of Russian industry in the first half of 1918. In few cases was this the product of anarchist inspiration, as the committees often looked to the state to step in, formally nationalise their enterprises, and help to manage them **(Smith 1983: 236–8)**. As we shall see in Chapter 13, until the summer of 1918 Lenin and the majority of Bolsheviks resisted nationalisation as they sought to entice the industrialists to lend their expertise to assist with the restoration of industry (with the exception of the banks, where a general strike by their staffs had driven the Soviet government to nationalise them on 14 December 1917). On 28 June 1918, however, in response to continuing 'bourgeois sabotage', the growing seizure of factories and plants at the local level, and hastened by fears that the sale of industry to German firms would remove it forever from the clutches of the Soviet government, all large enterprises were nationalised. At first, as E.H. Carr remarked, it changed little in practice, as the Vesenkha was unable to administer them – and leased them back, at no cost, to the old capitalists who were to finance, manage and draw revenue from them. It was the Civil War, and the imperative of producing the means with which to wage it, that increasingly drove the Bolsheviks to assume 'responsibility for administration' **(Carr 1966: 104–5)**.

Paradoxically, nationalisation did not lead to greater workers' control. Lenin and many other Bolsheviks had come to see it as a major cause of the continuing rapid decline of industry. The report of Aleksandr Shliapnikov, Commissar of Labour, to the CEC on 20 March 1918, focused on its destructive impact on the railways (ironically, he was to become a major advocate of workers' management, as we shall see in Chapter 13).

Document 10.6 The Impact of Workers' Control

The picture which presented itself . . . is one that produced very sad thoughts. It places before us the necessity of taking the most strict measures for re-establishing labour discipline at any cost and above all else on the railways. For instance, trains nowadays often go unlighted, without observing any signals . . . while the cars are not cleaned . . . . The usual explanation is that there is no kerosene or candles. In fact . . . both these commodities are available but are being pilfered in the most shameless manner. Besides, as a result of the complete lack of interest of the railway crews in running their lines it turns out that the conductors refuse to man the trains . . . . [B]oth cars and locomotives on occasions may be available, but there are no engineers or conductors . . . they either feign illness or refuse to go. . . . The disorganisation and demoralisation that exist in the repair shops defy description . . . . [F]rom the moment the railwaymen were guaranteed a

minimum wage they failed to guarantee the minimum of effort . . . .
[A]long all the railways we hear from all the class-conscious elements . . . the
same complaint: we must at any price get our railwaymen interested in
running their lines. There may be only one way to do this, by the introduction of piecework . . . for the repair and maintenance of locomotives and
payment per *verst* for the crews. This is the only painless method to raise the
productivity of the railway employees.

Source: Protokoly zasedanii Vserossiiskago Tsentral'nago Ispolnitel'nago
Komiteta. 4-go sozyva: Stenograficskil atchet *(Moscow: Gosudarstvennoe
izdatel'stvo, 1920), pp. 44–5*

Shliapnikov was far from alone in presenting a such damning indictment of workers'
control. Many agreed with him, including Leonid Krasin, one of the few Bolsheviks
with technical qualifications and managerial experience. In a letter to his wife in May
1918 he wrote that in many enterprises 'nobody [was] getting any work done'
(Krassin 1929: 86). Critically, Lenin, too, as we shall see in more detail in Chapter
13, had concluded much the same. Whether their condemnations of workers'
control were fully justified is a moot point. Many on the Left of the Party alleged
that many cases existed where the workers' management had been successful in
restoring discipline and production: N. Osinskii referred to the mines of Donbass;
A.L. Lomov pointed to the rise in productivity in numerous enterprises of the
Central Industrial Region around Moscow; while M.A. Savel'ev cited the Urals as a
shining example of the capacities of the workers to run industry efficiently.
Moreover, the research of Smith and Carmen Sirianni, among others, has indicated
that many workers were aware of the need for discipline if their enterprises were
to survive and, as we have seen above, sought the active intervention of the
government to help them to restore production. Industrial output in general,
however, continued to fall. But it remains difficult to assess to what extent it was
a product of the inabilities and foibles of the workers, or of circumstances outwith
their own control, such as lack of materials and food and the obstruction of the
capitalists **(Kowalski 1991: 116–17)**. Whatever the truth of the matter, by
the spring of 1918 Lenin and his fellow-thinkers attributed industrial collapse to
the effects of workers' control and acted to curb it. It was abolished on the
railways on 26 March 1918. One-man management (the employment often of old
capitalists to run the various industrial enterprises) was restored, as was strict
discipline over labour, principles that gradually yet inexorably were extended to all
of industry during the Civil War. Industrial democracy was increasingly curtailed,
but not without opposition.

Rumblings of dissatisfaction had been steadily growing since the beginning
of 1918. It found expression in the Assembly of Factory Representatives, an
organisation self-avowedly independent of the increasingly Bolshevik-dominated
Soviets, factory committees and unions. It held its first conference in Petrograd
on 13 March, with delegates from many metallurgical plants, the railways and the
print works present. Similar organisations soon sprang up in other cities, including

Kolomna, Samara, Tambov, Tula and Moscow **(Bernshtam 1981: 66–7, 110–11)**. The Petrograd Conference issued a declaration outlining the grievances of many workers and their objectives.

Document 10.7 Declaration of the Petrograd Assembly of Factory Representatives, March 15, 1918

The new power calls itself soviet, workers' and peasants'. But in reality the most important questions of state are decided without the paticipation of the soviets; generally the CEC does not meet or meets in order silently to approve steps . . . autocratically adopted by the People's Commissars. Soviets which do not agree with the government's policy are unceremoniously dissolved by armed force. Everywhere the voice of the workers and peasants is drowned by the voice of delegates allegedly representing the 10-million strong army . . . which exists only on paper, an army which in part has been demobilised and in part independently has abandoned the front . . . . In reality, any attempt by the workers to express their will in the soviets by means of re-elections is suppressed and more than once already the Petrograd workers have heard from the lips of the representatives of the new authority threats of machine guns.

We were promised a speedy peace, a democratic peace, concluded by the people above the heads of their governments. In fact, we were given a shameful capitulation before German imperialism. We were given a peace which deals the severest blow to the entire Workers' International and strikes to death the Russian workers' movement. We were given a peace which ensures the collapse of Russia and which makes it the prey of international capital, which destroys our industry and shamefully betrays the interests of all nationalities, committed to the Russian Revolution.

We were promised bread. But in fact we were given unprecedented hunger. We were given civil war, which lays waste our country and finally destroys our industry. Under the guise of socialism we were given the final destruction of industry and financial chaos . . . We were given the kingdom of bribery and speculation, which assumed unheard of proportions. We were faced with the horrors of lengthy unemployment, deprived of any means of actually fighting against it. Our trade unions have been destroyed, the plant committees cannot defend us . . . . Fleeing Petrograd, the Council of People's Commissars leaves us to the mercy of fate, closing the factories and plants, casting us on the street without money, bread, work, organs of self-defence, without any hopes for the future.

We were promised freedom . . . . Where is freedom of speech, assembly, unions, press, peaceful demonstration? Everything has been crushed under the heels of the police.

We, workers of the factories and plants of Petrograd, demand from the [Third All-Russian] Congress [of Soviets]:

I   A refusal to ratify the shackling and perfidious peace.

II A resolution on the dismissal of the Council of People's Commissars.

III The immediate convocation of the Constituent Assembly and the transfer of all power to it.

Source: Reprinted in M.S. Bernshtam (ed.), Nezavisimoe rabochee dvizhenie v 1918 godu. Dokumenty i materialy, *volume 2 (Paris: YMCA Press, 1981), pp. 88–9*

One major cause of disillusion clearly was economic. The material gains and economic security that the workers had sought in 1917 had become even more elusive after October. Food shortages grew. The demobilisation of industry brought sharply rising unemployment for those engaged in the defence industries, chiefly the formerly relatively privileged workers in the chemical and metal industries. Many workers also felt that the separate peace of Brest–Litovsk had betrayed their comrades abroad, German workers in particular, while the territorial losses that had ensued had severely worsened Russia's economic plight – though relatively few, it appears, were prepared to come forward and fight **(see Chapter 13)**. Resentment at the 'autocratic' political practices of the Bolsheviks was also evident, and justified. It had become more difficult to voice dissent against Bolshevik actions; recalcitrant soviets increasingly were dissolved; and the trade unions and factory committees more and more had become the 'transmission belts' of Bolshevik policy, not the defenders of workers' rights. Within the Assembly Menshevik and SR influence was evident, as the final demand, for the convocation of the Constituent Assembly, then was a fundamental part of their programmes. It remains difficult, however, to assess precisely what motivated rising worker opposition. While conceding that political issues did loom larger in the minds of many workers in the spring and early summer, William Rosenberg concludes that economic issues, in particular, growing unemployment (in Petrograd alone, 130,000 lost their jobs between January and April), probably was 'more important than politics *per se* as an underlying source of protest' **(Rosenberg 1985: 233–5)**. On the other hand, Vladimir Brovkin claims that political issues, such as the absence of free elections, increasingly lay at the root of the movement **(Brovkin 1985: 244–50)**. As yet no conclusive answer can be given, although Mary McAuley appears to imply that ordinary workers were more concerned with bread and butter issues than 'political demonstrations' **(McAuley 1991: 96)**.

In the final analysis, the Bolsheviks survived the challenge posed by the workers in the summer of 1918. Repression certainly played its part. The leaders of the opposition were arrested. The Mensheviks, SRs and, finally, Left SRs were expelled from the soviets and their press was closed down **(see Chapter 7)**. Many workers, too, ultimately remained loyal to the regime, possibly in the hope that soviet democracy would be restored in the future, perhaps in fear that the collapse of soviet power would lead to even greater economic chaos and, as the Civil War escalated in June, the return of the old order. The underlying sources of worker protest, however, were not removed. The material position of those workers left in the cities continued to deteriorate (many, 50 per cent in Petrograd, 40 per cent in Moscow, who had retained their ties with the countryside had fled the factories to seek survival in the villages). Food was particularly in short supply, shortages of fuel and materials disrupted production, while authoritarianism, not just in the state but in industry itself, was intensified. One-man management first introduced on the railways was imposed elsewhere while workers increasingly became subject to military discipline in the factories **(White 1994: 230)**. It was little surprise when worker resentments flared up again in the first half of 1919, when a new wave of strikes enveloped the major industrial regions of the country, in the provinces as well as Moscow and Petrograd **(Brovkin 1994: 57–89)**. An indication of the mainsprings of worker protest can be gleaned from the resolution of the workers of the massive Putilov engineering works in Petrograd.

Document 10.8 The Putilov Workers' Demands, March 10, 1919

We, the workers of the Putilov works . . . declare before the labouring classes of Russia and the world, that the Bolshevist government has betrayed the high ideals of the October Revolution and thus betrayed and deceived the workmen and peasants of Russia; that the Bolshevist government, acting in our name, is not the authority of the proletariat and peasants, but an authority and dictatorship of the central committee of the Bolshevist Party, self-governing with the aid of extraordinary commissions [the Cheka], Communists and police.

We protest against the compulsion of workmen to remain at factories and works, and attempts to deprive them of all elementary rights: freedom of the Press, speech, meetings, and inviolability persons, etc.

We demand:

1 Immediate transfer of authority to a freely elected Workmens' and Peasants' Soviets.
2 The immediate re-establishment of elections at factories and plants, barracks, ships, railways, and everywhere.
3 Transfer of wholesale management to released workmen of the professional union.
4 Transfer of the food supply to workmen's and peasants' cooperative societies.
5 The general arming of workmen and peasants.
6 The immediate release of members of the original revolutionary peasants' party of Left [Socialist] Revolutionaries.
7 The immediate release of Mari[ia] Spiridonova.

Source: The Times, *4 April 1919*

This report is based on that of an unnamed 'reliable source' (either a British official in, or a British citizen recently returned from, Russia) and is confirmed by other accounts **(Brovkin 1994: 66–70)**. As in 1918, workers again railed against the Bolsheviks' betrayal of the libertarianism promised in 1917. They demanded the restoration of basic civil liberties and genuine elections to the soviets and factory committees, as well as freedom for socialist opposition parties (the SRs had been legalised in February, only for Spiridonova and other leading Left SRs to be re-arrested at the end of the month). More particularly, they appear to have sought the reintroduction of some form of workers' management (point 3) and the end to labour militarisation ('the compulsion of workmen to remain at factories and plants'). Point 4 suggests that they also opposed the compulsory grain requisitioning which the Bolsheviks had introduced **(see Document 9.9)**. While briefly stating that the Putilov strike at first was 'economic rather than political', this report makes little detailed reference to the broader economic roots of worker protest in Russia in the first six months of 1919. Contrary to Brovkin, McCauley emphasises that hunger, not politics, was at the root of the strikes in Petrograd in the early months of 1919 **(McCauley 1991: 251–2)**. The following reports, this time from the towns of provincial Russia, reveal the parlous lives of the workers.

Document 10.9 Worker Protest in Provincial Russia

'We had a general strike caused by hunger. The factories were closed for seven days, and also the trams, plants and waterworks. But it has ended now' (Tver', 25 July 1919).

'The old women burst into the plant, forbade anyone to work and began to seek bread from the administration; for two days the plant did not operate; they issued each of us two funts of bread; soon a strike will erupt again. When comrade Kalinin was here four workmen were brought out of the place dead from hunger; a day does not pass when someone has not died from hunger, while the Bolsheviks each have 20 poods of white flour. In all probability the government will be overthrown soon' (Orel guberniia, Bezhitsa, no date).

'The chairman of the CEC, comrade Kalinin, visited us . . . . About 8,000 workers gathered at the Briansk plant . . . . [I]n response to the workers' request for bread comrade Kalinin replied that within two months we all shall have our fill . . . . Then voices rang out: "Away with him"' (Briansk, 26 July 1919).

'Hunger is starkly present among us. The factories went on strike for days because of this hunger . . . . In the meantime the needs of the factories have been satisfied, but it is rumoured that soon they will face shortages again. The factories are gradually closing. A "Congress of Soviets" took place, which the Bolsheviks very much feared and which at first was anti-Bolshevik; above all it demanded an end to the war but comrade Sosnovskii, a splendid orator from Moscow, explained everything: a resolution was passed to continue the war to a victorious conclusion; the Jews again came to life, and everyone hung their heads' (Tver', 26 June 1919).

'In Kaluga there was a three-day strike . . . because food was not supplied. Here in Riazan' strikes are expected in a day or two . . . everyone anticipates something will happen, but if only this damned war would end, whatever the cost, since we are sick of it . . . . ' (Riazan', 29 June 1919).

Source: I. Davidyn and V. Kozlova (eds), 'Chastnye pis'ma epokhi grazhdanskoi voiny', Neizvestnaia Rossiia, XX, II (1992), pp. 212–13

The material in Document 10.9 also has been taken from extracts from letters compiled by the local departments of the office of the Military Censor during the Civil War **(cf. Document 9.10)**. Food shortages patently were the cause of many strikes. The report from Bezhitsa also highlights another important source of worker protest, common, according to Brovkin, across Soviet Russia: namely, the fact that while the workers went hungry the Bolshevik functionaries enjoyed privileged rations. The hint of anti-Semitism in the report from Tver' is intriguing. It is difficult to gauge how widespread it was. The Putilov workers upbraided Zinoviev for being a Jew, while Brovkin remarks that slogans directed against Jewish Commissars were also reported from Briansk **(Brovkin 1994: 80)**. Finally, many workers, it seems, craved the end of the Civil War, seen as a prime cause of their suffering. They were to be disappointed, as it continued until the autumn of 1920.

The Bolsheviks typically responded to mounting worker unrest by adopting a 'carrot and stick' approach. As well as promising (if not always delivering) better rations for the workers, the Cheka was unleashed. Thousands of workers were arrested, and many (the precise number remains unknown) shot. Possibly, too, the escalation rather than cessation of the Civil War in the summer of 1919 helped mute protest as the prospect of the victory of counter-revolution rose. Life for the workers continued to be grim. Food shortages persisted and worsened dramatically in the winter of 1920–1; factories frequently closed due to irregular supplies of fuel and materials; the militarisation of labour grew; and in 1920 Trotsky's proposal to introduce, in effect, universal labour conscription was endorsed by the Party. The reality of the workers' position was in sharp contrast to the images presented in Bolshevik propaganda, as the following poster, produced by an unknown artist in 1920 to celebrate the third anniversary of the October Revolution, reveals.

Document 10.10 Labour will be the Master of the World

[see illustration on p. 164]

Source: S. White, The Bolshevik Poster *(New Haven: Yale University Press, 1988), p. 101*

The Russian workers certainly did not feel that they were the masters of anything. And as the Civil War ended resentments, provoked as much by their subjugated status as by material hardship, grew ever more bitter and labour militancy revived **(see Chapter 15)**.

11

The national minorities

Before 1917 the Russian Empire was a huge multi-national empire. It contained over 100 non-Russian peoples, including: Ukrainians and Belorussians who were closely akin to the Great Russians themselves; Poles, Finns and Balts; Azeris, Armenians and Georgians in the Transcaucasus; and the various Muslim peoples of Central Asia. By the end of the nineteenth century the Great Russians themselves had become a minority, totalling about 44 per cent of the population. The following table, based upon the 1897 census (the only comprehensive one before the Revolution), lists the major nationalities of the Empire, to which must be added the two and a half million Finns populating the Grand Duchy of Finland, then an autonomous part of the Empire.

Document 11.1 Major Nationalities of the Russian Empire

Nationalities	%	Nationalities	%
Slavs		**Lithuanians and Latvians**	
Great Russians	55.7	Lithuanians	1.7
Ukrainians	22.4	Latvians	1.2
Belorussians	5.9		
Poles	7.9		
Other Slavs	0.2		
Indo-European		**Caucasians**	
Moldavians	1.1	Georgians	1.4
Germans	1.8	Armenians	1.2
Jews	5.1		
Finno-Ugric		**Turkic**	
Estonians	1.0	Tatars	3.7
Mordvinians	1.0	Bashkirs	1.3
		Kirghiz	4.1
Other minorities	8.8		
Total	125.7		

Source: Based on table in V.I. Kozlov, Natsional'nosti SSSR *(Moscow: Statistika, 1975), pp. 34–5*

Although in the majority, from the late nineteenth century the non-Russian nationalities found themselves subject to increased repression, of varying degrees (the Jews, unsurprisingly, and the rebellious Poles suffered most severely, while the Muslims of Central Asia were least affected). Russification in all areas of life intensified: in education, with teaching increasingly conducted in Russian; in religion, with the non-Orthodox churches of the minorities subject to persecution; in the bureaucracy, where the influence of the Baltic Germans in particular was reduced; and even in the army. It is little wonder that the Empire had become known as 'the prison of nations'. Concessions during 1905, to assuage the Revolutionary upheaval in the non-Russian periphery of the Empire, proved to be short-lived and Russification soon commenced again **(Pearson 1989: 95–8)**.

The Bolshevik Party alone was prepared (at least in theory) to accommodate the aspirations of the oppressed minorities of the Empire. On the urging of Lenin it had revised the national section of its programme in 1913. The programme adopted in 1903 had subscribed to the view that the right of self-determination could be granted only to the proletariat of any oppressed nation. By 1913 Lenin had persuaded the Party to extend this right to embrace all oppressed nations. In a lengthy article published in the Bolshevik theoretical journal *Prosveshchenie* (*Enlightenment*) in the spring of 1914 he explained how the Party should address the problem of national oppression.

Document 11.2 Lenin's Defence of the Right of Nations to Self-determination

Even now, and probably for a fairly long time to come, proletarian democracy must reckon with the nationalism of the Great-Russian peasants (not with the object of making concessions to it, but in order to combat it). The awakening of nationalism among the oppressed nations, which became so pronounced after 1905 . . . will inevitably lead to greater nationalism among the Great Russian petty bourgeoisie in town and countryside. The slower the democratisation of Russia, the more persistent, brutal and bitter will be the national persecution and bickering among the bourgeoisie of the various nations . . . [and] give rise to (and strengthen) 'separatist' tendencies among the various oppressed nationalities which sometimes enjoy far greater freedom in neighbouring states.

In this situation, the proletariat of Russia is faced with a twofold or, rather, a two-sided task: to combat nationalism of every kind, above all, Great Russian nationalism; to recognise, not only fully equal rights for all nations in general, but also equality of rights as regards polity, i.e., the right of nations to self-determination, to secession. And at the same time, it is their task, in the interests of a successful struggle against all and every kind of nationalism among all nations, to preserve the unity of the proletarian struggle and the proletarian organisations, amalgamating these organisations into a close-knit international asociation.

Complete equality of rights for all nations; the right of nations to self-determination; the unity of the workers; the unity of the workers of all nations.

Source: V.I. Lenin, Collected Works, *20 (Moscow: Progress, 1964–5), pp. 453–4*

One element at the root of Lenin's conversion to the cause of national self-determination was the abortive revolution of 1905, which alerted him to the revolutionary potential of minority nationalism. By espousing the principle of self-determination, Lenin may have well have hoped to foment revolution on the periphery of the Empire that would help bring the autocracy down. But there was more to Lenin's change of heart than just *Realpolitik*. As Marx and Engels before him, he increasingly had come to realise the dangers to proletarian unity posed by the problem of national oppression. The proletariat of a dominant nation, he reasoned, must not deny the right of self-determination to a subjugated nation. Were it to do so, then the workers in the latter would doubt its commitment to freedom and democracy. In consequence, they would become vulnerable to the spell of nationalism and aspire to narrowly national, rather than socialist, objectives. The international proletarian unity vital to the success of socialist revolution, he concluded, could only be achieved by promising minority nations the right to secede. But Lenin's objective was not the break-up of the Empire. It was the task of the Party, which itself remained highly centralised (there were to be no national sections within it), to persuade the workers of the oppressed nations to reject secession and choose instead to struggle for a multi-national, ultimately pan-European, socialist state. Lenin's position on the national question provoked outrage on the Left of the Party, from Nikolai Bukharin and Iurii Piatakov in particular. They believed that the growth of imperialism had created an increasingly integrated international economy in which national boundaries counted for little. Imperialism also had established the prerequisites for socialist revolution on an international scale. In such circumstances, any concessions to national self-determination not only were redundant but would betray the cause of international socialism by diverting the workers from their proper objective of international revolution. Despite repeated and heated debates within the Party it was Lenin's thinking that determined the national policy first introduced by the Soviet government after the October Revolution, as we shall see shortly **(Carr, 1, 1966: 417–35)**.

The fall of the autocracy in 1917 was welcomed by those minorities with an awakened national consciousness (according to R.G. Suny, the Azeris, Belorussians and Lithuanians had scarcely awoken), in the belief that autonomy, political as well as cultural, would be granted to them by the new government. Only the Poles (and Finns) from the outset were bent upon complete independence from Russia. Their expectations, however, were to be dashed. Neither the Provisional Government, nor any major political party (except the Bolsheviks), were willing to grant any meaningful concessions to the minorities, lest this prefigure the disintegration of the Russian state. The Kadets, as William Rosenberg has remarked, were wedded to the maintenance, even expansion, of 'Great Russia, One and Indivisible'. Even the SRs, especially those on the Right of the Party, as Oliver Radkey concluded, were Great Russian nationalists at heart **(Radkey 1958: 479; Rosenberg 1974: 127)**. Admittedly, the Mensheviks in principle had conceded the right of national self-determination in 1917, but in practice did little to promote it. The position first adopted by the Provisional Government is by now familiar. Its programme of 3 March **(see Document 4.1)** made no reference to the national question, the solution of which (predictably) was to be deferred until the Constituent Assembly convened. The only actions that it took was to reaffirm, on 7 March, the autonomy of Finland which the tsarist government increasingly had circumscribed after 1905 and, on 16 March, to recognise the independence of Poland (an empty gesture as Poland was wholly occupied by Germany by then). This inaction spurred a number of the minorities to present increasingly urgent demands for autonomy at the very least. In March representatives of the Latvian and Lithuanian intelligentsia had demanded that their ethnic territories be granted some form of self-administration, but in vain. Muslim politicians sought the creation of a federal state. More important, on 10 June 1917, the Ukrainian Council (Rada), created in March by leading nationalist intellectuals, issued its manifesto, or First Universal (a name harking back to the proclamations once issued by independent Cossack leaders before the eighteenth century, the *hetmans*) **(Pipes 1995: 146–8)**.

Document 11.3 The First Universal of the Ukrainian Rada

Let there be a free Ukraine. Without separating from Russia, without breaking away from the Russian State, let the Ukrainian people on their own territory have the right to manage their own life. Let a National Ukrainian Assembly (Sejm), elected by universal, equal, direct and secret suffrage, establish order and a regime in the Ukraine. Only our Ukrainian assembly is to have the right to issue all laws which are to establish this regime. Those laws which will establish the regime throughout the entire Russian State must be issued by the All-Russian Parliament. No one knows better than we what we need and which laws are best for us. No one can know better than our peasants how to manage our own land. Therefore we desire that, after all lands throughout Russia are confiscated as national property, *pomeshchik*, state, crown, monastic and other lands, when a law is passed about this in the Constituent Assembly, the right to have control of our Ukrainian lands, the right to use them, belongs to us, to our Ukrainian Assembly (Sejm). . . . We had hoped that the central Russian Provisional Government would lend us a hand in this work . . . but the Russian Provisional Government rejected all of our demands; it has refused the outstretched hand of the Ukrainian people. We have sent our delegates to Petrograd to submit to the Russian Provisional Government our demands. And the chief demands were as follows:

That the Russian government publicly, by a special Act, declare that it is not against the national freedom of the Ukraine, against the right of the people to autonomy.

That the central Russian government have in its cabinet our commissar Ukrainian affairs for all matters related to the Ukraine.

That local authority in the Ukraine be united in one representative from the central Russian government, that is, commissar in the Ukraine elected by us.

That a certain portion of money collected by the central treasury from our people be returned to us, the representatives of this people, for their national and cultural needs.

All these demands of ours the central Russian government rejected. . . . And therefore we, the Ukrainian Central Rada, publish this Universal to all of our people and declare that from now on we shall build our own life. . . .

Source: R. P. Browder, A. F. Kerensky, The Russian Provisional Government, 1917: Documents, *i (Stanford: Stanford University Press, 1961), pp. 383–4.*

The Rada claimed, with some justification, that its Universal represented the wishes of the majority of Ukrainians. The First Ukrainian Military Congress which had met between 5 and 8 May had endorsed it, as had the All-Ukrainian Peasant Congress at the end of the month. Whether the still largely illiterate Ukrainian peasantry was as imbued with national consciousness, as later Ukrainian emigré historians alleged, remains less certain. While Marc Ferro has argued that the rise of nationalism 'absorbed political and social conflicts' in the Ukraine and other areas of the Empire, recent research has cast doubt on this conclusion. In many instances, ethnic and class loyalties reinforced each other. In the case of the Ukraine, the Ukrainian peasants arguably backed the Rada not because they were nationalists, but on economic grounds. Impatient at the Provisional Government's temporising on the issue of land reform, they hoped that the Rada would act more decisively – and also redistribute the land which it proposed to take from the largely Polish and Russian landlords amongst them alone, to the exclusion of the poor peasants from the north of the Empire **(Ferro 1980: 94; Jones 1992: 52)**. The Provisional Government, with the wholehearted support of the Kadets and the Right SRs, unsurprisingly rejected the Rada's claims out of hand, while the Soviet procrastinated. The Rada's response was swift. It set up its own administrative organ, the General Secretariat, under Volodymyr Vynnychenko, to control much of its own affairs. In an attempt to resolve this conflict a delegation comprising Kerensky, Tereshchenko and Tsereteli were despatched to Kiev to negotiate some compromise. On 2 July the Provisional Government issued a resolution in which it recognised the General Secretariat (if only in August to limit its powers severely). It also agreed that the Rada would be allowed to submit its proposals regarding the nature of land reform in the Ukraine, but their ratification must await the final decision of the Constituent Assembly. This retreat on the part of the Provisional Government precipitated the resignation of the Kadets from the First Coalition, though as we saw in Chapter 5 their opposition to Chernov's agrarian policy may have been a more important cause of their action **(Browder and Kerensky, I, 1961: 385–92)**.

In comparison with the dithering of the Provisional Government the Bolsheviks acted swiftly to appease the nationalities. On 1 November 1917, the Council of People's Commissars (Sovnarkom) adopted a decree which gave the various nationalities of the old Empire the right to self-determination.

Document 11.4 Rights of the Peoples of Russia to Self-determination

There remains now only the peoples of Russia who have suffered and are suffering under an arbitrary yoke. Their emancipation must be considered at once and their liberation effected with resoluteness and finality.

During the tsarist times the peoples of Russia were systematically incited one against another. The results of this policy are well known: massacres and pogroms on the one hand, slavery and bondage on the other.

There can be and there must be no return to this shameful policy of provocation. Henceforth it must be replaced by a policy of voluntary and honest co-operation of the peoples of Russia.

. . . after the March Revolution, when the government passed into the hands of [K]adet bourgeoisie the unconcealed policy of instigation gave way to one of cowardly distrust of the peoples of Russia, of caviling and provocation camouflaged by verbal declarations about the 'freedom' and 'equality' of peoples. The results . . . are well known – the growth of national enmity, the impairment of mutual trust.

Henceforth it must be replaced by an open and honest policy leading to complete mutual confidence among the peoples of Russia.

Only as the result of such a confidence can an honest and lasting union of the peoples of Russia be formed.

Only as the result of such a union can the workers and peasants of the peoples of Russia be welded into a revolutionary force capable of resisting all [counter-revolutionary] attempts on the part of the imperialist-annexationist bourgeoisie.

The Congress of Soviets in June of this year proclaimed the right of the peoples of Russia to free self-determination.

The Second Congress . . . reaffirmed this inalienable right.

In compliance with the will of these Congresses, the Soviet of People's Commissars has resolved to adopt as the basis of its activity . . . the following principles:

1 Equality and sovereignty of the peoples of Russia.
2 The right of free self-determination of peoples even to the point of separating and forming independent states.
3 Abolition of each and every privilege of limitation based on nationality or religion.
4 Free development of national minorities and ethnographic groups inhabiting Russian territory.

Source: J. Bunyan, H.H. Fisher, The Bolshevik Revolution 1917–1918: Documents and Materials *(Stanford: Stanford University Press, 1934), pp. 282–3*

This decree was based on the principles outlined by Lenin in Document 11.2. While granting self-determination to the minorities it also aspired to unite the workers (and peasants) of all nationalities of the old Empire in defence of the Revolution. Yet to Lenin's chagrin all that the October Revolution and the right to self-determination had achieved was to accelerate its disintegration in the winter of 1917–18. Finland became independent, under a conservative government; on 7 November the Rada declared the Ukraine a People's Republic and, despite calling for federation with Soviet Russia, in fact proclaimed its independence on 9 January 1918 (the Soviet regime created by force of arms on 2 March was promptly deposed by the Germans); the Menshevik government in Georgia allied with its neighbours, Armenia and Azerbaijan, in effect to create a separate Transcaucasian state; and national movements grew in strength in virtually all non-Russian areas of the old state. Only in Estonia and Latvia did Bolshevik governments in favour of union with Soviet Russia emerge, but they soon fell to the Germans. In an attempt to re-create the state within its previous borders, Lenin now advocated that it should be reconstructed on federal lines, an idea which he had hitherto treated as anathema **(Service 1991: 285–9)**. As we saw in Chapter 7, the principle of federation was incorporated in the Declaration of the Rights of the Working and Exploited People **(Document 7.4)** and, on Lenin's insistence, enshrined in the Constitution of July 1918 **(Document 7.7)**. In practice, however, what Lenin was proposing was, to quote Richard Pipes, 'a special form of pseudo-federalism'. Power in Soviet Russia resided in the Party. The Party would remain centralised and united, not federal. The Party would be dominant in the component states of the new federal Soviet Republic. In practice, federalism would be nothing but a fig leaf covering 'a rigidly centralised dictatorship centered in Moscow' **(Pipes 1995: 152)**. However, even federalism proved to have little appeal in the border republics and ultimately another solution had to be found.

The unintended consequences of the policy of self-determination prompted another development in Bolshevik nationality policy. In a speech to the Third All-Russian Congress of Soviets on 15 January 1918, Stalin, then Commissar of Nationality Affairs, declared that the right to self-determination had been exploited by 'bourgeois chauvinist elements' in the non-Russian border regions to establish reactionary, anti-Soviet regimes. In future, self-determination was to be granted not to the bourgeoisie but only to the 'labouring masses of the given nation', as the Party programme of 1903 had proposed. In an interview on 9 April 1918, he reiterated that in the Soviet Federation the vote would be given only to workers and poor peasants, not the bourgeoisie **(Wade 1991: 94, 125)**. This particular proposal was taken up by Bukharin, an ardent opponent of any truck with nationalism. In March 1919, at the Eighth Party Congress, he proposed that the principle of self-determination for the labouring classes alone be formally included in the revised party programme then under discussion. In this way, the potential conflict between nationalism and socialism could be reconciled. Lenin bitterly opposed this suggestion, reaffirming his support of the right of nations to self-determination. The debate became even more furious when Iurii Piatakov, leader of the Ukrainian Bolsheviks, entered the fray. Intensely anti-nationalist, he scathingly derided not just Lenin but also Bukharin. He began by condemning Lenin's policy which, in his opinion, had simply played into the hands of the forces of counter-revolution, in Finland, the Ukraine and elsewhere. While more sympathetic to Bukharin's position, in the final analysis he also found himself compelled to reject it. To justify his position he addressed the possibility of the workers of a nation seeking to exercise its right to secede from the Soviet state. His answer was unequivocal.

Document 11.5 Iurii Piatakov's Refutation of National Self-determination

In this case, an international party, the party of the proletariat, can in no way permit that a question [of secession] affecting the interests not only of the proletariat of these regions but to a considerable degree the interests of the proletariat of the whole capitalistically developed world be solved entirely by the working class of that country.

Let me give you a concrete example. At present a struggle for the establishment of the dictatorship of the proletariat is taking place in the Ukraine. You know perfectly well that the fate of the Ukraine is of immense interest not only to the working masses of that country but also to the working masses of Russia, Latvia, Belorussia and the other Soviet republics . . . . Can we permit that the form of existence of the proletarian-peasant Ukraine be determined solely and independently by the working masses of the Ukraine? Of course not! Here Comrade Lomov vainly disowned my point of view when he pursued the line of economic centralisation regarding the regions of the former tsarist empire. He said: 'one must bring together those material resources which these republics possess with the purpose of concentrating their management in a single economic centre.' It follows that once we unite economically, create one administrative machinery, one Surpreme Council for the National Economy, one railway administration, one bank, etc., then all this notorious 'self-determination' is not worth a farthing. It is either simply a diplomatic game which has to be played in certain cases, or it is worse than a game if we take it seriously. We, as members of the party of the proletariat, we must declare openly that, it stands to reason, we cannot permit independence of such a kind. Where the proletariat has been victorious, there immediate union must take place, and we must pursue one line.

Source: Vos'moi s''ezd RKP(b) mart 1919 goda. Protokoly *(Moscow: Gosudarstvennoe izdatel'stvo politicheskoi literatury, 1959), pp. 80–1*

Piatakov's argument was not without its logic. For example, the fate of the Ukraine, a major grain producing region and one rich in coal and other raw materials, was undoubtedly of major concern to the Russian proletariat. Should its 'labouring masses' decide upon independence, then Soviet Russia could find itself deprived of its vital resources. His own solution to this potential problem, while consistently internationalist, was certainly authoritarian: the Ukraine (or any other country for that matter) would be integrated within the existing Soviet state, regardless of the wishes of its own proletariat. Such brutal honesty proved to be too much for the Congress to endorse openly and his proposed amendment was decisively rejected. The section of the programme concerning the nationalities that was adopted was a compromise. The final goal remained the unity of all nations, with a federative union of states organised on the Soviet model as a transitional measure towards this end. More particularly, self-determination was limited to the 'colonies and dependent nations', that is, those without equal rights (which, in theory at least, could not apply to territory under Soviet control as the Constitution of 1918 guaranteed national equality). Accordingly, one is tempted to conclude that Piatakov had come very close to the truth. For many Bolsheviks, self-determination was increasingly little more than 'a diplomatic game which has to be played in certain cases'. But played it was for the duration of the Civil War, no doubt as a weapon against the Whites who remained wedded to a 'Russia, One and Indivisible' **(see Document 8.6)**. While efforts were intensified during 1919 to reincorporate the Ukraine, and other border republics, Lenin, if not Stalin, still attempted to appear receptive and conciliatory to minority opinion. Yet, as victory in the Civil War drew ever closer, so Bolshevik actions became less restrained. Soviet republics had been established in Azerbaijan in April 1920 (the Red Army had played a prominent role in this) and Armenia in November. Of the Transcaucasian republics Georgia alone survived, thanks to the Polish invasion deep into the Ukraine in early May, and its independence was formally recognised on 7 May 1920. After the end of the Soviet–Polish war it too soon fell. At a meeting of the CC on 14 February 1921, Lenin finally gave in to the repeated requests of Stalin and his henchman in the Caucasus, Sergo Ordzhonikidze, to allow the Red Army to invade Georgia, on the pretext of aiding a staged uprising, and re-establish Bolshevik power.

Document 11.6 The Invasion of Georgia

The Central Committee is inclined to allow the Eleventh Army to give active support to the uprising in Georgia and to occupy Tiflis provided that international norms are observed, and on condition that all members of the Military Revolutionary Council of the Eleventh Army, after a thorough review of all information, guarantee success. We give warning that we are having to go without bread for want of transport and that we shall therefore not let you have a single locomotive or railway track. We are compelled to transport nothing from the Caucasus but grain and oil. We require an immediate answer by direct line signed by all members of the Military Revolutionary Council of the Eleventh Army.

Source: J. Meijer (ed.), The Trotsky Papers 1917–1922, Volume 2: 1920–1921 *(The Hague: Mouton, 1971) p. 656*

By 1921 most of the territories of the old Russian Empire had been 'regathered' in the new Soviet state (Poland, Finland and the Baltic States had become independent, in large part thanks to the patronage of the West). In the final analysis it appears that doctrine of self-determination had played little part in the reincorporation of much of the old Russian Empire within the new Soviet state. As Horace Davis concluded, power politics determined this outcome **(Davis 1976: 32–3)**. By the end of 1920 none of the minorities, unaided, could hope to resist to the Red Army; none had the support of a major foreign power; and they remained divided amongst themselves.

12

The war and the army

Much has been said already on the issues of the army and war, especially during 1917. The main task of this chapter is to bring together the strands of the previous discussion, and amplify it where necessary, before concentrating on the formation of the Red Army and the heated debates which it provoked. As we saw in Chapter 3, the army, in Allan Wildman's opinion, 'the chief bulwark of the old order, its only major defense against revolutionary challenge', had played a crucial role in influencing the outcome of the February Revolution. In the final analysis the High Command had been prepared to abandon Nicholas II and accept the Revolution. In return, it expected the soldiers, and the population generally, to support the intensification of Russia's war effort. The Petrograd garrison too, increasingly reluctant to shoot unarmed workers demonstrating on the streets of the city, transferred its allegiances to the side of the Revolution, so aiding its victory. Yet February was neither simply nor solely a military revolution, despite Richard Pipes's claim that it 'was, first and foremost, a mutiny of peasant soldiers' **(Pipes 1992a: 278)**, as it was the workers of Petrograd who had precipitated the chain of events that led to the collapse of the autocracy.

However, the February Revolution had produced a number of unintended, and unwelcome, consequences from the point of view of the High Command. De facto Russia had been transformed into a republic, 'the freest country in the world', according to Lenin. Moreover, it also led to the proclamation of Order Number 1, adopted by the Petrograd Soviet of Workers' and Soldiers' Deputies on 1 March and printed in its newspaper, Izvestiia, on 2 March.

Document 12.1 Order Number One, 1 March 1917

Concerning the garrison of the Petrograd District. To all the soldiers of the guard, army, artillery and fleet for immediate and precise execution, and to the workers of Petrograd for information.

The Soviet of Workers' and Soldiers' Deputies has resolved:

1 In all companies, battalions, regiments, depots, batteries, squadrons and in individual units of military service of every kind, and in the ships of the navy immediately to select committees from elected representatives of the lower ranks of the above-mentioned units.

2 In all military units which have still not elected their representatives to the Soviet of Workers' Deputies are to elect one representative per company, who should report, with written credentials, to the state Duma at 10.00 a.m. on March 2.

3 In all political actions each military unit is subordinate to the Soviet of Workers' and Soldiers' Deputies and its committees.

4 The orders of the Military Commission of the state Duma must be carried out, excluding those cases which contradict the orders and decrees of the Soviet of Workers' and Soldiers' Deputies.

5 All kinds of arms, such as rifles, machine guns, armoured cars and others, must be put at the disposal and under the control of the company and battalion committees and are not in any case to be issued to the officers, even if they demand them.

6 While on duty and performing military responsibilities soldiers must observe the strictest military discipline, but when off duty, in their political, civil and private lives, in no way must soldiers be deprived of those which all citizens enjoy. In particular, standing at attention and compulsory saluting when off duty are abolished.

7 In the same way, the titles of officers (Your Excellency, Your Honour, etc.) are abolished and replaced by the following form of address, Mr General, Mr Colonel, etc.

Coarse address to soldiers of any rank whatsoever, in particular, addressing soldiers by *ty*, is prohibited, and any breach of this provision, as well as any misunderstandings between officers and soldiers, must be reported by the latter to the company committees.

This order is to be read to all companies, battalions, regiments, ships' crews, batteries and other combatant and non-combatant units.

Petrograd Soviet of Workers' and Soldiers' Deputies

Source: Sbornik dokumentove i materialov po istorii SSSR sovetskogo perioda (1917–1958 gg.) *(Moscow: Izdatel'stvo mosk. universiteta, 1966), pp. 21–2*

Document 12.1 was an expression of the demands made by the soldiers themselves, during the session of the Petrograd Soviet of 1 March, rather than being foisted on them by any particular party. Participation in the Revolution had created anxieties amongst ordinary soldiers. In particular, they were uncertain what the response of those officers who had 'disappeared' at the height of the Revolution would be. Fear of some form of retribution, combined with the desire to eliminate the tyrannical, often brutal, methods of maintaining discipline in the Imperial Army (methods which the Duma apparently wished to retain), prompted them to seek the series of checks on, and limitations of, the power of the officers contained in Order Number 1 **(Boyd 1968: 364–8)**. In theory, it was self-professedly to apply solely to the Petrograd Military District, but largely thanks to Bolshevik machinations it was widely distributed, in leaflet form, across the country, at the front as well as the rear. It was promptly accepted by the vast bulk of soldiers (and sailors) as the proper basis upon which the army of the Revolution should be restructured. However, contrary to a common misconception, it did not call for the election of officers, though undoubtedly there were instances where old officers were replaced by those chosen by the soldiers themselves. To counter this mistaken assumption the Petrograd Soviet was compelled to issue, on 5 March, Order Number 2. It unequivocally pointed out that there had been no provision for the election of officers in Order Number 1. It also stressed, in vain, that its provisions applied only to the Petrograd garrison **(Golder 1927: 388–9)**.

It would be unwise, however, to attribute the disintegration of the Russian army during 1917 solely to the impact of Order Number 1, and the proliferation of soldiers' committees that it spawned. While clearly reflecting the wishes of the soldiers for some form of democratic (soviet) control over the old officers, as well as the assertion of their civil rights, and their dignity (point 7), it was not an anarchistic charter. The soldiers remained prepared to carry out their military duties, as long as they were approved by the soviet. While desertion did markedly increase in the early months of the Revolution, the overwhelming majority of soldiers were committed to defending it from the threat posed by reactionary German imperialism. What they would not countenance, as we saw in Chapter 4, was the prosecution of war to a victorious conclusion, nor procrastination on the government's part in seeking a speedy, democratic peace.

The democratisation of the army was consolidated by the Declaration of Soldiers' Rights, approved on 11 May by Kerensky, Minister of War in the First Coalition Government. It was published in the government's official newsaper, *Vestnik Vremennago Pravitel'stva*, on 14 May. It began by affirming the civil liberties of the soldiers, including their right to join any political, national, religious, economic or professional organisation; to express, when off duty, their political and other views openly; and freely to receive any papers or journals, political or otherwise. But there was a twist in the tail of this Declaration. It did not propose the total abolition of the command power of the officers. On the contrary, certain points in it specifically reasserted the authority of the officers, especially in combat situations.

Document 12.2 The Declaration of Soldiers' Rights

14 No soldiers may be subject to penalty or punishment without trial. But in combat situations the commander has the right, on his own authority, to take all measures, including the application of armed force, against his subordinates who fail to execute his orders. These measures are not considered to be disciplinary punishments.

18 The right to determine the duties of, and, in those cases indicated by law, to remove temporarily from duties officers of all grades, belongs exclusively to the commanders. Similarly, they alone have the right to issue orders concerning combat actions and the preparation of a unit for combat, its training, its special duties . . . . The right of internal self-administration,

of the imposition of penalties and of control in precisely defined cases . . . belongs to elected army organisations.

Source: A.I. Denikin, Ocherki Russkoi Smuty: 1 *(Paris: Povolozky, 1921), pp. 44–5*

Despite these concessions, castigated by the Bolsheviks 'as transforming the Declaration into a "Declaration of Soldiers' Rightlessness'" **(Wildman 1987: 23)**, the old officers (more precisely, the senior officers, as a large proportion of the junior officers promoted from the ranks during World War I appear to have been sympathetic to reform of the army) remained intransigent. They, as many of the Duma politicians, considered that the civil freedoms granted to the soldiers, combined with the growth of their elected committees, had served simply to make the army vulnerable to political agitation from the left. In consequence, its discipline and fighting capacity had been severely eroded. The failure of the ill-conceived and ill-planned June offensive **(see Chapter 4)** simply confirmed them in their prejudices. Yet as Alan Wildman has recently argued, their analysis was fundamentally flawed. Temperamentally they were unable to accept any measures of democratisation in the army. They also shut their eyes to the fact that many elected committees, from the divisional level upwards dominated by members of the radical intelligentsia rather than ordinary soldiers themselves, had supported the offensive and in fact acted to maintain discipline and prop up the authority of the officers **(Wildman 1992: 79–82)**. They could not accept the fundamental problem facing them, that the majority of the rank and file was exhausted by three years of defeat and had no interest in their own cherished objective of war to a victorious conclusion. Their reaction was predictable: the restoration of the traditional powers of the officers who would be given absolute power to maintain discipline, by use of execution, if necessary **(see Document 5.3)**. Their attempts to implement this policy, by supporting the elevation of Lavr Kornilov to the position of military dictator, reinforced the growing radicalisation of the ordinary soldiers. They became increasingly susceptible to Bolshevik propaganda in favour of an immediate peace (as Robert Service has remarked, the Bolsheviks muted their commitment to waging a revolutionary war during 1917), though few then foresaw that it would be a separate, and costly, peace with Imperial Germany **(see Chapter 13)**. As the soldiers flocked to the Bolshevik cause, so too the senior officers deserted the Provisional Government led by the 'traitor' Kerensky. As the peasantry, the army was effectively 'neutralised' and remained largely passive in face of the Bolshevik seizure of power in October.

Yet the bulk of this democratised, and increasingly disillusioned, army did not desert before October. It was only the armistice with Germany on 4 December, and the prospect of imminent peace, that precipitated the return of the soldiers *en masse* to the countryside in late 1917, to take active part in the redistribution of the land also promised by the Bolsheviks **(Wildman 1987: 401)**. Ironically, the disintegration of the army posed massive problems for the Bolsheviks themselves. The lack of any credible military force compelled them, notwithstanding the protests of the Left Communists **(see Chapter 13)**, to accept the harsh peace conditions imposed by the Germans at Brest–Litovsk. The failure of a new volunteer army, drawn from the ranks of the workers and poor peasants, to emerge in any numbers in the early months of 1918 led many of them to reappraise their military strategy. Leon Trotsky was the driving-force behind this reappraisal, one that Lenin too came to endorse. He argued that the defence of the Revolution from external or internal attack could not be ensured by reliance on the creation of a popular militia. Instead, it demanded the creation of a new, regular army, organised on conventional lines: the gradual introduction of conscription; the creation of a single, unified, hierarchical command structure; and the replacement of elected officers by officers of the old imperial army, the so-called military *spetsy*, to provide efficient, professional leadership. The appointment of Trotsky, as President of the Supreme War Council on 4 March, and then as Commissar of War on 8 April, signalled a new departure in military policy. It became evident in the decree on compulsory military training issued by the All-Russian CEC on 22 April.

Document 12.3 On Compulsory Military Training

The Russian Soviet Republic, surrounded on all sides by enemies, must create its own powerful army, in order to defend the country as it completes the communist transformation of its social structure.

The Workers' and Peasants' Government . . . sets as its immediate task the recruitment of all citizens for universal labour conscription and military duty. This work is stubbornly opposed by the bourgeoisie, which is unwilling to surrender its economic privileges and seeks, by means of conspiracy, insurrections and traitorous deals with foreign imperialists, to recapture state power.

To arm the bourgeoisie would mean to introduce constant strife within the army and thereby paralyse its strength in the struggle against external enemies. The parasitic exploiters . . . who do not wish to assume the same duties and rights as others, cannot be allowed access to arms. The Workers' and Peasants' Government will seek ways of ensuring the bourgeoisie, in one way or another, bear part of the burden of the defence of the Republic . . . . But in the immediate transitional period military training and the arming of the population will be given only to workers and peasants who do not exploit the labour of others.

Citizens between the ages of 18 and 40, having undertaken a course of compulsory military training, will be registered as liable for military service. At the first call of the Workers' and Peasants' Government they will be obliged to take up arms and reinforce the ranks of the Red Army, which consists of the most devoted and selfless fighters for the freedom and independence of the Russian Soviet Republic and for international socialist revolution.

Source: Sbornik dokumentov i materialov po istorii SSSR sovetskogo perioda (1917–1958 gg.) *(Moscow: Izdatel'stvo mosk. universiteta, 1966), pp. 95–6*

This decree was followed by one five weeks later, on 29 May, which in fact conscripted the workers and peasants in the regions of the country deemed to be most threatened by counter-revolution, namely, Moscow, Petrograd, the Don and the Kuban. In the interim, Document 12.3 had provoked heated debate within the Party, especially as it had envisaged that compulsory military training should be undertaken by 'qualified teachers' (i.e., the old officers), so incorporating the plea made by Trotsky on 21 April that 'the better qualified and more honest of the old generals' be employed in this capacity **(Bunyan 1976: 267)**. The Left Communists led the attack, supported by many of the units of the slowly forming Red Army. At the end of April, in their journal, *Kommunist*, Karl Radek most fully articulated their objections. He began on a conciliatory note, conceding that Trotsky was correct in advocating the establishment of a much larger army. This was vital, he argued, not so much to combat counter-revolution within Russia itself (he patently misjudged the threat that it would come to pose), as to defend the Revolution against the pretensions of world imperialism, most recently confirmed by Japan's thrust into Siberia. He also welcomed the decision to exclude the bourgeoisie from the new army. He continued:

Document 12.4 Left Communist Military Policy

An army which would include the bourgeoisie and the *petty-bourgeois* mass, which trails behind it and in general is opposed to the proletarian revolution, would not be able to fulfil its revolutionary tasks . . . . The fact of the matter is that class divisions would fracture the army, wreck its internal unity, i.e., would destroy the main source of its strength – the consciousness of a common purpose, which unites all the soldiers . . . . [B]ut it is not such a simple matter to determine the paths which ensure this common purpose. It would be the simplest of all to train the the worker and peasant masses and immediately build the entire army from the lower classes. But in the meantime we are unable to carry out such a massive task as we have neither the registration boards in the localities . . . nor the cadres of instructors and leaders nor . . . finally, sufficient arms to do so . . . . A modern army is not simply a conglomeration of people, but a highly developed technical-administrative apparatus. The creation of such an army is the product of a lengthy process of consolidating and organising the victorious revolution. But this very process . . . demands an apparatus of compulsion which must play a primary role in the repair of transport and the creation of the prerequisites of all variety of creative work. Therefore the creation in the meantime . . . of a volunteer worker-peasant army is not only the first step towards the future arming of all the working class and poor peasantry but also the necessary prerequisite for the organisational consolidation of the Revolution. The Mensheviks point to the danger which is created by the separation from their social base of workers and peasants who volunteer for the Red Army. We do not deny that such a danger exists: any stratum of society which has arms is easily penetrated by its own special psychology, becomes a caste which demands privileges for itself, has its own interests, is easily transformed from an arm of the government into its conqueror. Agitation and revolutionary propaganda which strengthens the living relationship between the Red Army and its worker milieu may delay, but cannot eliminate this process . . . . The real means to preserve our Red Army cadres from degeneration into a praetorian clique, able to impose its demands on the Workers' and Peasants' Government, is the constant use of the Red Army . . . for the instruction of all the worker-peasant mass in military matters . . . . Only to the extent that these cadres help to create around themselves a people in arms will they in reality become a weapon of the Revolution, and not the basis of a counter-revolutionary movement . . . . [T]he leaders of the Soviet Republic do not realise sufficiently the looming danger . . . not only of the tendency of the cadres to separate themselves from the people, but equally that once having created an armed force they themselves easily will yield to the temptation to be satisfied by it alone . . . . In order to instruct the people in military science, one must not rely on the handful of military specialists that we possess. Lengthy, persistent work is necessary to ensure that military questions penetrate the consciousness of all democratic workers. An ideological interest in military matters must be created in the ranks of the workers. Given the colossal amount of work burdening the soviet leaders it can very easily transpire that the volunteer cadres push into the background their chief objective – the instruction of the toiling masses in military science.

Most attention was paid to the danger of the counter-revolutionary aspirations of the old officers which most of all troubles government circles . . . . We do not share the optimism of comrade Trotsky, who attests that among the officers he found a considerable number who understood the nature of the transformation that had taken place. There are very few officers who in the slightest understand the purposes for which our new army is created; officers who sympathise with these purposes are rare individuals. The majority coming to work for us are people seeking food . . . . They have no intention of playing an independent counter-revolutionary role, but they are convinced that we ourselves will proceed in the direction of creating a bourgeois republic. Therefore we consider that the old officers must play only a temporary role . . . . Understandably, as long as we do not have our own officers, officer-Communists, we are compelled to use the old officers not only as instructors but also as commanders. But we must make every effort to ensure that we get from them the opportunity to create cadres of our own officers: they must teach us the basics of military science which must become the property of Soviet democracy.

The fate of the Red Army is inextricably linked with the fate of the Revolution generally. The structure of an army always mirrored the structure of the society which created it. If the *petty-bourgeois* peasantry takes over the

Revolution, if the Workers' and Peasants' Government compromises with foreign and native capitalism, no organisational tricks, no protective measures can prevent the transformation of the Red Army into a weapon directed against the working class . . . . The task of proletarian [i.e., Left] Communists . . . by mobilising the proletariat, is to ensure that such a degeneration . . . does not occur. It will be easy to preserve the revolutionary army from [this danger] so long as its working-class character is strengthened.

Source: K. Radek, 'Krasnaia armiia', Kommunist, 2 (New York: Kraus, 1990; reprint of 1918 original), pp. 95–8

Hitherto untranslated, Document 12.4 is an important statement of the principles which many in the Party believed must determine the construction of a genuinely revolutionary army. It is also rather more complex than it might appear at first sight. The most easily understood part of it concerns the proposed role assigned to the military *spetsy* in the formation of the Red Army. While reluctantly conceding that they were necessary to teach the workers modern military skills, the Left Communists feared that they would abuse their positions to subvert the revolutionary ethos of the new army (a position which mirrored their fears about using the old technical *spetsy* to aid Russia's industrial reconstruction, as we shall see in Chapter 13). They also defended the principles then common amongst European socialists of all hues, and articulated most rigorously by the French socialist, Jean Jaurès, regarding the character of a socialist army. The standing army must be replaced by a locally trained, part-time militia, embracing all the workers. A regular conscript army, even if initially proletarian in composition, would become isolated from its class base. In turn, it would become transformed into a professional 'caste', with an increasingly weak commitment to the causes of the Revolution and vulnerable to manipulation by its officer class. Finally, despite formally conceding that the poor peasants had a role to play in the new army, consistent with their self-professed 'proletarian communist' principles and their suspicion of the '*petty-bourgeois*' peasantry **(see Chapter 13)**, they ultimately were convinced that the only sure means of ensuring the revolutionary character of the Red Army was by preserving, as Francesco Benvenuti has remarked, its 'proletarian purity' **(Benvenuti 1988: 32–5)**. How this was to be achieved in a predominantly peasant society, with a working class declining in numbers as industry continued to disintegrate, was never fully explained. As General Mikhail Tukhachevskii rather ironically pointed out in January 1921, admittedly when Soviet Russia was in the grip of waves of peasant insurrections **(see Chapter 15)**, '[i]t is completely incomprehensible how a militia army, which would be composed in its overwhelming majority of peasants, might become, immediately after its mobilisation, highly qualified politically, and prepared to take the field with Communist banners, ready for victory. It is quite clear that such a supposition is completely senseless' **(Tukhachevsky 1995: 168)**.

Circumstances, however, militated against any moves towards the creation of a purely workers' militia. The burgeoning Civil War, and the defeats inflicted on the Red Army in the summer of 1918 **(see Chapter 8)**, added weight to the increasingly urgent demands of Trotsky, and others, such as A.I. Egorov, Military Commissar at the recently formed All-Russian Main Staff, that a disciplined, mass conscript army, embracing peasants as well as workers, must be re-created. Moreover, in purely military matters, the authority of the commanders in the field, even if they were former tsarist officers, was to be paramount. Their orders were not to be interfered with by the political commissars, who had been appointed to every army unit to ensure that the old officers did not use their powers in ways harmful to the Revolution **(Meijer 1964: 93–7, 107–9)**. Trotsky himself was convinced that the officers had played a critical role in Red victories in the late summer and autumn of 1918. In December he issued an impassioned plea in their defence.

Document 12.5 Trotsky's Defence of the former Tsarist Officers

The frequent and often unjustified attacks on military specialists from the former officers' cadres now working for the Red Army have produced, in some units of the command, an uncertain and harrowing atmosphere . . . .

I therefore feel it necessary to issue the following declaration:

A general hostility to former regular officers is alien to both the soviet power and to the best units on active duty. Every officer who wants to defend our country against the invasion of foreign imperialists and its Krasnov and Dutov [Cossack leaders] agents is a welcome worker for the cause. Every officer who wants to and can co-operate in forming the internal structure of the army and thus help it to achieve its objectives with a minimum loss of workers' and peasants' blood, is a welcome collaborator with soviet power, has a right to be respected, and shall be respected in the ranks of the Red Army.

Soviet power will continue to bear down hard on rebels and to punish traitors . . . . Soviet power knows full well that many thousands of officers who graduated from the schools of the Old Regime and were brought up in a bourgeois-monarchist spirit cannot accustom themselves at once to the New Regime, understand it or respect it. But during the thirteen months of soviet power it has become clear to many, many officers that the Soviet regime is not an accident; it is a regularly constituted structure, based on the will of the working millions. It has become clear to many, many officers that there is now no other regime capable of securing the independence and freedom of the Russian people against foreign intervention . . . .

In the Ukraine . . . in Siberia . . . in the North, there are not a few former Russian officers who would be willing to submit to the Soviet Republic if they did not fear a drastic punishment for their previous activities. To them, the repentant apostates, applies what we said above about the general policy of the Workers' and Peasants' Government: it is guided in all its actions by its revolutionary objectives, not by blind vengeance, and it opens its doors to every honest citizen willing to work in soviet ranks.

Source: I. Howe (ed.), The Basic Writings of Leon Trotsky (London: Mercury, 1963), pp. 121–2

There was considerable truth in Trotsky's statement. By the end of 1918 there were 22,000 tsarist officers in the Red Army. Some had volunteered, if only to defend Russia from the continuing threat of German imperialism, while others had been subject to conscription after July. By the end of the Civil War, Evan Mawdsley has calculated that more than 48,000 had mobilised. Many, too, proved to be loyal and effective servants of the Soviet regime, in part since disloyalty was severely punished, by execution and, perhaps more importantly, by the threat of retribution against their families. But desertion remained more of a problem than Trotsky cared to admit. There was the famous case of Lieutenant-Colonel M.A. Muraviev, a Left SR himself, who led part of the Red Army in the Volga region to revolt on 10 July 1918, days after the Left SR rising in Moscow had been crushed **(see Chapter 7)**, while in the summer of 1919 the *spetsy* almost delivered Petrograd into the hands of the Whites **(Mawdsley 1987: 57–61, 179)**.

Critical voices within the Party, moreover, were not mollified by Trotsky's soothing words. Continuing suspicion of the *spetsy* was one catalyst behind the emergence of the so-called Military Opposition at the Eighth Party Congress in March 1919. It did not dispute the need to employ their services. However, it challenged the virtually autocratic powers given to these unelected officers, especially in combat situations. Equally, it opposed the material privileges granted to them. It insisted that the political commissars be given greater authority over them and, together with the elected soviets within the army, collectively determine operational decisions **(Service 1995: 75–82)**. While many in this opposition were former Left Communists, including its leading spokesman, Vladimir Smirnov, it was in fact a rather eclectic movement. Others, usually loyal to the 'party line', such as Joseph Stalin and his acolytes, K. Voroshilov and S. Budenny, adhered to it largely out of hatred towards the tsarist officers **(Benvenuti 1988: 3)**. At the Congress, Smirnov, himself a political commissar in the army, led the assault on the Trotsky's theses in defence of the existing structures within the Red Army. As Trotsky had departed to the Eastern Front his theses were presented by G.A. Soklo'nikov.

Document 12.6 The Military Opposition

I must state that the question of enlisting the services of military specialists, of the need to use them, does not cause us to disagree with the prevailing tendencies in military policy. Without doubt we need specialists but we must consider the difference which exists between the Red and White Armies. Regarding the Red Army we must remember that at present our policy is directed to recruiting the middle peasant . . . and that the survival of soviet power to a large degree depends on whether we succeed in this task or not . . . . We find ourselves in a more advantageous position than our opponents because the peasantry gravitates more towards the working class than the *kulaki* whereas the White Guards are forced to act solely by means of compulsion . . . . But as far as concerns the commanders, then on the contrary there are no doubts that the mass of old officers are inclined to the White Guards . . . . Therefore the question of specialists poses a great problem for us.

As far as concerns the commanders . . . political commissars, whose functions were not precisely defined, were created to control them. . . . In such a way a certain duality in administration was created. On the one hand - specialists, on the other - Communists, who watched over their political reliability . . . but the role of the political commissars . . . turned out to be broader, not just a supervisory one but to a great extent also an operational one. This is explained by the fact that at the beginning of the Revolution the vast bulk of the old officers went over to our enemies . . . . We were left, relatively speaking, with the poorest element and this explains . . . why the work of the military commissars was not only one of supervision but also of participation in operational matters, even in deciding questions of a strategic character. This was inevitable.

But . . . the decree on revolutionary military soviets [12 December 1918] . . . assigns to the army, front, etc. commander control of the army. The political commissar simply has the right in certain circumstances to countermand the decision of the commander . . . . In operational questions they do not even have the power to do this . . . . In point six [of Trotsky's theses] we read: 'In turn, the necessary condition of enlisting the specialists is to concentrate the general political leadership of the army and overall supervision of the commanders in the hands of the working class' . . . . In a word, the role of the political commissar is limited to measures of control. I assert that this decision is incorrect and does not correspond with our experience. On the contrary, right now when we already possess political commissars who have sufficient combat experience and who know not to intervene when it is not necessary to do so, we must assign to them broader rights, greater participation in the running of the army.

Commanders are given a series of privileges, viz. special pay . . . the right to live in separate billets when in barracks, the right in certain circumstances to have orderlies, etc.

Let me turn to the question of the operation of the army. Experience has shown that the commissar must participate in its operation, not be limited only to supervision. I personally defend the view that members of the revolutionary soviets must be given the deciding voice in the sphere of operational questions. I am told this contradicts military doctrine . . . . [which states] that the command must be responsible, that it must have the courage to take full responsibility for all those actions dictated by military

Source: S. White, The Bolshevik Poster *(New Haven: Yale University Press, 1988), p. 49*

imperatives. This will only be the case if operational responsibility is entrusted to the entire revolutionary soviet where there are Communists whose sense of duty . . . is higher than any other consideration.

Let me turn to political work. Despite its colossal importance in the organisation of the army, it is being conducted in a completely bureaucratic manner. I have in front of me a copy of *Voennaia mysl'*, the paper of the revolutionary soviet of the Eastern Front, which contains the draft of the instructions for the organisation of political departments in the army. What do we see? The political department consists of the head of the department and a whole series of departments under him . . . . There is no mention in the draft of collegiality [see Document 13.6], of the convening of Party conferences for the discussion of questions arising. Can such an institution actually work? Certainly not. This is is only an office for information and agitation. But it is not able to carry out any living party work as a result of which new forces can emerge from the ranks of the Party. And we need this very much because our reserves of old communists are being exhausted . . . . The only solution is to have done with bureaucratism and build political work in the army on the basis of the comradely union of Communists, by means of the combination of the principles of appointment and self-creativity.

Source: Vos'moi s"ezd RKP(b). Mart 1919 goda. Protokoly *(Moscow: Gosudarstvennoe izdatel'stvo politicheskoi literatury, 1959), pp. 154–8*

The minutes of the meetings of the sub-section of this Congress specially devoted to discussion of the military question, published in full for the first time in *Izvestiia TsK KPSS* (*News of the Central Committee of the CPSU*) in 1989, reveal that Smirnov's critique was widely supported, especially by delegates from the army itself. Trotsky's theses were rejected by a vote of thirty-seven to twenty. However, at the plenary session of the Congress on 21 March Lenin eventually 'waded in', as Robert Service expressed it, on the side of Trotsky. His theses were largely endorsed. Smirnov's plea for collegial decision-making in the army was emphatically rejected. But concessions were made. In particular, the need for greater party control in the army was accepted, as were the promotion of more workers to positions of command and greater powers for political commissars over the old officers. After the Eighth Party Congress, as we shall see in Chapter 13, the focus of intra-party debate largely shifted from the army to concerns about the increasing bureaucratisation and centralisation evident within the economy, party and state. However, rumblings of dissent regarding the structure of the army continued to be heard. At the Ninth Party Conference in September 1920 the old Left Communist, Ivan Mgeladze, criticised the military for disregarding the views of local party organisations and soviets, while Sergei Minin again vociferously attacked the powers of the military specialists **(Benvenuti 1988: 200)**.

Yet the mass conscript army, largely organised on conventional lines and led by former tsarist officers, played a major role in Bolshevik victory in the Civil War. Despite persistent problems of desertion, both by officers and peasant conscripts **(Adelman 1980: 49 estimated that 2.8 million peasants deserted during the Civil War)**, it had grown to number 5,300,000 by the autumn of 1920. Moreover, for all the recurring problems it faced in mobilising its forces (the initial successes enjoyed by Kolchak's and Denikin's armies in part were the result of a temporary numerical inferiority on the part of the Red Army), in the final analysis it provided the Bolsheviks with an overwhelming numerical superiority over the White armies. Trotsky's military strategy had been vindicated. Ironically, perhaps the most famous poster of the Civil War years, that created by Dmitrii

Moor in 1920 reproduced below (its affinities with that associated with Kitchener in World War I, 'Your country needs YOU', is obvious), had but little to do with the ultimate success of the Red Army.

Document 12.7 Have You Volunteered?

[See illustration on p. 187]

Opposition

Communist oppositions | 13

Perhaps 'the largest and most powerful Bolshevik opposition in the history of Soviet Russia' **(Cohen 1980: 63)**, the Left Communist movement of 1918 is equally important for the legacy that it bequeathed. The questions which the Left Communists raised regarding the growth of bureaucratic authoritarianism within Soviet Russia were at the root of the critiques put forward by later opposition factions, the Democratic Centralists and the Workers' Opposition. Accordingly, they will repay detailed examination.

The initial *raison d'être* of the Left Communist movement was to oppose Lenin's apparent reversal of agreed party policy. Rather than advocating revolutionary war against German (and world) imperialism after October he came to insist on the need to sign a separate, if Draconian, peace with Germany. The Left Communists coalesced into a distinct faction in late December 1917. At their peak, in January and February 1918, they won the support of the cream of the Party intelligentsia, including N.I. Bukharin, N. Osinskii, E.A. Preobrazhenskii and K.B. Radek; a majority of party organisations and local soviets; and most of the Party rank and file. After 18 February, however, this support rapidly crumbled in face of the renewed, and largely unopposed, German advance which followed the collapse of the peace negotiations at Brest–Litovsk. Grassroots support for revolutionary war had proved to be largely rhetorical, vindicating Lenin's hard-headed realism, his recognition that Soviet Russia had no effective military force with which to combat the German military juggernaut. On 7 March the Seventh Party Congress, by a majority vote, approved the punitive peace treaty that been signed on 3 March. This decision was ratified by the Fourth All-Russian Congress of Soviets eight days later **(Kowalski 1991: 11–19)**.

No doubt an emotional, even romantic, defence of revolutionary principles contributed to the Left Communists' opposition to a separate peace. Ivan Mgeladze declared that 'it [was] better to die in battle than to surrender all the positions of the Revolution without a struggle' **(Izvestiia Saratovskogo Soveta, 26 February 1918)**. Most Left Communists, however, strenuously denied that their opposition to the Brest peace was simply emotional. A separate peace on the terms dictated by the Germans, they argued, would suffocate the Revolution, left isolated in Russia, at birth. In particular, they emphasised its devastating economic impact. The loss of one-third of its grain-producing area, especially the Ukraine, and three-quarters of its grain surplus, threatened Russia, as G.A. Usievich sardonically remarked, with 'the bony hand of hunger'. Moreover, other losses (two-fifths of its industry and indus-trial work-force; nine-tenths of its easily exploitable coal reserves; and three-quarters of its iron production) precluded industrial recovery and any prospect of socialist construction within the truncated infant Soviet Republic **(Kowalski 1991: 72–3)**. In the Left Communists' *Theses on the Current Situation*, drawn up in early April by Osinskii and published in the first issue of *Kommunist*, their short-lived, theoretical journal, they offered a detailed (15-point), and gloomy, prognosis of the conse-quences for the Revolution of a separate peace with Germany.

Document 13.1 The Left Communists on the Consequences of Peace with Germany

9 . . . In view of the immediate, direct consequences of the peace . . . there arises the strong possibility of a tendency towards deviation on the part of the majority of the Communist Party and the Soviet government . . . into the channel of *petty-bourgeois* politics of a new type.

Should such a tendency materialise, the working class will cease to be the leader of, the dominant power in the socialist revolution leading the poor peasantry to destroy the rule of finance capital and the landowners; it will become a force scattered within the ranks of the semi-proletarian, *petty-bourgeois* masses, which sets as its task not proletarian struggle in alliance with the West European proletariat for the overthrow of the imperialist system, but the defence of the peasant-farmer fatherland from the oppression of imperialism . . . through compromise with the latter. In the event of a rejection of active proletarian politics, the conquests of the workers' and peasants' revolution will start to coagulate into a system of state capitalism and *petty-bourgeois* economic relations . . . .

10 Two paths stand open before the party of the proletariat. One path is to preserve and strengthen the surviving part of the soviet state which now from the economic point of view – given the incompleteness of the Revolution – is only in transition to socialism (given the incomplete nationalisation of the banks, the capitalist methods of financing industry, the partial nationalisation of industry, the domination of small-scale farming and property in the countryside, the peasants' aspiration to resolve the land question by its division), while politically it can be transformed from a dictatorship of the proletariat supported by the poor peasantry into the instrument for the political domination of the semi-proletarian, *petty-bourgeois* masses and turn into only a transitional stage to the complete supremacy of finance capital.

11 . . . The economic policy corresponding to such a course must develop towards agreements with capitalist crooks, both native and . . . foreign, and with representatives of 'solid' elements in the countryside ('cooperators'). The denationalisation of banks, in some concealed way, is logically linked with such agreements . . . . Instead of the transition from partial nationalisations to total socialisation of large-scale industry, agreements with the 'captains' of

industry must lead to the formation of large trusts directed by them and embracing the basic branches of industry . . . . Such a system . . . creates the social base for evolution towards state capitalism.

. . . the management of enterprises on the principle of broad participation of capitalists and of semi-bureaucratic centralisation naturally ties in with a labour policy aimed at the establishment of workers' discipline under the banner of 'self-discipline', the introduction of compulsory labour (such a project had been proposed by the right Bolsheviks), piece wages, extension of the working day, etc.

Government administration must develop towards bureaucratic central-isation: the supremacy of various commissars; the loss of independence for local soviets; and in fact the rejection of the 'commune state' administered from below . . . .

12 . . . The line of policy outlined above may strengthen the influence of counter-revolutionary forces, foreign and native, in Russia, shatter the revo-lutionary power of the working class and, by cutting off the Russian from the international revolution, ruin the interests of both.

13 Proletarian Communists consider another course of policy essential. Not the path of preserving a soviet oasis in the north of Russia by means of concessions which cause its degeneration into a *petty-bourgeois* state. Not the transition to 'organic internal work', in the conviction that the 'acute period' of the Civil War is over.

. . . The end of the acute period of the Civil War cannot mean that deals with the remaining forces of the bourgeoisie are possible. The 'organic construction' of socialism, without doubt the urgent task of the moment, can be completed only by the efforts of the proletariat itself, with the participation of qualified technicians and administrators, but with no form of collaboration with 'privileged elements' as such.

The Russian workers' revolution cannot 'save itself' by deserting the international revolutionary path, consistently avoiding a struggle and retreating before the pressure of international capital, making concessions to 'native capital' . . . .

The nationalisation of the banks must be completed . . . . [together] with the socialisation of industrial production and the complete elimination of capitalist and feudal remnants which obstruct its planned and extensive organisation. The administration of enterprises must be transferred into the hands of mixed *kollegii* of workers and technical personnel, under the control and direction of local economic councils. All economic life must be subordinated to the organising influence of these councils, elected by the workers without the participation of 'privileged elements', but with the participation of the unions of the technical and service personnel of the enterprises.

Not capitulation to the bourgeoisie and its *petty-bourgeois* intellectual minions, but the destruction of the bourgeoisie and the final smashing of sabotage . . . . The introduction of compulsory labour for qualified specialists and intellectuals, the introduction of consumer communes, the limitation of consumption for the wealthy classes and confiscation of their surplus property. The organisation in the countryside of an attack by the poorest peasants on the rich, the development of large-scale, socialised agriculture and support for forms of working the land by the poorest peasants which are transitional to socialism.

Source: 'Tezisy o tekushchem momente', Kommunist, 1 (New York: Kraus, 1990; reprint of 1918 original), pp. 16–23

Document 13.1 illustrates the Left Communists' fears of what a separate peace would entail and outlines, in broad terms, their own programme for the construction of socialism in Russia. Let us turn first to their critique. Theses 9 and 10 reveal a fundamental motif of Left Communist thinking. Professing themselves to be 'proletarian Communists', they were convinced that it was largely peasant pressure which had compelled the Party to abandon its commitment to revolutionary war and accept peace **(see Document 13.7)**. There was much truth in this allegation. Lenin himself admitted at the Seventh Party Congress that peace had been the price of securing peasant support for Bolshevik power. Having compromised over revolutionary war, they continued, the revolutionary state would find itself inexorably drawn to further compromises. In particular, the assault on capitalism within Russia would be halted and attempts made to enlist the services of the old capitalists in the reconstruction of industry. Such a policy would imply the dissolution of all forms of workers' democracy in industry (for them, an essential feature of socialism) and the restoration of the old bureaucratic and hierarchical methods of control over the workers. In turn, state administration would be recast on authoritarian lines, with power in the hands of centrally appointed officials, not the various local organs of the workers, as the experience of the Paris commune much lauded by Marx suggested. Rather than preserving Soviet Russia as an island of socialism in a hostile imperialist world, such a policy could lead only to the degeneration of the Revolution and the re-emergence of a real capitalist, or state capitalist, system. These forebodings were not without foundation, as an examination of Lenin's own thinking in the spring of 1918 confirms.

Document 13.2 Six Theses on the Immediate Tasks of the Soviet Government

1 The international position of the Soviet Republic is extremely difficult and critical, because the deepest and fundamental interests of international capital and imperialism induce it to strive not only for a military onslaught on Russia and the strangulation of soviet power, but also for . . . the strangulation of the soviet power.

   Therefore, the tactics of the Soviet Republic must be, on the one hand, to exert every effort to ensure the country's speediest economic recovery, to increase its defence capacity, to build up a powerful socialist army; on the other hand, in international policy, the tactics must be those of manoeuvring, retreat, waiting for the moment when the international proletarian revolution . . . fully matures.

2 In the sphere of domestic policy, the task that comes to the forefront at the present time . . . is the task of organisation.

3 . . . The organisation of proper administration, the undeviating fulfilment of the decisions of the Soviet government – this is the urgent task of the soviets, this is the condition for the complete victory of the soviet type of state, which it is not enough to proclaim in decrees . . . but which must also be practically organised and tested in the course of the regular, everyday work of administration.

4 In the sphere of the economic building of socialism, the essence of the present situation is that our work of organising the country-wide and all-embracing accounting and control of production and distribution, and of introducing proletarian control of production, lags far behind the direct expropriation of the expropriators.

From this basic fact follows . . . the explanation as to why the Soviet government was obliged in certain cases to take a step backward, or to agree to a compromise with bourgeois tendencies. Such a step backward and departure from the principles of the Paris Commune was, for example, the introduction of high salaries for a number of bourgeois experts. Compromises of this kind will be necessary until . . . the accounting and control of production and distribution is fully introduced.

5 Particular significance now attaches to measures for raising labour discipline and the productivity of labour . . . . This includes, for example, the introduction of piece-work, the adoption of much that is scientific and progressive in the Taylor system, the payment of wages commensurate with the general results of the work of a factory, the exploitation of rail and transport, etc.

6 The proletarian dictatorship is absolutely indispensable during the transition from capitalism to socialism . . . . Dictatorship, however, presupposes a revolutionary government that is really firm and ruthless . . . . Obedience, and unquestioning obedience at that, during work to the one-man decisions of soviet directors, of the dictators elected or appointed by the soviet institutions, vested with dictatorial powers (as is demanded, for example, by the railway decree) is far, very far from being guaranteed as yet. This is the effect of the influence of *petty-bourgeois* anarchy, the anarchy of small-proprietor habits . . . which fundamentally contradict proletarian discipline and socialism.

Source: V.I. Lenin, Collected Works, *27 (Moscow: Progress, 1964–5), pp. 314–17*

These *Theses* summarise the strategy that Lenin had been developing since late

March. They were published on 4 May and sent to all the local soviets, with the instruction that their policies should be based on them. They reveal quite unequivocally the measures that Lenin believed to be vital if the weak and isolated Soviet Republic was to survive. Economic recovery was paramount. Without it, Soviet Russia would be unable to rebuild a viable military force, either to defend the Revolution from attack or to aid the proletariat of Europe when it rose, as Lenin still felt it would. To achieve this recovery he was prepared to go to virtually any lengths, candidly conceding that retreats from the principles of the Paris Commune would be necessary. For instance, in 1917 he had argued in *State and Revolution* that in socialist society all administrators would be paid no more than an average worker's wage. Now he accepted that the old bourgeois experts (*spetsy*) must be paid much more if they were to be enticed to work for the new state. Underlying this renewed emphasis on the *spetsy* were Lenin's growing reservations about the abilities of the workers (which he had praised during 1917) independently to run the state and economy after the Revolution. Undoubtedly, his reservations were reinforced by the report of Aleksandr Shliapnikov, Commissar of Labour, on the economic chaos on the railways, which he attributed to the baneful consequences of workers' control **(see Document 10.6)**. One-man management had been restored first on the railways on 26 March. Here Lenin was urging its widespread extension to other industries. He now regarded such a system, together with other measures – the replacement of pay per hour regardless of output (introduced after October) by piece-work, to provide material incentives to impel the proletariat to work; traditional hierarchical forms of labour discipline; and, by implication, severe limits on the powers of the factory-plant committees to countermand managerial orders – as the prerequisites to restoring industrial production. He had retreated far from his position in 1917 when he had claimed that after the Revolution 'every cook can learn to administer the state'. In a highly polemical series of articles published in *Pravda* in early May, *'Left-Wing' Childishness and the Petty-Bourgeois Mentality*, he also directly confronted the Left Communists' accusation that these policies would lead to state capitalism, not socialism.

Document 13.3 Lenin's Defence of State Capitalism

State capitalism would be a gigantic step forward . . . because it is worthwhile paying for 'tuition', because it is useful for the workers, because victory over disorder, economic ruin and laxity is the most important thing; because the continuation of the anarchy of small ownership is the greatest, the most serious danger, and it will *certainly* be our ruin . . . whereas not only will the payment of a heavier tribute to state capitalism not ruin us, it will lead to socialism by the surest road. When the working class has learned . . . to organise large-scale production on a national scale, along state capitalist lines, it will hold . . . all the trump cards, and the consolidation of socialism will be assured.

In the first place, *economically*, state capitalism is immeasurably superior to our present economic system.

In the second place, there is nothing terrible in it for soviet power, for the soviet state is a state in which the power of the workers and the poor is assured . . . .

Source: V.I. Lenin, Collected Works, *27 (Moscow: Progress, 1964–5), pp. 338–9*

Document 13.3 is interesting on many grounds. First, in it Lenin tacitly admits that the arguments he had presented in September and October 1917 in defence of an immediate seizure of power had been exaggerated **(see Document 6.4)**. He concedes that the economic preconditions for socialism did not exist in Russia. Second, he defends measures to promote state capitalism as 'a step towards socialism', claiming that the existence of a proletarian state ensured that they would not result in the degeneration of the Revolution back towards capitalism itself. The implication of this argument is a curious one for a Marxist. The proletariat, it seemed, could seize political power and then proceed to create the economic prerequisites for socialism **(cf. Documents 3.9, 3.10)**!

To the Left Communists, Lenin's rather sanguine defence of the virtues of state capitalism, or 'organic construction', as they had termed it in their *Theses* **(Document 13.1)**, was arrant and dangerous nonsense. Nikolai Bukharin presented their analysis of the inevitable political consequences of the promotion of state capitalism in the economy.

Document 13.4 Bukharin's Critique of Lenin's Defence of State Capitalism

We will look at the matter concretely: let us suppose that soviet power (the dictatorship of the proletariat, supported by the poor peasants), while organising in name . . . state regulation, in fact transfers the business of administration to the 'organisers of trusts' (i.e., to the capitalists). What happens in that case? The real power of capital in the economy grows and becomes consolidated. Meanwhile the political superstructure either little by little degenerates beyond recognition, or at a certain point 'bursts', because the protracted 'command power' of capital in the economy is incompatible with the 'command power' of the proletariat in politics.

Source: N.I. Bukharin, 'Nekotorye osnovnye poniatiia sovremennoi ekonomiki', Kommunist, 3 (New York: Kraus, 1990; reprint of 1918 original), p. 149

Osinskii explained their fears in a little more detail than Bukharin. He too argued in a rather determinist Marxist fashion that, in the final analysis, 'politics is based upon economics, and whoever possesses the power of command over production sooner or later will lay hold of political power'. He insisted that the old 'captains of industry' were so immured in the mores of capitalism that they could not but act in a counter-revolutionary manner: 'our "teachers" will not help us to build socialism, but, on the sly, they will create a real capitalist trust, they will conduct their own *class* policy.'

Accordingly, October would be reduced to nothing but a bourgeois revolution, one which had served merely to sweep away all vestiges of feudalism in Russia **(Osinskii 1918: 32; and *Kommunist* 1: 41)**. More positively, it also fell to Osinskii to explain how the Left Communists believed socialism should be constructed.

Document 13.5 The Construction of Socialism

We stand for the construction of *proletarian socialism* by the class creativity of the workers themselves, not by orders on high issued by the 'captains of industry'. How do we envisage the tasks and methods of such construction? . . . Not only the Russian but even the Western European proletariat lacks the technical knowledge . . . to create a socialised economy . . . . Without engineers and other trained specialists it is impossible to organise large-scale industry on socialist lines . . . . Therefore we must put them to work. But . . . in such a way that real 'command power' in production remains in possession of the working class . . . . The proletariat must *buy* the talents of the intelligentsia . . . . But this remuneration must be strictly *personal*, simply payment for skilled work. It must in no way be in the form of transferring shares or bonds to engineers or assigning to them a 'profit share' in the formation of a semi-state, semi-capitalist trust. This means not only to build a bridge to state capitalism but also to sustain within the intelligentsia its material and psychological link with finance capitalism . . . . The working class *as a whole* must remain the master of production. The workers of a *given* enterprise certainly must not be owners of this enterprise . . . . Let us also underline that the organisation of labour must in no way transform the worker simply into an appendage of the machine, into a mechanical force, the main task of which is to work more . . . . From the point of view of the socialist organisation of labour, piece-work and time and motion studies [the Taylor system] is completely inadmissible. But the establishment of output norms, related to hourly pay which guarantees a normal existence, is . . . admissible . . . . Non-fulfilment of these established norms by the workers' organisations is the conscious or unconscious sabotage of socialism and must be punished most severely.

Considering the question in such a way, we proceed from faith in the class-consciousness, in the active class initiative, of the proletariat. It cannot be otherwise. If the proletariat itself does not know how to create the necessary preconditions for the socialist organisation of production, then no one can do this for it nor compel it to do this. A stick raised above the workers will be in hands of such a social force which either finds itself under the influence of another social class or must fall under its influence. If the stick is in the hands of the Soviet government, then the Soviet government will be forced to rely upon another class (e.g., the peasantry) and therefore will destroy itself as the dictatorship of the proletariat. Socialism, and the socialist organisation of production, must be constructed by the proletariat itself, or not at all, and something else will be constructed – state capitalism.

Source: N. Osinskii, 'Stroitel'stvo sotsializma', Kommunist, 2 (New York: Kraus, 1990; reprint of 1918 original), pp. 68–72

Document 13.5 begins rather negatively, reiterating the measures that the Left Communists believed it necessary to avoid. There was to be no truck with state capitalism, and all its trappings (including one-man management and authoritarian discipline over the work-force). Piece-work and the Taylor system, of time and motion studies, also were an anathema to them. They would exhaust and dehumanise the workers by converting them into mindless appendages of machines, routinely performing fragmented tasks decreed from above. In all, such policies would transform the proletariat into passive cogs in the production process and deprive it of the opportunity to participate actively in the administration of industry. For the Left Communists the principle of the conscious participation of the proletariat in the construction of the new socialist order was an essential part of its emancipation from the habits of the capitalist past **(Kowalski 1991: 107–8)**. In his classic work of the mid-1920s (still untranslated into English), *The Heroic Period of the Russian Revolution*, Lev Kritsman (a Left Communist himself in 1918) retrospectively offered a more philosophical justification of this principle, essentially one of workers' self-management. In language reminiscent of the young Marx, he emphasised that the fundamental objective of socialism, 'the further conquest and transformation of nature (the progress of technology) . . . and the further conquest and trans-formation of the nature of man himself . . . [was] a creative task'. To achieve this goal it was imperative that the proletariat, consciously and collectively, undertake the socialist transformation of society. It could do so, however, only if it was given the freedom to exercise its latent creative abilities and learn how to harness them in the very process of socialist construction. For Kritsman and his comrades 'mass creativity [was] the basic characteristic of communism' **(Kritsman 1924: 86–7)**. He also explained why collegial, or collective, administration, a principle defended by the Left Communists (and by subsequent oppositions), was necessary to unleash this creativity.

Document 13.6 Kritsman on the Virtues of Collegial Administration

In just the same way the fourth organisational principle of the epoch [of socialist revolution] follows from the character of the ruling class – the principle of collectivism. Its most profound manifestation, of course, was the nationalisation of the means of production and exchange. As the specifically distinctive characteristic of the proletariat, distinguishing it from *all* other social classes, the principle of collectivism becomes . . . the most popular principle of construction, permeating all spheres of social life. Nothing . . . is so characteristic . . . as the desire to eliminate individualism and implant collectivism. It was manifest in the organisation of administration (collegiality), in the ways of paying labour (collective supply and reward) . . . and in the attempts to replace petty agriculture by large-scale. collective agriculture (agricultural collectives and communes) . . . . The external expression of this principle was the universal supremacy in all organs of administration, including economic organs, of the system of *collegiality*, the direct link of all organs of administration (in one form or other, especially electivity) with the broad proletarian organisations, trade unions . . . . Every individual member of society was linked, by ever new paths, with society as a whole. In opposition to bourgeois society . . . in the newly forming society every member of it everywhere acted as a member of a broader or narrower collective.

Source: L. Kritsman, Geroicheskii period russkoi revoliutsii *(Moscow: Gosudarstvennoe izdatel'stvo, 1924), pp. 80–1*

The same ideas underlay Left Communist thinking on how to allow full play to proletarian 'mass creativity'. The banks and large-scale industry, the 'commanding heights of the economy', were to be nationalised and the old capitalists totally expropriated. Once nationalised, they were to be administered 'on socialist principles', that is, by a system of workers' management. They did accept, however, as Document 13.5 makes clear, that the old *spetsy* still had a vital, if subordinate, role to play until a new socialist intelligentsia was trained, and they were prepared to pay them more than an average worker's wage for their services. Moreover, workers' management was to be constructed from the level of the individual enterprise upwards. They were quick to add that this would not be tantamount to syndicalism whereby the organs of workers' management would convert enterprises into their own property and run them in their own narrow interests. Central planning, they argued, would prevent the atomisation of Russia into a myriad of self-governing, anarcho-syndicalist communes. What they were seeking to create was a genuinely democratic centralist system, which would combine workers' management at the enterprise, or micro- , level with central control of the economy at the national, or macro- , level. The problem was to provide mechanisms to reconcile conflicts, actual or potential, between the enterprises and the Supreme Economic Council (Vesenkha), the central planning agency. Osinskii, for one, rather optimistically assumed that such conflicts would be resolved by negotiation. However, if negotiation failed, then in the final analysis the decision of the centre would take precedence, so overriding the authority of the workers at the enterprise level. Ultimately, the Left Communists did not stand quite as 'uncomprisingly for the democratisation of industry' as Maurice Brinton has suggested **(Brinton 1970: 43)**. **(Kowalski 1991: 109–13 provides a more detailed account of this dilemma facing the Left Communists.)**

Lenin's espousal of state capitalist methods to restore Russia's ailing economy was not the sole focus of the Left Communists' critique. They were also plagued by concerns about political and military developments within Soviet Russia in the spring of 1918 **(for the military see Document 12.3)**. At the end of March, in face of virtual anarchy in much of the country, Lenin also demanded a return to 'businesslike methods' in state administration, an end to 'the overlapping of authority and irresponsibility [within the soviets] from which we are suffering incredibly at the present time . . . .' Coercion was required, not just against 'our enemies' but also 'all waverers and harmful elements in our midst'. '[T]he revolution', he continued, would be crushed 'if we do not counter ruin, disorganisation and despair with the iron dictatorship of class conscious workers'. The Party, 'the disciplined and class conscious vanguard of the proletariat', he now asserted, alone had the political nous to run the state. Yet the Party itself did not possess skilled administrators in sufficient numbers to cope with the range of tasks before it. Therefore, there was little choice but to employ the bureaucracy from the old regime, and to 'pay a very high price for [its] "services"', to assist the Party in restoring order to state administration. The outcome of this policy was an ever greater centralisation of power in the hands of the Sovnarkom and its spawning bureaucracy, at the expense of the power of the local soviets **(Kowalski 1991: 132–4)**. In response, the Left Communists railed against Lenin's abandonment of the model of egalitarian workers' participation that, as Bukharin sarcastically commented, he had so splendidly outlined in *State and Revolution*. They leapt to the defence of the vision of proletarian democracy contained within it. Mass participation was as essential in political as economic administration for the construction of socialism. Otherwise the Revolution would degenerate. Their own position, however, was not without its flaws, as Vladimir Sorin's critique of bureaucratisation reveals.

Document 13.7 On the Question of Soviet Power

Who composed the vast army of soviet workers who rushed into the various commissariats and commissions, departments and offices, bureaus and committees? Obviously, old, experienced party workers above all entered; however . . . we must admit that only an insignificant minority is sufficiently active and indefatigable to think about the further development of the Revolution; the majority, exhausted . . . by a revolutionary life full of danger . . . now aspire to quiet and peaceful work in the construction of socialism . . . and involuntarily begin to react with hostility and unconcealed fear to any extreme measures which may destroy the peace that has been achieved after such toil. Thanks to the sabotage of the well-qualified technical personnel, a rather ignorant semi-intelligentsia also entered the soviet organisations . . . . Anyone who . . . knew how to count and read became a valuable and needed person whom we seized with both hands . . . . they, as a whole . . . are interested in the preservation of their privileged position . . . decent pay, a greater guarantee of food . . . all this . . . does not dispose them to revolutionary boldness . . . . it is necessary still to include that impudent group which is prepared to serve anyone and under any system . . . and finally . . . a multitude of technicians and specialists of all sorts who undoubtedly do not sympathise with soviet power and went to serve it only for more money . . . . This group is, I suppose, the most reactionary . . . Since the leading circles take the opinions of this group into consideration, value them . . . then it has the opportunity from within to exert pressure on the policy of the soviets in a . . . conservative, even a reactionary direction . . . . Given the low cultural level and backwardness of Russia and the poverty of its intellectual forces it could not be otherwise . . . . It is clear from our analysis that the personnel of the soviets are interested wholly in the preservation of their privileged position . . . and are inclined to act as a *conservative* social group; from this flows a distinct distrust of the working masses . . . the feeble impulse to escape the control of the Party . . . . We are far from asserting that the soviet employees already have been transformed into a new bureaucracy . . . but undoubtedly this tendency exists . . . it is necessary to combat this tendency . . . and there is only one method to do so: the involvement of the broad working masses in social work and . . . the strengthening of the control of the workers called up to serve their needs, the limitation of all privileges for public workers. Finally, the Party itself, considerably better protected against degeneration, must strengthen its control over the soviet factions and make public workers responsible and accountable. It has often been pointed out that the power of the soviets . . . is the highest achievement of our revolution. This certainly is true but one must not forget that *the Party . . . is in every instance and every place superior to the soviets.* This is fully understandable. Only the Party acts as the defender of the interests . . . of the international working class; the soviets represent *the democratic toilers generally* and its interests, especially the interests of the *petty-bourgeois* peasantry, do not always coincide with those of the proletariat. The Left Communists are the most passionate proponents of soviet power but, of course, only so far as this power undeviatingly pursues a proletarian line and does not degenerate . . . in a *petty-bourgeois* direction. Our comrades like to reproach us for being . . . enemies of the soviets 'from the Left'. This, certainly, is utter stupidity. A real dictatorship of proletarian soviets, with no policy compromises, the rejection of any whatsoever opportunist steps - these are the demands of the Left Communists. We do not conceal the fact that the undeviating introduction of a proletarian line . . . is fraught with great dangers and . . . even temporary destruction, but we assume that . . . it is preferable . . . to perish as a *real government of the proletariat* than to preserve our existence at the price . . . of rejecting the principles of communism, of the degeneration of soviet power . . . .

Source: V. Sorin, 'K voprosu sovetskoi vlasti', Kommunist, 4 (New York: Kraus, 1990; reprint of 1918 original), pp. 193–6

The criticism of the old bureaucrats employed by the soviet state made by Sorin in Document 13.7 was not without foundation. From a series of questionnaires completed by them several years later Kritsman concluded that the majority of them had remained implacably hostile to soviet rule and hankered after the restoration of capitalism. At best, they fulfilled their duties without commitment; at worst, they sabotaged the construction of socialism **(Kritsman 1924: 93)**. To ensure that they in fact worked to serve the Revolution, not their own narrow self-interests, Sorin proposed that the soviets, more reliable repositories of revolutionary *élan*, be reinvigorated (precisely how was not explained in detail) in order to be able to control them. However, the soviets, as representatives of 'the *petty-bourgeois* peasantry' as well as the workers, themselves were not immune from corruptive and demoralising influences. The only reliable bastion of proletarian interests was the Party. In Sorin's view, it must be 'superior to the soviets', to ensure the latter carried out undeviating proletarian (i.e., Left Communist) policies. Ironically, the Left Communists' plea for a revived soviet democracy was becoming diluted by the dominant role assigned to the Party. But there was more. Other Left Communists, including Bukharin, Osinskii and Radek, doubted the health of the Party itself. Before it could effectively control the soviets it had to be purged itself of all non-proletarian elements which had flocked to it since the autumn of 1917. The problem remained of defining such non-proletarian elements. In the final analysis, the only solution that they could offer was to deem those who opposed their own policies to be non-proletarian. Beneath their defence of proletarian democracy lay an intolerance of views that conflicted with their own and a latent authoritarianism.

The final element of Left Communist ideology that requires elaboration, one that permeated their thinking but often is neglected, was their profound suspicion of and antipathy to the peasant majority in Russia. In their eyes the peasantry was an inherently reactionary class which would oppose all attempts to transform Russia into a socialist society. Karl Radek articulated their fears.

Document 13.8 Left Communist Attitudes to the Peasantry

... and the victory of proletarian revolution in Europe may allow the proletarian minority in Russia to place the peasantry on socialist rails. The absence of this revolution can cast the proletariat from power. If the Soviet government, standing on the point of view of a dictatorship of the proletariat and the peasantry ... takes into account the numerical and social preponderance of the peasantry, then it will proceed to a compromise with capital, a compromise acceptable from the point of view of the peasantry, but one which destroys the socialist character of the Revolution is and therefore unacceptable to the proletariat.

Source: K. Radek, 'Posle piati mesiatsev', Kommunist, 1 (New York: Kraus, 1990; reprint of 1918 original), pp. 6–7

Document 13.8 adds to our understanding of the reasons for the Left Communists' opposition to separate peace with Germany. It would place the Revolution, confined to Russia, at the mercy of its vast peasant masses. Revolutionary war, which they over-optimistically calculated would help to provoke revolution across Europe, alone would provide the proletarian support required to counter the weight of the peasant majority in Russia itself. But even had international revolution occurred, the problem of how to deal with the peasantry would not have been resolved. The Left Communists' objective was to transform the peasants from petty proprietors into rural proletarians working in large, collective farms. This objective underlay their critique of the agrarian policy proposed by Lenin himself from the summer of 1917. Then he responded to peasant aspirations **(see Document 9.1)** and argued for the divison of the bulk of the land amongst them, to ensure at least that they did not oppose the Bolsheviks. For the Left Communists such a policy would be economically retrogressive. Breaking up the large capitalist estates that existed would only destroy the most productive sector of Russian agriculture and exacerbate the problems of feeding urban Russia. It also would have fatal political consequences. By providing land for the farm labourers (*batraki*) it would convert them into propertied peasants and so strengthen the forces opposed to socialism. The dilemma facing them was that their own proposals for the collectivisation of agriculture found virtually no support among the peasants. Their solution to this dilemma appears to have been coercion: soon after the October Revolution Bukharin is alleged to have professed, in virtually Stalinist terms, that force might have to be used against the peasants **(Koenker 1981: 345)**. Forced collectivisation, however, was not introduced and their protests were in vain. The Land Socialisation Law of February 1918, despite its rhetoric in favour of 'the collective system of agriculture', *de facto* sanctioned land division **(Kowalski 1991: 88–95)**.

By the summer of 1918 the Left Communist opposition had disintegrated. Circumstances militated against its success. First, its policies rapidly lost credibility. Just as revolutionary war had come to appear impractical, so too its defence of the devolution of economic and political power to the local soviets and other elected workers' organisations seemed to offer no realistic solution to the chaos gripping the country. Many within the Party, the trade unions and even the leadership of the factory-plant committees agreed with Lenin that centralised economic and political control, one-man management and traditional means of discipline and incentive had to be restored. The renewed outbreak of civil war in the summer, which demanded increased production and political order, reinforced this current of opinion, while the Left Communists themselves were prepared to suspend their opposition in face of the grave threat to Bolshevik rule. Second, measures were taken to increase discipline in the Party. Some members were expelled, though how many suffered this fate and how crucial such a purge was to the defeat of the Left Communists are difficult to gauge with any accuracy. Finally, changes in policy may have gone some way to appeasing them. By May Lenin's hopes of running industry in collaboration with the old capitalists had collapsed. The Left

Communists' grave doubts about the compatibility of state capitalism with socialism were not put to the test and large-scale industry was nationalised on 28 June. Moreover, the worsening food crisis in urban Russia led to an assault on the peasants (in theory, only the rich) and the encouragement of communal agriculture, as the Left Communists had sought.

However, the questions raised by the Left Communists about whether post-revolutionary Russia was developing in a socialist direction had not been adequately answered, as the future was soon to reveal. As we have seen, at the Eighth Party Congress in March 1919 serious concerns about the military policy of the regime emerged **(see Document 12.5)**. Thereafter, the focus of intra-party debate largely shifted from the army to renewed criticisms of the increasing bureaucratisation and centralisation evident within the economy, the Party and state. During 1919 and 1920 the Democratic Centralists, led by Osinskii and the 'irreconcilable' Timofei Sapronov, both former Left Communists, more and more vociferously challenged the persistence of bureaucratisation, centralisation and hierarchy in all spheres of soviet life, the soviets, industry and the Party. The critique presented by Sapronov at the Ninth Party Conference in September 1920 is perhaps the most comprehensive statement of the grounds of their opposition.

Document 13.9 The Democratic Centralists' Critique of Bureaucratic Centralisation

I wish to talk about the sources of the emergence of that sore which is eating away at our party . . . . It is perfectly true that ideological differences do not exist, but disagreements on one fundamental question do . . . concerning the way in which soviet construction has been organised. Those forms and methods of administration which exist among us give birth to a bureau-cratism . . . which eats away at the body of our party . . . this system does not bring the organs of power closer to the masses but on the contrary isolates them from it. You remember the Eighth Congress . . . then the Seventh Congress of Soviets and a whole series of meetings, conferences, etc., between them at which the unsuitability of a system of bureaucratic centralism was pointed out, a system isolating the central organisations from the local executive committees . . . and the entire mass of workers generally. I think that it is not without purpose to recall those warnings made at the Eighth Congress concerning the dangers of building our soviet organism on so-called columns . . . central boards or people's commissariats from Moscow administered, for example, a small sanatorium in Samara *guberniia*, while the executive committee of the provincial soviet . . . had no right to inspect or even to enter the territory of this sanatorium; in return the right was granted to officials from Moscow, often not Communists, to live in their own state, fenced off by barbed wire from the local executive committee, to do what they liked . . . and to give sumptous meals . . . . Let us also take the organisation of Soviet farms where . . . even still in certain places the old *pomeshchiki* are retained as administrators and on their estates as of old assemble guests, hold balls . . . the results of such a policy are known to all . . . . All workers from the localities spoke firmly against the bureaucratic system. Our CC for long was for the system of bureaucratic centralism, or vertical centralism . . . but thanks to extensive pressure by the workers from the localities the CC was forced to take it into account and at the Seventh Congress [of Soviets] agree that it was necessary to end bureaucratic methods of soviet construction. It is necessary to give scope to local workers, to the creativity which is growing in the ranks of workers and peasants . . . . The Seventh Congress introduced a resolution which gave broad scope for the development of the creative forces of local organisations . . . . But, alas, even after the Seventh Congress the system of centralism remained as of old . . . . At the Ninth [Party] Congress a point was adopted which reads: 'to instruct local and central workers that in soviet construction they should be guided by the resolution of the Seventh Congress'. The resolutions, as you see, were fine, but everything remained as of old.

Let us now turn to the question of the administration of industry. Comrades, a debate about one-man management and collegiality took place at the Ninth Congress . . . . In many factories . . . a specialist is in charge of the enterprise, often the former director of the factory and often one whom the workers in 1917 and 1918 jailed for counter-revolutionary activity . . . . He carries out his work and, certainly, zealously introduces labour discipline, by imposing fines or often by arresting workers . . . for no cause. Of course, discipline is necessary, comrades, but when a *spets* introduces it, without a workers' commissar over him who would be able to control and inspect his actions, then it is natural for the workers to develop a negative attitude to that system of administration.

What are the causes of these signs of degeneration which exist in our party? One of the main causes is the incorrect organisation of soviet construction while the second is that our party . . . only had a thin proletarian stratum and certainly could not but fall under the influence of bourgeois elements, could not but succumb to the influence of the bourgeois *spetsy*.

. . . the broad influx to our party of workers and peasants also had undesirable consequences. These new comrades, . . . often incapable of critically reflecting on all the questions thrust before them . . . remained silent . . . . This created . . . the separation of comrades in high positions who can look down on the lower ranks, on the rank and file members of the Party as a subordinate element . . . at times with scorn . . . . we have party discipline which is degenerating into the most abnormal forms . . . if one or another comrade puts forward any criticism he is subject to repression . . . . We must combat this most decisively, but we will be able to do so only if the CC actively supports the elimination of repression not in words, but in deed. And, however strange it seems, we must defend actual freedom of criticism within our party – a freedom which at present is absent. Thanks to such abnormalities we have various sorts of ugly occurrences, for example, mass exoduses of workers from our party, the alliance of Communists with non-party members against the so-called commissars.

All these phenomena are threatening enough and must be eliminated . . . . Many put forward the slogan that at present one can only reform, make the Party healthy when we 'workerise' our apparatus at the centre and the grassroots. This slogan is also incorrect: it is impossible to put on one level all the workers and on another the intellectuals and say that the latter must be replaced, whatever the cost, by workers.

Source: Deviataia konferentsiia RKP(b). Sentiabr' 1920 goda. Protokoly *(Moscow: Izdatel'stvo politicheskoi literary, 1972), pp. 156–61*

It is widely recognised that the criticisms presented in Document 13.9 were not without foundation. Much of the power of the local soviets had been stripped away, to be replaced by that of various plenipotentiaries appointed from the centre. In industry, nationalisation had not led to greater workers' control. On the contrary, enterprises had been increasingly subjected to directives issued by the Vesenkha, and the central boards (*glavki*) it had appointed to run each separate branch of industry. Fifty-two such boards had been created by the end of 1920, according to James White **(White 1994: 223)**. Within individual enterprises, too, there was no opportunity for the workers to participate in their management, as they increasingly were administered by centrally appointed *spetsy*. Echoing the fears of the Left Communists about the wisdom of utilising the old administrators in positions of power, Sapronov had argued previously, at the Seventh Congress of Soviets in December 1919, that 'the specialist . . . [would] work not for the Revolution, but for the counter-revolution'. The Party as well had become increasingly subordinate to the decisions of its burgeoning central apparatus, with prominent dissenters frequently 'exiled' to positions of obscurity in the provinces. Such developments, they argued, again in terms reminiscent of the Left Communists, were stifling the 'self-creativity' of the masses. Their own proposals did call for devolution of effective economic and political power to the various local organs of the workers. All interference in the work of the local soviets, and party organisations, by centrally appointed commissars must cease. In particular, collegial administration of industry by the workers themselves **(see Document 13.6)**, which alone would provide them with opportunity of 'learning the art of self-administration', and at the same time enable them to supervise the activities of the *spetsy*, must be restored. How these laudable objectives were to be achieved in what remained a one-party state, immune to the pressures of demo-cratic election of its governing bodies, remained unarticulated. Their opposition to 'workerisation' of the Party and state divided them sharply from the Workers' Opposition which also had emerged as a distinct faction during 1920. Composed largely of disgruntled trade unionists (unlike the more intellectually based Democratic Centralists) it had coalesced in response to the efforts of Leon Trotsky to militarise labour, that is, to subordinate the unions in all industries to centrally appointed *spetsy*, as he had done on the railways. Their critique was most famously presented by Alexandra Kollontai, herself a former Left Communist, and the only prominent intellectual in their ranks. Her pamphlet, *The Workers' Opposition*, was published in limited quantities (1,500 copies, not 1,500,000 as her critics charged) before the Tenth Party Congress met in March 1921.

Document 13.10 The Workers' Opposition

Why was it that only the unions stubbornly defended the principle of collective management, even without being able to adduce scientific arguments in favour of it? And why was it that the specialists' supporters at the same time defended 'one-man management'? The reason is that in this controversy . . . two historically irreconcilable points of view had clashed. The 'one-man management' is the product of the individual conception of bourgeois class rule . . . disconnected from the collective.

Rejection of a principle – the principle of collective management in the control of industry – was a tactical compromise on behalf of our party . . . it was, moreover, an act of deviation from that class policy which we so zealously cultivated and defended during the first phase of the Revolution.

Why did this happen? . . .

Beside peasant-owners in the villages and burgher elements in the cities, our party . . . is forced to reckon with the influence exerted by the representatives of wealthy bourgeoisie now appearing in the form of specialists, technicians, engineers and former managers of financial and industrial affairs . . . . The more Soviet Russia finds itself in need of specialists . . . the stronger becomes the influence of these elements, foreign to the working class, on the development of our economy.

And let us, comrades, ponder whether it is possible to attain and build a communist economy by the hands and creative abilities of scions of the other class, who are imbued with their routine of the past? If we begin to think as Marxists, as men of science, we shall answer categorically and explicitly: 'No!'

The solution of this problem, as proposed by the industrial unions, consists in giving complete freedom to the workers as regards experimenting, class training, adjusting and discovering new forms of production, as well as expression and development of their creative abilities – that is, to that class which alone can be the creator of communism . . . . 'Organization of control over the social economy is a prerogative of the All-Russian Congress of Producers . . . which elect[s] the central body directing the whole economic life of the republic' (*Theses of the Workers' Opposition*). This point would ensure freedom for the manifestation of class creative abilities, not restricted and crippled by the bureaucratic machine.

Distrust toward the working class . . . is the whole essence of the theses signed by our party leaders. They do not believe that by the rough hands of the workers, untrained technically, can be created those foundations of the economic forms which, in the course of time, shall develop into a harmonious system of communist production.

There can be no self-activity without freedom of thought and opinion . . . . We give no freedom to class activity, we are afraid of criticism, we have ceased to rely on the masses: hence we have bureaucracy with us . . . our enemy, our scourge, and the greatest danger for the future existence of the Communist Party itself.

In order to do away with the bureaucracy that is finding its shelter in the soviet institutions, we must first get rid of all bureaucracy in the party itself.

The second condition . . . is the expulsion from the Party of all non-proletarian elements.

The third decisive step towards democratisation of the Party is the elimination of all non-working class elements from all the administrative positions.

The fourth basic demand . . . is that the Party must reverse its policy to the elective principle.

Source: A. Kollontai, The Workers' Opposition *(London: Solidarity, no date), pp. 5–7, 12–13, 20–21*

The criticisms in Document 13.10 require little further explanation. The attack on one-management, by the old *spetsy* appointed from above rather than elected from below, as corruptive of socialism and the source of bureaucratism has been well rehearsed. The fact that elsewhere the Workers' Opposition also argued for equal wages should come as no surprise. However, the solution proposed by them was less nebulous than that of the Democratic Centralists, with whom they had little sympathy. The implication of their argument that control of the economy, from the centre down to the grassroots, should be in the hands of 'the All-Russian Congress of Producers' was nothing less than a call for the restoration of workers' management, vested in the trade unions. But to ensure that this objective was realised it was necessary, they continued, that all organisations in the soviet state, including the Party, be 'workerised', that is, that they be purged of all non-proletarians **(see Document 13.6)**. This proposed solution to the problem of bureaucratisation itself begs several questions. In the circumstances of 1921 'workerisation' was a rather Utopian remedy to the ills of the Soviet state as the working class itself had been considerably reduced in numbers by the rigours of the Civil War and the calamitous decline in industrial production **(see Chapter 10)**. Much of it too was less than committed to supporting the Communist Party. Moreover, as with the Left Communists, their defence of democracy, of 'freedom of thought and opinion', was limited. It was to be confined to the ranks of the Party, but not extended to the 'non-party masses' (Kollontai's pamphlet was strictly for circulation within the Party). Nor had they any solution to the methods whereby central planning, in which they too believed, could be reconciled with worker power at the enterprise level. At the same time, Kollontai and her fellow-thinkers, such as Shliapnikov and S.P. Medvedev, the leaders of the Union of Metal Workers, totally disregarded the wishes of the peasant majority, which they regarded, as all oppositions did, as an obstacle to socialist transformation in Russia **(Sirianni 1982: 234–5)**.

The Workers' Opposition suffered a crushing defeat at the Tenth Party Congress, its programme being supported by only 18 of the almost 400 delegates present. At the same time, proposals for the militarisation of labour were also decisively rejected, in favour of Lenin's compromise position that the unions be granted sufficient autonomous power to defend the rights of the workers against a state which remained far from being a pure proletarian one. However, this concession was not to be the harbinger of any future democratisation, as other measures adopted by this Congress in face of the grave crises then threatening Communist rule considerably increased the power of the central party bureaucracy **(see Chapter 15)**.

The Mensheviks and the Social Revolutionaries 14

The Mensheviks

The Second Congress of the Russian Social Democratic Workers' Party (RSDWP) in 1903 had witnessed the division of the Party into two factions, the Bolshevik (the 'majoritarian') and the Menshevik (the 'minoritarian'). The Mensheviks opposed the model of party organisation proposed by Lenin. Rejecting his conclusions that a highly centralised and disciplined conspiratorial party was necessary to further the cause of revolution in Russia, they espoused the creation of a mass democratic party, embracing all who broadly shared the Party's objectives. Before 1917 they also repeatedly argued that the forthcoming revolution in Russia would be bourgeois-democratic, not socialist (Lenin himself, as we saw in Chapter 3, had argued similarly). This revolution would result in democratic transformation of the country and its industrial development along capitalist lines. The task of the Mensheviks was to defend democracy and the rights of the workers, while organising them to be prepared to strike for power when the preconditions for socialist revolution finally matured. On no account, as Leopold Haimson has affirmed, should they seek to seize, or even share, power at this first stage of the Revolution **(Haimson 1974: xviii)**. Consistent with this strategy, the majority of Mensheviks were prepared to support the Provisional Government, from a distance, in so far as it acted to further the democratisation of Russia **(see Document 3.9)**. Moreover, the February Revolution also served to heal (temporarily) the split that had emerged in Menshevik ranks during World War I. The Internationalists, whose views were most cogently articulated by Iulii Martov, refused to support Russia's, or any other country's, participation in the war. Instead, they advocated the speedy negotiation of a democratic peace, without annexations and indemnities. On the other hand, the Defencists, whose opinions were voiced by Aleksandr Potresov and even more extremely by Georgii Plekhanov, believed that workers and socialists had a duty to defend Russia from German aggression. The fall of the autocracy led many former Internationalists, most prominently Fedor Dan and Irakli Tsereteli, to adopt the strategy known as 'revolutionary defencism'. Now that Russia was a democratic state, socialists legitimately could countenance a defensive war against reactionary German imperialism while at the same time pressuring the Provisional Government to begin negotiations to conclude a democratic peace **(Brovkin 1987: 3–4)**. However, this unity was to be short-lived. The crisis of 20–1 April provoked by Miliukov's note to the Allies **(see Document 4.4)** compelled the Revolutionary Defencist majority, reluctantly, to enter the First Coalition **(see Document 4.7)**. Solomon Shvarts defended this decision at a conference of the Petrograd Mensheviks that began on 3 May.

Document 14.1 Menshevik Reasons for Entry into the First Coalition

The condition of the country in respect of food, industry, the war, etc., is extremely grave. There is disorganisation at the front, the inability not only to attack, but also to defend ourselves . . . . Democracy is beginning to drift away from the soviet: the question is whether the country and the Revolution can be defended. The government must be reorganised, to give it authority in the eyes of democracy. In order to prevent the government seeking the support of the moderate strata of society, it must be given support within the ranks of democracy. The Mensheviks do not doubt that they must support the government (with the exception of certain comrades). The only question is whether to support the government from outside, or to enter it. The first path has been tried by the soviet. Certainly, it is the most acceptable, if only it were possible. But political life of the last two months, especially the events of 20–21 April, have shown that the soviet in fact did not support the Provisional Government but undermined its authority. This path proved to be unsuccessful. Now there is no third way. . . . One path is that of Lenin: seizure of power by the soviets. The second path is to take responsibility upon ourselves, to enter the Provisional Government. How will the entry of socialists into a coalition ministry affect the approach of peace? Does it not mean the prolongation of the war? These are exceptionally important questions which demand the greatest attention. Our refusal to enter the Provisional Government will force it to seek support in those circles which supported the imperialist policy of the tsarist government. This will lead to the war dragging on. We will find ourselves in a blind alley from which there is no escape. By entering the Provisional Government we will force it to abandon its imperialist policy and by so doing promote the cause of peace.

Source: Z. Galili and A. Nenarokov (eds), Men'sheviki v 1917 godu. Tom 1: Ot ianvaria do iiulskikh sobyti' *(Moscow: Progress-Akademiia, 1994), pp. 257–8*

The thinking behind Document 14.1 is quite clear. Entry into a coalition (though one presumably that would not include 'comrades' Miliukov and Guchkov!) alone would provide the Mensheviks with sufficient influence to ensure that the government did not take decisions provocative to 'democracy', that is, the workers, soldiers and peasants. In particular, Shvarts held out the prospect that this action would help to ensure that the Provisional Government adhered to its declaration in favour of a democratic peace **(see Document 4.2)**. But, as we saw in Chapter 4, such sanguine hopes were soon to be dashed. Not only was the First Coalition unable to do much to improve the lot of the workers and peasants but it also sanctioned, with Menshevik approval, the ill-fated and deeply unpopular June offensive. The Internationalists, including Martov, who had only just returned to Russia at the beginning of May, opposed this policy, but vainly, as they remained very much a minority then. Martov too became increasingly sceptical of the consequences of coalition with the Kadets. The political crisis provoked by the Kadets' resignation from the First Coalition on 2 July led him to re-evaluate the strategy which the Mensheviks should adopt. In a speech delivered to the CEC of the Soviet of Workers' and Soldiers' deputies on 16 July he began by stressing the dangers posed by the growing organisation of the forces of counter-revolution. He continued in the following vein.

Document 14.2 Martov's Conversion to the Need for Soviet Power

Being opposed in principle to the premature transfer of power to the organs of revolutionary democracy, at the present moment we consider such a transfer to be necessary since the question is posed so – either revolutionary democracy assumes total responsibility for the Revolution, or it loses its voice in determining its future fate.

We must oppose the will of the revolutionary majority against the clear attempt to tear power from the hands of revolutionary democracy by the artificial creation of a crisis. We must declare that revolutionary democracy cannot accomplish its tasks if it becomes a dictatorship of only ten men. It must be supported by the entire forces of revolutionary democracy across the country.

Allow me to say a few words about the indecisive programme developed by Prime Minister Kerenskii [his speech on July 13 … when he first publicly declared the intention of the Provisional Government to summon an All-Russian Conference in Moscow to save the state and revolution]. I am talking of the aforementioned Moscow Conference which gathers together not only the living forces of the country but which also reanimates the dead forces of counter-revolution. Regarding this Conference, in which the voice of democracy, the voice of all the peasantry and workers, may be stifled, we must in time say that it is unnecessary, that it must not come about.

Source: Z. Galili and A. Nenarokov (eds), Men'sheviki v 1917 godu, Tom 2: Ot iiul'skikh sobytii do kornilovskogo miatezha *(Moscow: Progress-Akademiia, 1995), pp. 158–9*

In insisting that power be transferred 'to the organs of revolutionary democracy', that is, the soviets, Martov had abandoned the policy of broad coalition which he defended throughout May and June **(Getzler 1994: 432–3)**. Convinced that the Kadets had gone over to the side of counter-revolution, he now believed that what in fact would be an all-socialist government alone would be able to carry out the measures desired by the majority of ordinary Russians. Pressure was to be put on the Allies to begin negotiations for a democratic peace immediately, or else Russia would pull out of the war. Domestically, legislation was to be introduced to control prices, curb war profits and speed up land reform. The state too should take control of the production and distribution of goods and even seize those factories and plants where the bourgeoisie was seeking to sabotage production **(Ascher 1976: 102–3)**. At the so-called Unification Congress of the RSDWP (Mensheviks) which convened on 18 August he explained his change of heart. Intent to preserve the coalition at all costs, the socialist Ministers (SRs as well as Mensheviks) in effect had given the Kadets the power to veto all meaningful attempts to end the war and to implement agrarian and economic reforms. This tactic had produced nothing but growing popular disillusion with the Mensheviks, as the rapid rise in Bolshevik support in June (and its equally rapid recovery after the July Days) confirmed. Moreover, now that it was increasingly clear that the Kadets (and the bourgeoisie generally) had gone over to the camp of reaction **(see Documents 5.2, 10.4)** there was no possibility of a lasting coalition. When the Second Coalition collapsed, as it inevitably would, it must be replaced by an all-socialist government **(Lande 1974: 16–18)**. However, only one-third of the delegates at the Unification Congress supported Martov's strategy. The majority continued to favour the policy of coalition. Refusing to split from the Party and seek a bloc with the Left SRs and Right Bolsheviks (such as Kamenev and Zinoviev), Martov remained in it, in the hope that the Internationalists would soon gain the upper hand. His hopes were realised, in part. On 24 October he won over Dan and other Revolutionary Defencists to agree to the formation of a Left bloc, of Internationalists, Left SRs and some Revolutionary Defencists, in order to establish an all-socialist government, with Bolshevik participation. Yet his victory had come too late. The Bolshevik rising that had begun on the same day was to deepen irreconcilable fissures within the Menshevik Party. These divisions were evident at the Menshevik Extraordinary Congress which convened on 30 November. On the Right, speaking for the Defencists, Mark Liber dismissed the October Revolution as an 'adventure'. The Bolsheviks, he argued, could only sustain themselves in power by dictatorial measures. In these circumstances the Mensheviks must have no truck with them. Martov urged a different strategy. He began by reiterating that it was the fruitlessness of coalition politics that had driven the proletariat, and the mass of soldiers, to support revolution.

Document 14.3 Martov's Response to the October Revolution

As a party of the proletariat the basis of our policy should not be to strive to retreat from the Bolshevik revolution back to coalition . . . but to advance, to realise the tasks that we mapped out, but did not achieve, by re-creating revolutionary unity, the unity of the proletarian movement. . . . The choice is only between coalition with the Bolsheviks or coalition with census society (i.e., the bourgeoisie), but . . . the latter is only possible at the price of the death of the proletarian movement.

Source: Cited in V.I. Miller, 'Po goriachim sledam (Men'sheviki ob Oktiabr'skoi revoliutsii', Kentavr, 1994, 2), p. 73

The task of the Mensheviks, he concluded, was to re-educate the proletariat, to persuade it of the virtues of a democratic, all-socialist government, a task which did not exclude attempts to come to some understanding with the Bolsheviks in the meantime. With the support of Dan and other Revolutionary Defencists, who, after the failure of General Krasnov's forces to oust the Bolsheviks, had come to accept the futility of armed resistance, his strategy was approved. On the Right of the Party, the Defencists were unmoved, insisting that such a strategy would come to naught in face of the Bolsheviks' intransigent authoritarianism. The dissolution of the Constituent Assembly **(see Chapter 7)** appeared to vindicate their arguments. The Left Internationalists joined in their condemnation of it. An uneasy unity emerged by the spring of 1918 when all factions agreed that they should rejoin the CEC (which they had boycotted since November), campaign to recapture control of the soviets and then bring pressure to bear on the Bolsheviks to reconvene the Constituent Assembly. This course of action met with considerable success. More and more workers, disillusioned by continuing economic hardship and the increasing Bolshevik repression of all protest **(see Chapter 10)**, increasingly re-elected Mensheviks to the urban soviets in the spring and early summer. Paradoxically, this very success reopened splits within the Mensheviks as the Bolsheviks forcibly disbanded those soviets opposed to them. The Right saw this as confirmation of their prognosis that it would prove impossible to work with the Bolsheviks **(Dallin 1974: 146–7)**. In June it resolved to support the Komuch **(see Chapter 8)** in seeking to overthrow the Bolsheviks by force and restore the Constituent Assembly. The Menshevik leadership, however, afraid that support for the Komuch would lead ultimately to the victory of White counter-revolution, resolved to remain neutral. In a letter written on 25 October 1918, to a Menshevik emigré, A.N. Stein, Martov justified the leadership's decision.

Document 14.4 Martov's Rejection of Armed Opposition to the Bolsheviks

[At the end of the summer of 1918] the situation had become clearer in those areas where there were no Bolsheviks. It turned out that the weak, *petty-bourgeois* democracy was incapable of channelling its struggle with Bolshevism into the stream of struggle for the Revolution. In the East and in the North, it is hopelessly pulling toward a 'national' alliance, that is, a coalition with the clearly counter-revolutionary bourgeoisie. As a result, it is steadily losing credibility in the eyes of the working masses after the Bolsheviks had been chased away with the approval of, even with the help of these same masses. This factor explains, to a considerable extent, the Bolsheviks' quick successes at retaking Simbirsk, Kazan and Samara [see Chapter 8].

This is getting worse and worse because an ever-greater role in the anti-Bolshevik struggle is being played by all sorts of officers' and cadets' units, with sympathies ranging from Kornilovite at best to monarchist at worst. They are becoming a more decisive factor in the 'national' coalition than the Committee of the Constituent Assembly [Komuch] and similar elements. Furthermore, it is likely that, with . . . Wilson's victory . . . the divisions amongst the propertied classes . . . will disappear and they will all become Allied supporters. In such conditions, the 'Thermidor' [counter-revolution] to which our Robespierres [the Bolsheviks] are leading will acquire an all the more ominous, restorationist, and Black Hundred-like character . . . .

All this caused a great turmoil in the Party. At first, our Right elements . . . took the next step and openly identified themselves with the foreign occupation . . . and with the struggle against the Bolsheviks as part of a 'coalition'. They proclaimed it to be a 'national task' to restore capitalist order. Headed by Liber, they organised the Committee for Active Struggle for the Regeneration of Russia. This created a *de facto* split in the Party, which did not become *de jure* only because terror put such pressure on all of us that any public debate . . . or convocation of a conference or congress to judge any rebellious elements became impossible . . . .

Source: V.N. Brovkin, Dear Comrades: Menshevik Reports on the Bolshevik Revolution and Civil War *(Stanford: Stanford University Press, 1991), pp. 125–6*

As we saw in Chapter 8, Martov's forebodings were well founded. Allied intervention in the North, at Murmansk in March and Archangel in July, led to the fall of soviet power, to be replaced initially by an SR government under N.V. Chaikovskii. In turn, it gradually became transformed into little more than a military dictatorship. Similarly, the authority of the Komuch in the East ultimately was usurped by a military dictatorship under Admiral Kolchak on 18 November 1918. The Allies too, as German defeat drew ever nearer, increasingly came to support the Whites, instead of the socialist opposition to the Bolsheviks. For Martov, and the Left Mensheviks, the primary objective remained the defeat of counter-revolution. The Right, according to Vladimir Brovkin, grudgingly concluded that a White victory would be in Russia's interests. It would restore capitalism, which alone could produce economic recovery. It also believed, over-optimistically, that democratic capitalism would result if the bourgeoisie and workers united to restrain the more authoritarian impulses of the officers **(Brovkin 1994: 169–74)**.

These different evaluations of what would best serve the interests of the country fuelled Menshevik divisions during 1919. The Right was increasingly forced underground while the Left was legalised in the first three months of 1919, although hardline Bolsheviks (and Chekisty) in much of provincial Russia refused to permit it any freedom **(Brovkin 1994: 29–31)**. Despite suffering renewed repression (its just reopened press was closed down) in face of Bolshevik fears of rising worker protest in the spring **(see Chapter 10)**, in the summer the Left endorsed the Bolsheviks as the lesser of two evils, as the dreaded Whites advanced on all fronts. But it also continued to seek ways to ameliorate the harsher and more authoritarian aspects of Bolshevik policy which, it felt, had contributed greatly to White success. To this end the Menshevik CC assigned its leading economists to elaborate a programme of reform. The fruits of their labours, *What Is To Be Done?*, was ready by July but apparently was not published at the time. It began by reaffirming that the main task remained that of defeating the Whites. To do so required not just military force. It also demanded economic and political reforms, to provide the despairing workers and peasants with a better material life and an end to the repressive, often brutal, actions taken against them. This alone would prevent them welcoming (for a time) the White forces as liberators.

Document 14.5 What Is To Be Done?

ECONOMIC MEASURES

1 The peasants should retain . . . the public and privately owned lands which they seized and parcelled out at the time of the Revolution.

2 The present food supply system should be replaced by one on the following basis:

　a The state should purchase grain at agreed prices . . . it should then be sold at low prices to the poorest dwellers in town and country, with the state making up the difference.

　b The state should purchase, at a price equal to the cost of production, a certain proportion of the grain surpluses held by the better-off peasants.

　c Grain should be purchased by cooperatives and workers' organisations, who should . . . make over the stocks they have procured to government organs concerned with food supply.

3 The state should retain control of major industrial enterprises that are fundamental to economic life . . . . All other large industrial enterprises . . . should as a rule be gradually transferred into private hands.

4 Small-scale industry should in no case be nationalised.

5 The state shall regulate the distribution to different areas . . . the chief articles of mass consumption such as textiles, farm implements, salt . . . with the aid of cooperatives and private traders.

6 As regards trade in other articles . . . the state should . . . allow cooperatives and private enterprise to function freely.

8 The repression of speculation and trading abuses should be left to the

courts and governed by specific legal provisions. All arbitrary acts of requisition, confiscation . . . should be punished.

9 Workers' unions . . . should be wholly independent of any state bodies.

10 Wage rates in state enterprises should be raised and minimum rates fixed for private enterprises.

POLITICAL MEASURES

1 The right of voting for . . . soviets should be extended to all workers . . . town and village soviets should be elected freely by all workers, with a secret ballot and freedom of canvassing by word of mouth and by the press.

2 The CEC . . . should once more function as the supreme legislative and administrative body.

3 Freedom of press, of assembly and of association should be restored, and any party representing the workers shall have the right . . . to use premises for meetings, paper supplies, printing works, etc.

4 Terror shall be done away with as an instrument of government; the death penalty shall be abolished, and likewise all investigatory and punitive organs independent of the courts, such as the Extraordinary Commission (Cheka).

5 Party institutions and cells should be deprived of state authority, and party members of all privileges.

7 A policy of understanding should be pursued *vis-à-vis* the nationalities . . . in order to put a speedy end to the Civil War and restore the unity of the state on a basis of national self-determination.

Source: A. Ascher (ed.), The Mensheviks in the Russian Revolution *(London: Thames & Hudson, 1976), pp. 113–17*

This document prefigured the New Economic Policy which Lenin was to introduce in 1921 **(see Chapter 15)**. It called for the end to grain requisitioning and the introduction of a considerable degree of free trade. Equally, while the state should retain control of the 'commanding heights' of the economy it also advocated the return of the rest of industry to private hands, to promote the recovery. However, the political freedoms demanded in it were not to be realised. Undeterred, the Menshevik CC persisted with its tactic of 'legal opposition', even after Kolchak's and Denikin's forces had been defeated. In fact, in April 1920 it went as far as to recognise the inevitability of the October Revolution and the dictatorship of the proletariat established by the Bolsheviks, provided it was a democratic dictatorship of all the workers. It paid dividends, in one respect, as Bolshevik repression eased and Mensheviks won an increasing number of seats in the soviets. Negatively, more and more Mensheviks began to defect to the Bolsheviks, now that the gulf between them had closed, and many workers, despite voting for the Mensheviks, despaired of their ability to defend them from the militarisation of labour **(see Chapter 10)**. The Right remained intransigently opposed to the dictatorship of the proletariat, if not unanimously prepared to seek to foment its overthrow, lest this bring further suffering to the workers. They also categorically rejected the possibility that socialism could be constructed in such a backward, peasant society as Russia, even if international revolution were to be victorious. In the spring of 1920 a group of Right Mensheviks reiterated their long-standing fears of the inevitable consequences of premature socialist revolution.

Document 14.6 Report of the Right Mensheviks

When some groups of the population were openly, though passively hostile, when others were indifferent . . . it was only possible to rule by repression. That is why the overall policy of soviet power emerges more and more as a struggle against any manifestations of democracy, a curbing of political rights, a liquidating of civil liberties, a suppressing of the activities of all those who are not regime supporters, a bureaucratising of government, a militar-ising of the entire social order that combines bureaucratic rule with the absence of civil rights for the entire population. What is being created now is a new form of barrack-like socialism – unforeseen by Marxism – which is reminiscent of the Jesuits' experiments in Paraguay in the sevententh century.

Source: V.N. Brovkin, Dear Comrades: Menshevik Reports on the Bolshevik Revolution and Civil War *(Stanford: Stanford University Press, 1991), p. 230*

This analysis was uncannily prescient. Increasingly, Soviet Russia was to become a highly centralised, bureaucratic state, in which the population was coerced to carry out the objectives determined by the Party. One might even argue that this document was one of the earliest predictions of Stalinism.

Whether the Mensheviks adopted a conciliatory approach to the Bolsheviks or not, their fate ultimately was to be the same. From August, 1920, all were subject to intensified repression at the hands of the Cheka. Many were arrested and flung into prison. The mounting challenges to the regime, from the workers, the peasants and even the Kronstadt sailors that erupted in the winter and spring of 1921 **(see Chapter 15)**, sounded their death knell. Many remained imprisoned and often were sent to the new camps in the north of the country; others, including Martov, emigrated; while some were prepared to work for the regime once the New Economic Policy was introduced, if only to suffer an even worse fate in the reign of terror implemented by Stalin in the late 1920s and 1930s.

The Social Revolutionaries

The Social Revolutionary Party (SRs) was founded, illegally, in 1901. It is widely regarded as the heir to the populist movement of the 1870s which had envisaged the creation of a socialist society in Russia, based on the village commune. Legalised after the 1905 Revolution, the programme adopted at its First Congress in 1906 proposed that Russia should be transformed into a federal republic, with the various minorities granted the right to national self-determination. Socialisation of the land was also advocated **(see Chapter 9)**, an ill-defined policy, according to Oliver Radkey, which entailed the expropriation of the land, without compensation, and its equal division (somehow defined) among the peasants. This particular proposal led to a split in the Party, with those opposed to expropriation forming the Popular Socialist Party in 1907. Another ultra-revolutionary faction, embittered that the Party had refused to sanction the socialisation of industry too, also broke away, to form the Union of Maximalists (SR-Maximalists). It also advocated the immediate overthrow of the autocracy, by terrorist tactics if need be, and the swift introduction of socialism in agriculture and industry **(Radkey 1953: 26–31)**. As the Mensheviks, the SRs too were to be riven by increasing, even more bitter, internal splits during and after 1917. They mirrored the division that had emerged during the war. The Right, led by N.D. Avksentiev, had supported a defensive war on Russia's part, while the Left, headed by Maria Spiridonova and Boris Kamkov, condemned all warring powers equally and sought a democratic peace.

The rapid collapse of the autocracy caught the SRs unaware. However, their leaders, drawn from the Right and Centre of the Party, swiftly agreed to support the Provisional Government, in so far as it implemented the democratic transformation of the country. They were not yet prepared to go as far as Kerensky, a leading member of the Trudoviki (Labour Group) affiliated to the SRs, who entered the government as Minister of Justice. However, the April crisis also produced a change of heart on the part of the SRs who, as the Mensheviks, entered the First Coalition **(see Chapter 4)**.

Document 14.7 Right SRs' Defence of Coalition

Not so long ago the participation of the socialists in the Provisional Government seemed to many almost a betrayal of all the hopes of international socialism.

At the extraordinary conference of Socialist Revolutionaries . . . a minority – a small one to be sure – did voice opposition to the SRs' participation in the revolutionary government.

Perhaps, of course, this minority was not worth taking into account inasmuch as its resolution was a slavish copy of the Lenin-anarchical models. But undoubtedly some confusion on this question still exists in the socialist camp.

. . . many of the socialists have not as yet learned that basic difference which exists between the Provisional Revolutionary Government and any coalition cabinet of a nonrevolutionary period.

A properly organised popular rule does not as yet exist at the present moment in Russia. In the name of democracy and for the sake of its interests spontaneous revolutionary organisations talk and act.

That is their right, their responsibility.

And we, Socialist Revolutionaries, have no reason to maintain the former halfway policy of semitrust and semisuspicion toward the government. The Russian socialists must from now on see in the government the sole revolutionary power which is in intimate contact with the Soviet . . . .

. . . We have the right to expect of the Provisional Government that it will prove to be the genuine power; that it will vigorously combat tendencies toward anarchy; that it will restore . . . civil and military discipline; and that it will create conditions favourable to a planned and organised expression of the people's will in the Constituent Assembly.

Source: R.P. Browder and A.F. Kerensky, The Russian Provisional Government 1917: Documents, *Volume III (Stanford: Stanford University Press, 1961), pp. 1281–2*

This defence of coalition was published on 5 May, in *Volia Naroda* (*Freedom of the People*), first issued on 30 April as the voice of the Right SRs. It clearly captures their reasons for joining the First Coalition. They saw it as a means of maintaining order in Russia, both in the rear and, equally important, at the front, as they were ready to support an offensive by the Russian army. At the SRs' Third Congress in May the Left SRs (still a minority) insisted that coalition was a mistake, but did little to fight their corner. Instead, a muddled compromise was agreed between Avksentiev and Viktor Chernov, the leader of the so-called Left Centre. By a large majority the Congress accepted that coalition was necessary, but only as a transitional step towards an all-socialist government – though no attempt was made to specify under what conditions this transition should be completed. A similarly muddled compromise committed the Party to the continuation of the war, though few were prepared to support an offensive. Curiously, little attention was paid to the question of land, bar approving the Party's traditional policy of socialisation. The details of how this was to be implemented were to be left to the Constituent Assembly. In the interim, land committees, democratically elected by the peasants themselves, were assigned the duty of preserving the land, and its livestock and equipment, from arbitrary seizure by the peasants, pending its redistribution by the Constituent Assembly. Finally, the Congress also agreed to Mark Vishniak's proposal that in the new Federal Republic autonomy, but not self-determination, be granted to all nations in it (excluding the Poles whose independence was recognised). As Oliver Radkey has remarked, this was an astonishing *volte-face* for a party that 'prided itself on its belief in the brotherhood of nations', **(Radkey 1958: 198–220)**.

The fragile unity achieved at the Third Congress did not endure. The failure of the First Coalition to carry out any significant reform underlay the growing divisions. Even the modest efforts of Chernov, now Minister of Agriculture, to prohibit the sale of *pomeshchik* land met with opposition, not just from the Kadets but also from the Right of the Party, reinforced since February by an influx of provincial gentry **(see Chapter 9)**. More important, however, was the offensive, and the subsequent reintroduction of the death penalty, which outraged the Left. Surprisingly muted at the Third Congress, its opposition steadily mounted from July. It increasingly called for an end to coalition politics; for immediate land socialisation (which the Constituent Assembly could ratify); and an immediate democratic peace. Yet it did not form its own party. Its thinking, apparently, was analogous to that of Martov: to conquer the Party from within. Given that it was winning increasing support from the SRs' main constituency, the soldiers and peasants, themselves increasingly radicalised by the actions and inactions of the government, its tactics were not without sense. However, it failed to 'swallow the whole party' **(Radkey 1958: 369–74)**. In September, the Left SRs were expelled from the Party. They formed their own organisation in November and entered into a coalition government, as junior partners of the Bolsheviks.

The mainstream SRs, as we saw in Chapter 7, opposed the Bolshevik seizure of power. In alliance with the Right Mensheviks they formed the Committee for the Salvation of the Fatherland and the Revolution, which tried to organise the overthrow of the Bolsheviks by force. They supported the abortive rising of the officer cadets in Petrograd on 29 October. Its failure, combined with the defeat of Krasnov's troops despatched to restore Kerensky to power, led them to reappraise their strategy. At the trial of the SRs staged by the Bolsheviks in 1922, Abram Gots, former leader of the so-called Right Centre of the Party, recalled the new strategy which they had adopted in November 1917.

Document 14.8 SR Rejection of Armed Struggle against the Bolsheviks

We began to fight, but when we realised the failure of our action we shifted to the tactic of isolating the Bolsheviks from the proletariat and the broad masses of toilers, an isolation which naturally was provoked by the very policy of the Bolsheviks. We were not the only ones to evaluate the state of affairs in this way, but some of your own comrades did so too.

Source: M. Jansen (ed.), Partiia Sotsialistov-Revoliutsionerov posle Oktiabr'skoi perevorota 1917 goda. Dokumenty iz arkhiva P.S.-R. *(Amsterdam: Stichting Beheer IISG, 1988), p. 26*

Document 14.8 is brief, but important. SR tactics had affinities with those of Martov and Dan explained above. Having rejected armed struggle it was now incumbent on the SRs to convince those workers (and peasants) wary of a purely Bolshevik government to throw their weight behind the soon to be elected Constituent Assembly. Gots himself, with Avksentiev's support, continued to oppose the formation of an all-socialist government and effectively sabotaged Chernov's efforts (backed by the All-Army Committee, which represented the views of the soldiers' committees) to construct one as an alternative to the Bolshevik 'dictatorship'. His reference to disquiet within Bolshevik ranks was apt, as many moderates (Kamenev, Zinoviev, Riazanov and Rykov, among others) feared that unless a broad socialist government was formed the Bolsheviks would have to resort to terror to maintain themselves in power. Yet his judgement that the 'masses' would soon split away from the Bolsheviks was over-optimistic, as the Bolsheviks were to give them what they wanted: peace (at a price); land; and workers' control.

SR policy was now effectively established for the next eight months. It did not rule out civil war but this could only be waged successfully when the majority of soldiers, peasants and workers had rallied behind the SR cause. The focal point for rallying the 'masses' was to be the Constituent Assembly. Even when it was forcibly dispersed the SRs refrained from calling for civil war against the Bolsheviks, no doubt chastened by the ruthless suppression of the (small) demonstrations against its dissolution in Petrograd. To promote their objective of peaceful political competition with the Bolsheviks the SRs followed the Mensheviks and re-entered the CEC in the spring, notwithstanding their bitter opposition to the peace of Brest–Litovsk concluded by the Bolsheviks. Much more aggressively than the Mensheviks, they sought to utilise control of the soviets as a means of reconvening the Constituent Assembly. Indeed, growing disillusion with the Bolshevik government also was translated into increased support for the SRs, in the villages and even in the urban soviets **(Brovkin 1987: 220–1)**. However, this revival of the political fortunes of the SRs, together with the creation of the Komuch on 8 June **(see Chapter 8)**, provoked a Bolshevik backlash. The SRs too found themselves expelled from the CEC, and all local soviets, by the decree of 14 June **(see Document 7.8)** and the various assemblies of factory workers which had offered them succour were repressed. The Left SRs too, as we saw in Chapter 7, were ejected after their assassination of Mirbach. In the circumstances they had little choice but to urge an armed struggle to oust the Bolsheviks.

However, the intensification of the Civil War, the defeat of the Komuch and the overthrow of the Directorate by a military *coup* **(see Chapter 8)** precipitated fresh divisions within the SRs. The Right was prepared essentially to close its eyes to the reactionary tendencies within the White movement and collaborate with it in an armed struggle against the Bolsheviks. On the Left the so-called Ufa delegation, headed by V.K. Vol'skii, formed. Shocked by the *coup* against the Directorate it expressed a readiness to ally with the Bolsheviks to fight the forces of White counter-revolution. The majority in the Centre meanwhile had remained suspicious of the White officers and the bourgeosie, and had refused to join the Directorate. Yet, at the same time, it was not prepared to join with the Bolsheviks against the Whites and remained 'neutral'. E.M. Timofeev explained its thinking in January 1919.

Document 14.9 SR Pursuit of a 'Third Way' between Reds and Whites

The fall of the Ufa Directorate marks a grievous defeat for democracy. The ease with which Kolchak and his associates managed to liquidate the Directorate and disperse the Committee of the Constituent Assembly

[Komuch], reveals with an oppressive clarity the almost boundless disorganisation, atomisation and apathy of toiling democracy, which is powerless to defend its interests.

Propelled to power by the mass of soldiers yearning for peace and supported by the maximalist sentiments of part of the proletariat, Bolshevism increasingly has degenerated into an essentially counter-revolutionary force . . . and revived mediaeval forms of political despotism and lawlessness. On the other hand, as democracy grows weaker, smashed and overwhelmed by the Maximalists of the left, so maximalism of the right grew stronger. *Pomeshchik*-bourgeois reaction became ever more determined and naked, openly dreaming of the complete liquidation of the conquests of the Revolution and the restoration of the monarchy.

Both these forces are objectively and equally hostile to the interests of the toiling masses. And Social Democracy – above all the Party of Social Revolutionaries – clearly realised the necessity of opposing them with a third force, the force of united democracy.

The Siberian events [the overthrow of the Directorate] clearly revealed the complete weakness of toiling democracy at the present moment. But at the same time . . . they demonstrated that the middling and *petty-bourgeois* strata had finally resolved their waverings and thrown themselves into the arms of reaction . . . . The efforts to attract elements of census society to democracy were at an end.

Related to this, considerable circles within the Party intelligentsia have begun to talk about the need to come to an understanding with the Bolsheviks . . . . [But] the whole intrinsic sense of Bolshevism does not allow it to deviate from its chosen path and embark on the path of democracy and creative and constructive social work so necessary for Russia and its toiling masses.

Soviet power is deeply anti-democratic and cannot cease to be so. Objectively it is counter-revolutionary and completes the preparations for the triumph of Black Hundred reaction . . . . The vital interests of toiling democracy compel it to struggle against both these forces. The toiling masses represent the huge majority of the people and the future belongs to them. But at present they are disorganised, overcome with apathy and weariness, and therefore temporarily powerless . . . . Insurrections and armed struggle at present are senseless . . . . The fundamental task standing before the Party . . . is to overcome this apathy and atomisation . . . and to unite and rally the working class in the towns and countryside into strong class organisations.

Source: M. Jansen (ed.), Partiia Sotsialistov-Revoliutsionerov posle Oktiabr'skoi perevorota 1917 goda. Dokumenty iz arkhiva P.S.-R. *(Amsterdam: Stichting Beheer IISG, 1988), pp. 142–5*

Document 14.9 is important as it outlines the strategy that the majority of SRs consistently were to pursue during the rest of the Civil War, and even in the spring of 1921 when the country was in the grip of a wave of peasant insurrections. Admittedly, it is probable that some SRs (a minority) did help these (Green) movements. Equally, Volskii's group, now renamed 'Narod' (The People), split from the Party after its Ninth Conference, in June 1919, and aligned itself with the Bolsheviks in October of the same year. And the Right, under Avksentiev, continued to be more hostile to the Bolsheviks than the Whites. But the majority adhered to the line of action advocated by Timofeev, the so-called 'third way'. Its thinking was similar to that of the Right Mensheviks (if not of Martov and the Menshevik majority). As the Bolshevik regime was essentially unreformable it was not possible to cooperate with it (nor with the Whites who were considered to be as dictatorial). Yet to foment at present an armed struggle against it would be fool-hardy at best, and at worst invite brutal reprisals. Insurrection, however, was not completely ruled out, but must wait until such time as the workers and peasants were sufficiently organised to carry it out with good prospects of success. Such a time, in the eyes of the majority, never came.

The subsequent fate of the SRs paralleled that of the Mensheviks. The end of their open opposition was 'rewarded' by a brief period of legalisation in February and March 1919. The Left SRs were treated similarly. However, evidence of their growing popularity, combined with swingeing criticisms of Bolshevik policy in their newly opened papers (and virulent opposition from provincial Bolshevik organisations), soon led to renewed suppression. Their press was swiftly closed down. They did maintain a perilous, semi-legal existence, always at the mercy of arbitrary harassment, until the autumn of 1920. Then, as the Civil War drew to a close, and opposition to Bolshevik policies mounted in the towns and countryside, they were subject to arrest and increased persecution. Some were imprisoned, subject to a show trial in 1922 and sent to the camps in the north; others were exiled; and those who had allied with the Bolsheviks suffered grievously under Stalin.

The Communist autocracy challenged
The crisis of 1921

The victory over Wrangel's forces in the autumn of 1920 **(see Chapter 9)**, which marked the final defeat of White counter-revolution, failed to secure the Bolsheviks in power. Ironically, now that fear of the restoration of the old order had been removed once and for all, waves of popular opposition gripped the countryside and cities, as N.I. Podvoiskii and other leading members of the Party conceded in a hitherto unpublished memorandum to the CC on 13 February 1921. They also added their doubts about the Red Army which, unless reinforced by the creation of special detachments of reliable Communists, was unlikely to prove capable of suppressing peasant and worker revolts **(Naumov and Kosakovskii 1994, 4: 12–13)**. Events were soon to confirm their fears when at the end of February even the Kronstadt sailors of the Baltic fleet (the 'pride and glory' of Bolshevism during 1917 and the Civil War) rose in revolt against the Bolsheviks. I.S. Agranov, assigned by Feliks Dzerzhinskii, head of the Cheka, to investigate the causes of the Kronstadt rising filed the following, hitherto secret, report on 5 April 1921. In it he outlined the sources of the unrest in Petrograd as well as Kronstadt itself.

Document 15.1 Unrest in Urban Russia

The counter-revolutionary insurrection of the Kronstadt garrison and workers (1/III – 17/III inclusive) was the direct and logical development of the disturbances and strikes in certain plants and factories in Petersburg [sic] which erupted in the last days of February. The concentration in the industrial enterprises of Petersburg [sic] of a considerable number of workers subject to labour conscription and the sudden closure of the majority of only just reopened enterprises as a result of a fuel crisis at the beginning of February caused dissatisfaction and irritation in the ranks of the most backward Petersburg [sic] workers. Those subject to labour mobilisation brought with themselves from the countryside the corruptive attitudes of petty proprietors, infuriated by the system of grain requisitioning [razverstka], by the prohibition of trade and by the actions of the anti-profiteer detachments.

The reduction of the food ration which followed in the middle of February provided the immediate impetus for the open manifestation of the dissatification which had grown in part of the Petrograd workers and provoked strikes in a series of plants: the Baltic and Tube plants, the 'Laferm' [tobacco] factory and others. One of the fundamental causes of this movement undoubtedly was the fierce debate in the ranks of the RKP before the [Tenth] Party Congress, the weakening of intra-party cohesion and the decline in discipline in the broad ranks of party members. The striking workers did not confine their demands to an increase in the bread ration and the removal of the anti-profiteer detachments. In the most backward ranks of the workers demands even were heard for the convocation of the Constituent Assembly. But all in all the movement proceeded under the slogan of the elimination of the dictatorship of the Communist Party and the establishment of a government of freely elected soviets. If the movement in Petersburg [sic] did not assume an organised character and failed to become general, then this was due to a considerable extent to the timely and speedy liquidation of the Petrograd organisations of the SRs, Mensheviks, Left SRs and Anarchists, which straight away deprived the movement of organised leadership.

Similar conditions and attitudes were present in Kronstadt too on the eve of the revolt.

Source: 'Kronshtadt v marte 1921 g.', Otechestvennye arkhivy, *1996 (1), pp. 54–5*

Document 15.1 is particularly revealing both of the nature of the grievances and the demands of the workers of Petrograd (and of other industrial cities). They opposed the policy of the militarisation of labour that Trotsky had been bent on implementing since the spring of 1920. Growing unemployment, as industry ran out of fuel and materials, added to their discontent. Hunger, too, fuelled their anger. In large part it was the product of renewed peasant resistance to grain requisitioning; it was severely exacerbated by the drought and consequent disastrous harvest of 1920; and it could not be resolved by buying food directly from the peasants (the anti-profiteer detachments' task was to stamp out such direct trade). However, the workers, whose political backwardness Agranov exaggerated, did not simply seek economic amelioration. They too, as the Kronstadters and the Green movement as we shall see below, sought the restoration of soviet democracy and an end to the Bolshevik monopoly of power which they held responsible for their sufferings. The Bolsheviks themselves tried, with some success, to appease the workers by issuing them with additional food rations. But no political concessions were made, and a Politburo decision of 28 February ordered the arrest of the most active and overt opponents of the regime by the Cheka **(see Document 15.4)**. Reliable military units were also concentrated in the city, to deter the workers from taking to the streets.

The crisis facing the regime deepened when opposition erupted in the naval base of Kronstadt in late February, apparently precipitated by (false) rumours about the brutal repression of the strikes in neighbouring Petrograd. It was motivated by similar concerns to those of the Petrograd workers. In early March the newly elected Kronstadt Military Revolutionary Committee, established to maintain order in the town in face of Bolshevik threats of using force, issued an appeal to the railway workers. This recently released document contained the most comprehensive statement of the reforms desired by the Kronstadters.

Document 15.2 The Demands of the Kronstadters

Brother railway workers!

The day of judgment has come. The Kronstadt sailors have raised the banner of freedom against tyrants, oppressors and speculators. We have sacrificed our blood and lives at the altar of freedom, [for the] happiness and great future for the Russian worker and peasant.

For three years we have observed the debauchery of tyrants and speculators; for three years we have observed hunger and cold, the death and exhaustion of the Russian people; for three years our fathers in the countryside have sweated for tyrants; for three years we have died at the fronts. The time has come to say to the tyrants: 'Enough!' Let our death give the people freedom. We have resolved to die, but brother railway workers, if you will not support us, then our blood will be on your consciences . . . . Dying as slaves you will regret your lack of resolve. Support us. Only the railway workers can save the Russian people.

We ask you to support these modest demands presented to the soviets:

1 Equal electoral rights for all, peasants and workers.
2 Secret voting, so that the voter can participate in soviet elections in accord with his or her conscious convictions, and not under constraint. Then scoundrels will not get into the soviets.
3 Freedom in law to seek food through free cooperatives in order that the state does not have the possibility to exploit the hunger of the workers.
4 Freedom of the press, to expose the crimes of officials and the abuses of the speculators.
5 Freedom of expression and agitation so that every honest worker without fear can speak the truth.
6 Freedom of assembly.
7 Abolition of the death penalty, this vile institution of tyrants.
8 Closure of all commissions of the secret police, and the retention of only a criminal police and judges.
9 Abolition of all privileges for Communists.
10 Freedom to move from one place of work to another.
11 Demobilisation of the army, which is needed in the countryside.
12 Dissolution of the labour army – of this new form of enserfment of the worker and peasant . . . .
13 Freedom of travel for all citizens on the railways and rivers.

14 The right for workers to engage in direct commodity exchange with the peasants and the removal of the anti-profiteer detachments – these new highway robbers.

15 Freedom for worker cooperatives to buy goods from abroad, in order to escape the mediation of government speculators who make millions from the sweat of the workers.

16 To ensure this payment of wages in gold, not in paper rubbish.

17 Destruction of political departments – these surveillance organisations of the tyrants.

18 The immediate re-election by secret ballot of all soviets and the government.

Our demands are modest. We want less freedoms than there were in 1917. We will die for this. But we hope that our sacrifices should not have been suffered in vain. Whether we die in battle or are executed in the cellars of the Chekisty, we will curse you if you do not help us.

Support our demands. Stop the movement of . . . the military and you will see that the tyrants, these cowardly monsters who bought the tsarist generals in order to destroy the workers will flee and leave the exhausted people in peace . . . . Join up with the plants, stand firmly together and all the self-appointed little tsars will flee like church mice.

Source: 'Kronshtadtskaia tragediia 1921 goda', Voprosy istorii, *1994 (4), pp. 18–19*

Document 15.2 indicates the broad nature of the demands of the Kronstadters. The coercive, one-party dictatorship of the Bolshevik Party, and all its organs of control and repression, especially the Cheka, were to be eliminated (points 8 and 17). Civil liberties (points 4, 5 and 6) were to be restored to the workers and peasants, as were free elections to the soviets – there was no support for a reconvened Constituent Assembly, which suggests the absence of SR influence (points 1, 2 and 18). Grain requisitioning was to be ended (points 3 and 14), together with labour militarisation (points 10 and 12). Point 11 implied that equal rations, except for those employed in heavy manual labour, were to be provided for all workers. Elsewhere, they called for the release of all political prisoners, but not those who had supported the Whites. Such a demand belies the myth of Bolshevik propaganda that the Kronstadt insurrection was a White Guard conspiracy, although the old tsarist general, A.N. Kozlovskii, then in command of the artillery at Kronstadt, did agree to serve the insurgents. Nor was it simply a movement of 'declassed' workers and peasants recently recruited to the base to replace the proletarian sailors who had perished in the Civil War, as Trotsky and others charged **(Avrich 1991: 88–9, 99–100)**. What the Kronstadters were seeking was the fulfilment of the libertarian and egalitarian promises of 1917, the creation of some form of democratic socialist society that they perceived to have been increasingly crushed under the iron heel of Bolshevik authoritarianism. In this there is little doubt that their aspirations were shared by the majority of Russian workers and peasants **(Brovkin 1994: 397–8)**. Their hopes, however, were to be dashed and many of them in fact did sacrifice their lives in vain.

But perhaps the greatest challenge to the Bolsheviks in the winter of 1920–1 was the Green movement. A series of armed peasant insurrections, in West Siberia, the Middle Volga region, the Don and Kuban and particularly the Ukraine, where Nestor Makhno's forces continued to harry the Red Army, threatened to deprive the Bolsheviks of the grain which they needed to feed the already hungry towns. In turn this could only exacerbate the opposition already evident within them and ultimately lead to the collapse of Bolshevik power. The most famous manifestation of the Green movement was the peasant insurrection which had been simmering since the autumn of 1919 in Tambov province. Its fundamental cause was the policy of grain requisitioning, carried out with particular severity, brutality and incompetence (much of the grain collected simply rotted) in Tambov. Peasant resentment was heightened by more thorough efforts to introduce collective agriculture in the province, especially as the collective farms often were administered by the old landlords and their managers. The final spark, after the defeat of the Whites, was the continuing drought which had destroyed the winter grain crop and promised to reduce markedly the summer one. As hunger spread in Tambov the Bolsheviks refused to reduce the levies imposed on the peasants. In these circumstances the appeals of the Union of Toiling Peasants, led by S.A. Antonov, found a ready response, especially in the south-east of the province **(Radkey 1976: 20–35)**. Its first, self-professed, task was 'the overthrow of the government of the Communist-Bolsheviks'. Its other demands are outlined in Document 15.3, which again draws on recently published archival material.

Document 15.3 The Programme of the Antonov Movement

. . . Political equality of all citizens, without class distinctions; convocation of the Constituent Assembly on the basis of equal, universal, direct and secret ballot, without limiting its liberty to determine the political system; freedom of speech, press, conscience, associations and assembly; the actual implementation of the law on the socialisation of the land [see Chapter 9]; supplying with food and items of prime necessity the population of town and countryside; the regulation of wages and prices of goods produced by state factories and plants; partial denationalisation of factories and plants, with large-scale industry, especially the mining and metallurgical industries, remaining in the hands of the state; the admission of Russian and foreign capital to restore the economic life of the country; freedom of production for domestic [cottage] industry; the immediate restoration of political and economic relations with foreign powers; free self-determination for the nationalities . . . the end of Civil War and the establishment of a firm peace.

Source: Iu.I Korablev, 'Krest'ianskoe vosstanie v tambovskoi gubernii v 1919–1921 gg. "Antonovshchina": dokumenty', Otechestvennaia istoriia, 1996 (1), p. 179

The demands presented in Document 15.3 require little further explanation. In large part they mirror those of the Petrograd workers and the Kronstadters for economic and political freedom. However, rather than seeking a solution by restoring real power to the soviets, Antonov and his supporters, in a manner similar to the SRs **(see Chapter 14)**, argued that only a reconvened Constituent Assembly could re-establish democracy in Russia. This similarity in programme, and the fact that Antonov himself professed to be an SR, led the Bolsheviks to accuse the SR Party of organising and inciting the insurrection – and on this pretext to arrest its leaders. The SRs themselves denied this charge, claiming that their party conference in September 1920 had concluded that at present an insurrection in Tambov (and elsewhere) would have been premature. It did not rule out the possibility of revolt in the future, should changed circumstances make its prospects of success more likely. They also protested, in a highly elitist manner, that they could not have been involved as they would not have produced a programme as ungrammatical as that of the Antonov movement **(Jansen 1988: 547–55)**!

Many of the economic demands contained in the preceding three documents were to be met as the Bolsheviks responded to the crises facing them by a series of economic concessions. But they were to be accompanied by a policy of brutal repression and the intensification of dictatorship, both within and without the Party **(Brovkin 1994: 400–1)**. In a speech at the Tenth Party Congress in March 1921 Lenin hurried to announce the introduction of economic measures designed to appease the peasantry and prevent insurrection spreading to other regions of the countryside (and repetitions of Kronstadt elsewhere within the army or navy).

Document 15.4 Lenin's Defence of the Abolition of Grain Requisitioning

Comrades, the question of replacing requisitioning with a tax is above all and most of all a political question, for it is essentially a question of the relationship of the working class to the peasantry . . . . We know that so long as there is no revolution in other countries, only an agreement with the peasantry can save the socialist revolution in Russia . . . . We must try to satisfy the demands of the peasants who are dissatisfied and discontented, and rightly so . . . it will take essentially two things to satisfy the small farmer. First, a certain freedom of exchange is essential, freedom for the small private proprietor, and second it is necessary to obtain commodities and products.

Why must we replace requisitioning by a tax? Requisitioning implied confiscation of all surpluses and establishment of a compulsory state monopoly. We could not proceed otherwise, for our need was extreme. Theoretically speaking, state monopoly is not necessarily the best system from the point of view of socialism. A system of taxation and free exchange can be employed as a transitional measure in a peasant country which possesses an industry . . . and if there is a certain quantity of goods available. Exchange itself is a stimulus, an incentive, a spur to the peasant. The proprietor can and surely will make endeavour to promote his own interest when all his surplus produce will not be taken away from him, but only a tax, which should as far as possible be fixed in advance . . . . We must adapt our state economy to the economy of the middle peasant, which we have not managed to remake in three years, and will not be able to remake in another ten . . . . This is the task confronting our propaganda among the peasants. If there is a fair harvest then we will have a surplus of up to 500 million poods. This will cover consumption and provide a certain reserve. The fact of the matter is to give the peasants an economic stimulus, an incentive. The small proprietor must be told: 'you, as owner, must produce goods while the state will take the minimum in tax.'

The fundamental task to bear in mind at the moment is that we must broadcast to the whole world, by radio, about the decision taken this evening; we must announce that this Congress . . . is, in the main, replacing requisitioning by a tax, so giving the small farmer a whole series of incentives to expand his farm and increase the area sown; that by embarking on this course the Congress is correcting the system of relations between the proletariat and the peasantry and expresses its conviction that in this way these relations will be made more durable.

Source: Desiatyi s″ezd RKP(b). Mart 1921 goda. Stenograficheskii otchet *(Moscow: Gos. izd. pol. lit., 1963), pp. 403–14*

This speech signalled a retreat on the part of the Party in the face of widespread peasant hostility (the Bolshevik, David Riazanov, is alleged to have dubbed it the 'peasant Brest–Litovsk', comparing it to the retreat made in face of German military superiority in 1918) and ushered in the era of the NEP (New Economic Policy). Its objectives were self-professedly political as well as economic. Politically, Lenin sought to neutralise the mass peasant opposition to Bolshevik rule by ending the universally hated system of grain requisitioning and replacing it by a fixed tax on the peasantry, initially in kind, and only later commuted to money. Economically, by allowing the peasants to sell freely any surpluses remaining to them after taxation he hoped to raise the production of grain desperately needed to feed the towns and the drought-stricken regions of the country in the grip of a growing famine. The attempt to centralise in the hands of the state the distribution of all food, with armed roadblocks preventing private trade, was also ended. Other concessions were made. Small-scale industry, itself subject to increasing nationalisation under War Communism, along with retail trade, was returned to private hands (the banks, transport, and large-scale industry remained in the possession of the state), in the expectation that such privatisation would stimulate a rapid increase in the production of consumer goods demanded by the peasants – and provide them with incentives to market their surpluses. To a large extent, the NEP did succeed in its objectives. Opposition rapidly declined and where it survived it was mercilessly crushed, as we shall shortly see.

However, the introduction of the NEP came too late to save the country from famine. It was precipitated by the continuing drought, particularly severe in the lower Volga region. However, its underlying cause was Bolshevik grain requisitioning which had deprived much of the peasantry of the reserves of food necessary for survival. It is estimated that over five million died from the famine and the number would have been much greater but for the international aid offered to the Soviet government, most notably from the American Relief Administration **(Pipes 1995: 411–19)**. The crisis also inspired one of the great works of poster art, Dmitrii Moor's stark depiction (in black and white) of an old peasant crying for help. The one-word caption reads simply 'Help'.

Document 15.5 Help

[See illustration on p. 236)

The economic concessions of the NEP prevented the recurrence of famine (the forced collectivisation introduced by Stalin in 1929 led to an even worse catastrophe in the countryside in the early 1930s). But there were no commensurate political concessions. All surviving opposition, real or potential, be it strikers in the cities, insurgents in the countryside, the Kronstadters, the Mensheviks and SRs, and even distressing voices within the Party itself, was subject to repression in varying degrees. In a leaflet of 8 March 1921, recently republished in a leading Russian journal, *Voprosy istorii* (*Questions of History*), the Petrograd Committee of the Mensheviks described their own fate.

Document 15.6 Repression of the Mensheviks

Searching for a scapegoat the Bolsheviks made our party [the Mensheviks] the favourite object of its mendacious and slanderous agitation. The Mensheviks support the intervention, the Mensheviks incite the peasants to revolt, the Mensheviks provoked strikes in Petrograd and the insurrection in Kronstadt. So the bureaucratic literateurs write day after day, day after day trying to 'please' their masters and 'honourably' earn their crust.

And following these literary brigands come the real robbers from the Cheka. At night they burst into the rooms of our party members, and of workers sympathetic to us, turn everything upside down and arrest everyone whom they found. Dozens of our comrades have been arrested in recent days, including Dan, Rozhkov, Kamenskii, Nazar'ev, Chertkov and others.

And all this is being done in the name of the Petrograd proletariat.

We know that the Petrograd workers certainly have nothing to do with it. We know that in a whole series of factories and plants the workers are striking, demanding the release of those who have been arrested.

Source: S. White, The Bolshevik Poster *(New Haven: Yale University Press, 1988), p. 50*

It is not our fault if the government responded to the unanimous demand of the Petrograd and Moscow workers to change its policy by the arrest of workers' delegates, and to the resolution of the Kronstadt sailors and garrison in favour of free elections to the soviets by salvoes of heavy artillery.

There is no bad without good. Now everyone, even the most ignorant worker, will understand that Bolshevik power is based not on the soviets of the workers and peasants, but solely on naked force. Now every worker will understand that the only solution is the transfer of power into the hands of really freely elected soviets – will understand and together with us will fight for the abolition of martial law, for freedom of expression, press, association and assembly for all toilers, for free elections to the soviets and other workers' organisations, and for the release of all socialists and non-party workers and peasants arrested for their political convictions.

Source: 'Kronshtadtskaia tragediia 1921 goda', Voprosy istorii, 1994 (4), pp. 15–16

There is no reason to doubt that the Mensheviks, and those workers who supported them (the numbers of which grew rapidly in the winter of 1920–1 in most cities), were subject to arbitrary arrest for voicing demands for genuine elections and other freedoms. They were not alone. Many SRs remaining at liberty were also arrested, as we have seen, on the dubious charge that they had fomented and organised the Antonov movement. Many, tens of thousands, according to Vladimir Brovkin, soon were to find themselves in concentration camps in the north of the country. But the repression that they suffered was mild in comparison to that meted out to the Kronstadters and the peasants of Tambov. Alexander Berkman, a Russian Anarchist, who had been in Petrograd in March 1921, had discovered from his various contacts the fate of the Kronstadters. Writing from his self-imposed exile in Stockholm in early 1922, he recounted his impressions of their brutal suppression.

Document 15.7 The Suppression of the Kronstadt Mutiny

On the morning of 17 March a number of forts had been taken. Through the weakest spot of Kronstadt – the Petrograd Gates – the Bolsheviki broke into the city, and then there began most brutal slaughter. The Communists spared by the sailors now betrayed them, attacking them from the rear . . . . Till late in the night continued the desperate struggle of the Kronstadt sailors and soldiers against overwhelming odds. The city which for fifteen days had not harmed a single Communist, now ran red with the blood of Kronstadt men, women and children.

An orgy of revenge followed, with the Tcheka claiming numerous victims for its nightly wholesale *razstrel* (shooting).

For several weeks the Petrograd jails were filled with hundreds of Kronstadt prisoners. Every night small groups of them were taken out by order of the Tcheka and disappeared – to be seen among the living no more. Among the last to be shot was Perepelkin, member of the Provisional Revolutionary Committee of Kronstadt.

The prisons and concentration camps in the frozen district of Archangel and the dungeons of far Turkestan are slowly doing to death the Kronstadt men who rose against Bolshevik bureaucracy and proclaimed in March, 1921, the slogan of the Revolution of October, 1917: 'All Power to the Soviets'.

Source: A. Berkman, The Russian Tragedy *(Sanday: Cienfuegos Press, 1976 – translation of 1922 original), p. 104*

While personally hostile to the Bolsheviks there is no reason to doubt the veracity of Berkman's account of the savage treatment meted out to the insurgents. The Bolsheviks had ruled out any negotiated settlement from the outset, perhaps fearing that negotiation would be construed as a sign of weakness which would precipitate further rebellions. Perhaps too negotiation would be seen as an admission that there was considerable substance to the Kronstadters' claim that the Bolshevik government in fact had betrayed the ideals and principles of 1917 and so weakened it further at a time of crisis. Finally, negotiation would take time, time which might prevent the speedy recapture of Kronstadt as the ice over the Gulf of Finland melted. In retrospect, the insurrection seemed to have been doomed to failure. Critically, it remained isolated, lacking in food and fuel. It received no support from the workers of Petrograd whose own opposition had disintegrated in response to a combination of Bolshevik 'bribes' of food and the arrest of their most active leaders. The peasant rebellions were too remote, and too localised, to offer any prospect of effective assistance. And no aid was forthcoming from any of the foreign powers that earlier had supplied the Whites.

General M.N. Tukhachevskii, who had commanded the forces that had suppressed Kronstadt, was then despatched to crush the Antonov movement, with repeated instructions from Lenin to stop at nothing. The measures taken in Tambov were, if anything, even more barbarous: mass executions; the creation of concentration camps, into which women, children and old men were consigned too; the destruction of entire villages by artillery fire; the use of poison gas, to flush the insurgents out of the forests; and sophisticated tortures which even some Chekisty rather censoriously compared to the horrors of the Inquisition **(Korablev 1996: 180)**. The practice of taking hostages in order to break the insurrection was also widely applied. The following report by the chairman of the political commission of the fourth military section which was intimately involved in the Tambov campaign, drawn from recently published archival materials, illustrates the arbitrary nature of Bolshevik actions.

Document 15.8 Bolshevik reprisals in Tambov

. . . if the population refused to surrender the bandits and their weapons . . .
then hostages were taken . . . given 30 minutes to think and if they did not
give up [the bandits], the hostages were shot, and this continued as long as
the population remained silent. Together with men women too were taken
as hostages and they also were shot . . . a five-day operation in four villages
produced the following results: 154 bandits and hostages were shot; about
1,000 hostages were taken from the families of about 227 bandits; 17 homes
were burnt down; 24 homes were expropriated and transferred with all their
property to the poor.

*Source: Iu.I Korablev, 'Krest'ianskoe vosstanie v tambovskoi gubernii v
1919–1921 gg. "Antonovshchina": dokumenty', Otechestvennaia istoriia,
1996 (1), p. 180*

Without question such measures of 'pacification', carried out by vastly superior
Bolshevik forces, hastened the final collapse of the Green movement in Tambov.
However, military force alone is insufficient to explain its collapse. The introduction
of the NEP had gone far to satisfy the demands of the peasants, so removing the
basic cause of the movement, opposition to grain requisitioning. It also remained
localised. It was confined largely to the south-east of the province itself. Moreover,
it failed to unite with the peasant insurrections in neighbouring regions, relatively
nearby, either with that of Makhno in the Ukraine or of Sapozhkov in Samara.
Isolated, outnumbered, and weakened by the NEP its failure was no surprise
(Radkey 1976: 383–95).

The final victim of the crisis was the Party itself, more precisely, the opposition
factions within it. At the Tenth Party Congress Lenin moved to restore discipline
and unity by banning all factions.

Document 15.9 On Party Unity

1 The Congress draws the attention of all members of the Party to the fact
that the unity and solidarity within its ranks, the guarantee of complete trust
among Party members and of genuine harmonious work which in fact
embodies the unity of will of the vanguard of the proletariat, are vitally
needed at present when a series of circumstances intensifies the waverings of
the *petty-bourgeois* population of the country.
2 Meanwhile, even before the all-party discussion on the trade unions
certain signs of factionalism were revealed in the Party, i.e., the emergence
of groups with their own particular platforms, groups which sought to
a certain degree to segregate themselves and create their own group
discipline.

All conscious workers must clearly understand the damage done by and
impermissibility of factionalism of any kind, which inevitably leads in practice

to the weakening of harmonious work and to intensified and repeated efforts by enemies who have clung to the governing party to deepen the split in it and to use it for counter-revolutionary purposes.

The manner in which enemies of the proletariat exploit every deviation from a thoroughly consistent Communist line was most graphically revealed in the case of the Kronstadt mutiny, when bourgeois counter-revolution and the White Guards in every country of the world immediately expressed their preparedness to accept even the slogans of the soviet system, if only to overthrow the dictatorship of the proletariat in Russia, and when the SRs and bourgeois counter-revolution generally in Kronstadt made use of slogans of insurrection against the Soviet government . . . in the name, as it were, of soviet power. Such facts fully prove that the White Guards strive and are able to pass themselves off as Communists, even as the most 'Left' of them, if only to weaken and overthrow the bulwark of the proletarian revolution in Russia.

3 These enemies, convinced of the hopelessness of counter-revolution under an openly White Guard flag, exert all their efforts to exploit disagreements within the RKP in order to promote counter-revolution in one way or another by means of transferring power to political groups which in appearance are close to acknowledging soviet power.

4 Every party organisation must be most strict in ensuring that the unquestionably necessary criticism of deficiencies in the Party, that every analysis of the general line of the Party or evaluation of its practical experience, that verification of the implementation of its decisions and the means of correcting mistakes, etc., not be referred for discussion to groups formed on the basis of some 'platform' or other, etc., but that they be referred for discussion to all party members.

5 All members of the Party should know that . . . while rejecting unbusinesslike and factional criticism the Party will continue tirelessly . . . [and] in every way possible to fight bureaucratism, to extend democratism and initiative, and to discover, expose and drive from the Party those who have wormed their way into it.

6 The Congress orders the immediate dissolution of all groups without exception which have been established on the basis of one platform or another and instructs all organisations to take the strictest measures to ensure that no manifestations whatsoever of factionalism be permitted. Non-compliance with this resolution . . . must lead to unconditional and immediate exclusion from the Party . . . .

Source: KPSS v rezoliutsiakh i resheniiakh s"ezdov, konferentsii i plenumov TSK', *volume 2 (Moscow: izdatel'stvo politicheskoi literatury, 1970), pp. 218–20*

Document 15.9 marks a distinct turning-point in the history of the Bolshevik Party. Hitherto debate within it had been relatively free and open. Now, surrounded by enemies on all sides, Lenin convinced the Party that such freedom was a luxury that could not be tolerated, one in fact that gave succour to their opponents. This resolution, in conjunction with that *On the Syndicalist and Anarchist Deviation in Our Party* also adopted at the Tenth Party Congress, which depicted the arguments of the Workers' Opposition that the workers themselves (or their unions) would be able to manage the economy on their own initiative as 'a syndicalist and anarchist deviation', reaffirmed the leading role of the Party (or more precisely, of the Leninist faction within it) in the revolution, its right in effect to exercise total power. Those who refused to bow to these directives to abandon their factional struggle, as many of the Workers' Opposition did, found themselves purged, that is, expelled, from the Party. Later opposition voices which dissented from the 'general line' of the Party found themselves subject to the same disciplinary strictures which were used (or abused) by Joseph Stalin to promote his own rise to supreme power.

Conclusion

By 1921 the Bolsheviks had consolidated themselves in power in much of the old Russian Empire. The price of victory, however, had been very high. The Civil War exacted huge human costs. Evan Mawdsley estimates that possibly nine to ten million died during it, many directly in the fighting but the majority from hunger and disease in the towns and countryside. The economy suffered grievously too. Industrial production generally was one-sixth of its pre-war level; the rail network was severely dislocated; and grain production was less than half what it had been in 1913 **(Mawdsley 1987: 285–8)**. But there had been another price to pay. All opposition without the Party had been suppressed, often brutally, and critics within it silenced. The democratic and libertarian visions of 1917 touted by the Bolsheviks themselves had been dashed. Some explanation of why this was the case is merited. An entire book could be written on this subject (many have) but this discussion will focus on three possible causes: circumstances; Lenin and Leninism; and, finally, more general lacunae in Bolshevik ideology briefly alluded to in the introduction.

In his memoirs, Victor Serge, a former anarchist who had returned to Russia from exile in 1919 and joined the Bolshevik Party, subsequently to be hounded from it for his support of Trotsky, recalled the despair that he had felt in 1921.

Document 16.1 Serge's Explanation of Soviet Authoritarianism

What with the political monopoly, the Cheka and the Red Army, all that now existed of the 'Commune-State' of our dreams was a theoretical myth. The war, the internal measures against counter-revolution, and the famine (which had created a bureaucratic rationing-apparatus) had killed off Soviet democracy. How could it revive, and when? The Party lived in the certain knowledge that the slightest relaxation of its authority would give the day to reaction.

Source: V. Serge, Memoirs of a Revolutionary 1901–1941 *(Oxford: Oxford University Press, 1967), p. 133*

In the extract in Document 16.1 Serge appears to ascribe the demise of the 'Commune-State' (the libertarian vision of the egalitarian and self-governing post-revolutionary society sketched by Lenin when he wrote State and Revolution in exile in Finland in the summer of 1917) largely to circumstances. The Revolution, to the Bolsheviks' consternation, remained isolated in Russia; from the summer of 1918 they faced a range of internal foes, often aided by the capitalist powers of the West; their responses to the economic disintegration gripping the country – the restoration of harsh discipline within industry and especially forced grain requisitioning in the countryside – provoked widespread opposition amongst many workers and the vast bulk of the peasantry. In this parlous situation, with their own popular support fast eroding, it is little wonder that they resorted to dictatorial measures to stay in power, professedly to safeguard the gains of the Revolution.

Such an explanation in itself, however, remained insufficient, as Serge himself realised. He continued his argument by referring to the psychology, or ideology, of Bolshevism, the belief that '[t]he Party is the repository of truth, and any form of thinking which differs from it is a dangerous or reactionary error. Here lies the source of its intolerance'. He attributed this attitude to what he terms 'Lenin's "proletarian Jacobinism"' **(Serge 1967: 134)**. In truth, there is much substance to this argument. In *What Is To Be Done?*, published in March 1902, Lenin outlined what many consider to be the fundamental principles of Bolshevism. As we saw in Chapter 1, he argued that, left to its own devices, the proletariat would be unable to acquire the revolutionary consciousness necessary to overthrow capitalism. Only a self-selected elite, of revolutionary intellectuals, would be able to do so. The mission of this vanguard was to infuse this level of political consciousness within the mass of workers. Yet if this task was to be successfully accomplished, the vanguard must organise itself into a centralised, tightly disciplined, conspiratorial party, to protect itself from the *Okhrana* (tsarist secret police) – and the risk of ideological degeneration posed by the mass influx of politically backward workers. Admittedly, during 1917, especially in *State and Revolution*, Lenin came to extol the political nous of ordinary workers, their abilities to administer the post-revolutionary state. He soon reverted to type. From the spring of 1918 he again increasingly came to disdain them. He repeatedly claimed that the devolution of power into the hands of the workers themselves would have fatal consequences for the Revolution. The Party alone had acumen to carry out the socialist transformation of Russia.

At one level, there is some substance to Lenin's argument, particularly with respect to the post-October period. Russia's already small working class was in precipitate decline. Many, often the most politically conscious workers, were killed in the Civil War. Others were driven back to the countryside by hunger in the towns. Those that remained often were critical of the Bolshevik government. At another level, however, it would be unwise to ignore the profoundly authoritarian implications in Lenin's thinking. Long before the Revolution, in 1904, Trotsky, in a lengthy pamphlet entitled *Our Political Tasks*, had acerbically pointed to the dangers inherent in Lenin's strategy. By 'substituting' itself for the entire proletariat as the leading agency of revolution, by claiming for itself alone the right to define what the true interests of the proletariat were, the Party could not but become an instrument of oppression **(Knei-Paz 1979: 177–206)**. It would only succeed in creating a dictatorship over, not of, the proletariat.

Document 16.2 Trotsky's Critique of Leninist Organisational Principles

. . . the dictatorship over the proletariat [means] not the self-activity of the working-class which has taken into its hands the destinies of society, but a 'powerful commanding organisation', ruling over the proletariat and, through it, over society, thus securing presumably the transition to socialism.

Source: Cited in B. Knei-Paz, The Social and Political Thought of Leon Trotsky (Oxford: Oxford University Press, 1979), p. 204

By 1917 Trotsky apparently had forgotten this warning, as well as his prophetic conclusion that the application of Leninist principles would lead to 'the Party organisation substitut[ing] itself for the Party, the Central Committee substitut[ing] itself for the organisation and, finally, a "dictator" substitut[ing] himself for the Central Committee'. Indisputably, a dictatorship over, not of, the proletariat had come into existence after 1917, as no less an authority than Lenin frankly admitted in a speech delivered at the Eighth Party Congress in March 1919 **(Lenin, 29, 1964–5: 183)**. He explained that it had been necessary to act in such a way because of the 'low cultural level' of working people in Russia, itself the product of the country's economic, educational, political and social backwardness. The fears of Tsereteli and the Mensheviks, that the preconditions for socialism had not matured in Russia **(see Document 3.9)**, rather ironically were now endorsed by Lenin himself.

It is tempting to conclude here and provide a synthesis which embraces both preceding explanations. It would proceed along the following lines. Leninism clearly contained an authoritarian potential. The threats crowding in on the beleaguered Party after 1917 intensified its propensity to try to resolve them by increasingly dictatorial means. These means succeeded, in the sense that the Bolsheviks survived in power, but at the expense of democracy. Moreover, the brutalisation of this period of the Revolution left a permanent scar. It had led to the 'militarisation' of soviet politics, to the permeation throughout the Party and state machines after 1920 of veterans of the Civil War accustomed to resolve problems by force. Such a propensity surfaced violently in the late 1920s when the refusal of the peasants to surrender sufficient of their grain put the regime in peril again – until Joseph Stalin, with the willing support of these veterans, removed the danger by a bloody assault on the peasants euphemistically known as 'collectivisation' **(Fitzpatrick 1989: 391–7)**.

However, even had circumstances been less threatening, even had the authoritarian tendencies within Leninism been muted, there is still reason to doubt if a democratic socialist system would have emerged. Increasingly, historians (and others) also have come to emphasise more general flaws in the ideology of all Bolsheviks, of those on the Left as well as Lenin. In Chapter 13 we saw that the Left was as wedded to the idea of *partiinost'* (party spirit, implying belief in its leading role) as Lenin. Such thinking clearly did not bode well for political democracy.

Equally, their understanding of the economics of socialism would have precluded democracy. As the majority of Marxists of their time they were convinced that the transition to socialism must lead to the abolition of money, prices and commodity production, the characteristics of the market system that they detested and equated with capitalism. Under socialism, the market was to be abolished, with production and regulation now regulated by planning. The plan, however, if it was to satisfy the needs of society in general, rather than particular local demands, had to be drawn up by a central authority. It alone would possess the vision, and the information, necessary to determine what these general needs might be. This central authority would then instruct all enterprises under its purview what and how much they must produce; would distribute materials and labour amongst them to ensure that their production plans could be met; and would distribute the goods produced. Under such a regime of central planning there could not be any scope for meaningful workers' democracy, that is, real shop-floor power over the production process. As Alec Nove has pointed out, if the market was abolished, then the creation of a centralised bureaucracy to regulate production would become 'a *functional necessity*'. Accordingly, '[b]elow the centre there are bound to be severe limits placed on the power of *local* or regional authorities, in order to ensure the priority of the general over the particular' **(Nove 1983: 18, 34)**. A democratic form of socialism was unlikely to emerge under such a system. Even in the best of all possible worlds, it is likely that the ideological preconceptions of the Bolsheviks would have spawned a centralised, bureaucratic system, not an emancipated society in which power was diffused to the workers **(Kowalski 1991: 188)**.

Bibliography

Primary sources in Russian

Arsen'ev, V.S. (1994) '"Sud'by rodiny kazalis' v kakom-to tumane". Vospominaniia V.S. Arsen'eva 1917g.', *Istoricheskii arkhiv*, 2: 89–110.

Avdeev, N. (ed.) (1923) *Revoliutsiia 1917 goda (Khronika sobytii)*, I, II, Moscow, Petrograd: Gosudarstvennoe izdatel'stvo.

Balk, A.P. (1991) 'Poslednie piat' dnei tsarskogo Petrograda (23–8 fevralia 1917g.)', *Russkoe proshloe*, pp. 7–73.

Bernshtam, M.S. ed. (1981) *Nezavisimoe rabochee divizhenie v 1918 godu: Dokumenty i materialy* (volume 2), Paris: YMCA Press.

Bordiugova, G.A. (ed.) (1992) 'Pravda dlia sluzhebnogo pol'zovaniia: Iz dokumentov lichnogo fonda F. Dzherzhinskogo', *Neizvestnaia Rossiia: XX vek, 1*, pp. 28–55.

Bukharin, N.I. (1918) 'Nekotorye osnovnye poniatii sovremennoi ekonomiki', *Kommunist*, 3, Millwood: Kraus International (1990 reprint of 1918 original), pp. 145–54.

Dan, F. (1923) 'K istorii poslednikh dnei Vremennogo Pravitel'stva', *Letopis' revoliutsii*, 1, Berlin: Izdatel'stvo Z.I. Grzhebina.

Davidyn, I. and Kozlova, V. (eds) (1992) 'Chastnye pis'ma epokhi grazhdanskoi voiny: Po materialam voennoi tsenzury', *Neizvestnaia Rossiia: XX vek, II*, pp. 200–52.

Denikin, A.I. (1921) *Ocherki russkoi smuty: I*, Paris: Povolozky & Co.

—— (1930) *Ocherki russkoi smuty: V*, Berlin: Mednyi Vsadnik.

Desiatyi s''ezd RKP(b). Mart 1921 goda: Stenograficheskii otchet, Moscow: Gosudarstvennoe izdatel'stvo politicheskoi literatury, 1963.

'Dokumenty k "Vospominaniiam" gen. A. Lukomskago', *Arkhiv russkoi revoliutsii*, 1922: III, 247–70.

Fleer, M.G. (1925) *Rabochee dvizhenie v gody voiny*, Moscow: Voprosy truda.

Galili, S. and Nenarokov, A. (eds) (1994) *Men'sheviki v 1917 godu, Tom 1: Ot ianvaria do iiul'skikh sobytii*, volume 1, Moscow: Progress-Akademiia.

—— (1996) *Men'sheviki v 1917 godu, Tom 2: Ot iiul'skikh sobytiia do kornilovskogo miatezha*, volume 2, Moscow: Progress-Akademiia.

Grave, B.B. (1927) *Burzhuaziia nakanune fevral'skoi revoliutsii*, Moscow–Leningrad: Gosudarstvennoe izdatel'stvo.

Guchkov, A.I. (1991) 'Aleksandr Ivanovich Guchkov rasskazyvaet', *Voprosy istorii*, 7–8: 191–216; 9–10: 186–211.

Gurevich, B. (1923) 'Vserossiiskii Krest'ianskii S"ezd i pervaia koalitsiia', *Letopis revoliutsii* 1, Berlin: Izdatel'stvo Z.I. Grzhebina.

Iakhontov, A.N. (ed.) (1926) 'Tiazhelye dni. (Sekretnye zasedaniia Soveta Ministrov 16 Iiulia–2 Sentiabria 1915 goda)', *Arkhiv russkoi revoliutsii*, XVIII: 5–137.

Izvestiia soveta rabochikh i soldatskikh deputatov, August 8, 1917.

Izvestiia TsK KPSS, 1989–91.

Jansen, M. (1988) *Partiia Sotsialistov-Revoliutsionerov posle Oktiabr'skogo perevorota 1917 goda: Dokumenty iz arkhiva P.S.-R.*, Amsterdam: Stichting Beheer IISG.

Koenker, D. (ed.) (1982) *Tret'ya vserossiiskaya konferentsiya Profes-sional'nykh Soyuzov 3–11 Iyulya (20–28 st.st.) 1917 goda. Stenograficheskii Otchet*, New York: Kraus (reprint of 1927 original).

Kommunist: Ezhenedel'nyi zhurnal ekonomiki, politiki i obshchvennosti, nos 1–4, 1918 (1990 reprint, edited by R.I. Kowalski), Millwood: Kraus International.

KPSS v resoliutsiakh: resheniiakh s"ezdov, konferentsii i plenumov TSK', 2, Moscow: Izdatel'stvo politicheskoi literatury.

Kritsman, L. (1924) *Geroicheskii period russkoi revoliutsii*, Moscow: Gosudarstvennoe izdatel'stvo.

'Kronshtadt v marte 1921 g.', *Otechestvennye arkhivy*, 1996, 1: 48–76.

Lukomskii, A.S. (1922a) *Vospominaniia generala A.S. Lukomskago*, Berlin: Otto Kirkhner.

—— (1922b) 'Iz vospominanii gen. Lukomskago', *Arkhiv russkoi revoliutsii*, II: 14–44.

Osinskii, N. (1918) Stroitel'stvo sotsializma, *Kommunist*, 2, Millwood: Kraus International (1990 reprint of 1918 original), pp. 65–77.

Protokoly zasedanii Vserossiikago Tsentral'nogo Ispolnitel'nago Komiteta 4-go sozyva: Stenograficheskii otchet, Moscow: Gosudarstvennoe izdatel'stvo, 1920.

Radek, K. (1918a) 'Posle piati mesiatsev', *Kommunist*, 1, Millwood: Kraus International (1990 reprint of 1918 original), pp. 1–8.

—— (1918b) 'Krasnaia armiia', *Kommunist*, 2, Millwood: Kraus International (1990 reprint of 1918 original), pp. 94–101.

Remizova, I.A. (ed.) (1954) *Agrarnaia politika sovetskoi vlasti (1917–1918 gg.). Dokumenty: moterialy*, Moscow: Izdatel'stvo academii nauk SSSR.

Revoliutsionnoe dvizhenie v Rossii posle sverzheniia samoderzhavie, Moscow: Izdatel'stvo akademii nauk SSSR, 1957.

Revoliutsionnoe dvizhenie v Rossii v mae–iiune 1917g.: Iiunskaia demon-stratsiia, Moscow: Izdatel'stvo akademii nauk SSSR, 1959.

Revoliutsionnoe dvizhenie v Rossiia v iiule 1917g.: Iiul'skii krizis, Moscow: Izdatvel'stvo akademii nauk SSSR, 1959.

Revoliutsionnoe dvizhenie v Rossii v avguste 1917g.: Razgrom kornilovskogo miatezha, Moscow: Izdatel'stvo akademii nauk SSSR, 1969.

Revoliutsionnoe dvizhenie v Rosii nakanune Oktiabr'skogo vooruzhennogo vostaniia (1–24 oktiabria 1917g.), Moscow: Izdatel'stvo akademii nauk SSSR, 1962.

Saratovskii sovet rabochikh deputatove (1917–1918): Sbornik dokumentov. Moscow, Leningrad: Gosudarstvennoe sotsial'no-ekonomicheskoe izdatel'stvo, 1931.

Sbornik dokumentov i materialov po istorii SSSR sovetskogo perioda (1917–1958 gg.), Moscow: Izdatel'stvo moskovskogo universiteta, 1966.

Shestakov, A.V. (ed.) (1929) *Sovety krest'ianikh deputatovi drugie krest'ianskie organizatsii (mart–noiabr' 1917g.)*, Moscow: Izdatel'stvo Kommunisticheskoi akademii.

Shestoi s"ezd RSDRP (Bol'shevikov) Avgust 1917 goda: Protokoly, Moscow: Gosizdat, 1958.

Shliapnikov, A.G. (1923–5) *Semnadtsatyi god*, 4 volumes, Moscow–Leningrad: Gosudarstvennoe izdatel'stvo.

Sorin, V. (1918) 'K voprosu sovetskoi vlasti', *Kommunist*, 4, Millwood: Kraus International (1990 reprint of 1918 original), pp. 191–9.

Sukhanov, N.N. (1991) *Zapiski o revoliutsii*, 3 volumes, Moscow: Izdatel'stvo politicheskoi literatury.

'Tezisy o tekushchem momente', *Kommunist*, 1, Millwood: Kraus International (1990 reprint of 1918 original), pp. 8–24.

Tsereteli, I.G. (1963) *Vospominaniia o fevral'skoi revoliutsii*, Paris: Mouton.

Vakunova, S. (ed.) (1992) '"Zato teper' svoboda . . . " Pis'ma krest'ian i gorodskikh obyvatelei v Uchreditel'noe sobranie i obzor khoda izbiratel'noi kampanii 1917g.', *Neizvestnaia Rossiia*, XX, II: pp. 176–99.

Voitinskii, V.S. (1990) *1917-i, God pobed i porazhenii*, Benson, Vt.: Chalidze.

Vos'moi s"ezd PKP (b). Mart 1919 goda. Protokoly, Moscow: Gosudarstvennoe Izdatel'stvo, 1959.

Vospominaniia o Vladimire Il'iche Lenine, volume 2 (5 volumes), Moscow: Izdatel'stvo politicheskoi literatury, 1959.

Secondary sources in Russian

Burdzhalov, E.N. (1971) *Vtoraia russkaia revoliutsiia. Moskva. Front. Periferiia*, Moscow: Nauka.

Burganov, A.Kh. (1993) 'Byla li vozmozhnost' sozdaniia demokraticheskogo pravitel'stva posle oktiabr'skoi revoliutsii', *Otechestvennaia istoriia*, 5: 26–38.

Fel'shtinskii, Iu.G. (1985) *Bol'sheviki i Levye Esery: Oktiabr' 1917–Iiul' 1918*, Paris: YMCA Press.

Gaponenko, L.S. (1970) *Rabochii klass Rossi v 1917 godu*, Moscow: Nauka.

Grunt, A.Ia. (1976) *Moskva 1917-i revoliutsiia i kontr-revoliutsiia*, Moscow: Nauka.

Gusev, K.V. (1993) 'V zaschite "shtreikbrekherov revoliutsii"', *Otechestvennaia istoriia*, 2:142–8.

Igritskii, Iu.I. (1993) 'Snova o totalitarizme', *Otechestvennaia istoriia*, 1: 3–18.

Ioffe, G.Z. (1992) 'Posleslovie: N. Avksent'ev, "Bol'shevistskii perevorot"', *Otechestvennaia istoriia*, 5: 143–54.

Iurchenko, V.V. (1993) 'Oktiabr'skaia revoliutsiia: ozhidaniia i rezultaty. Nauchnaia konferentsiia v Moskve', *Otechestvennaia istoriia*, 4: 212–16.

Korablev, Iu.I. (1996) 'Krest'iansko vosstanie v tambovskoi gubernii v 1919–1921 gg. "Antonovishchina": dokumenty', *Otechestvennaia istoriia*, 1: 177–84.

Kornev, V.V. (1994) 'Krizis v istoricheskoi nauki v Rossii', *Kentavr'*, 4: 87–93.

Kozlov, V.I. (1975) *Natsional'nosti SSSR*, Moscow: Statistika.

Kulegin, A.M. (1993) 'Dokumenty revoliutsii', *Otechestvennaia istoriia*, 2: 91–9.

Miliukov, P.N. (1921) *Istoriia vtoroi russkoi revoliutsii*, Sofia: Rossiisko-bolgarskoe knigoisdatel'stvo.

—— (1927) *Rossiia na perelome: Bol'shevistskii period russkoi revoliutsii*, volume 1, Paris: Voltaire.

Miller, V.I. (1993) 'Vserossiskoe Uchreditel'noe Sobranie i demokraticheskaia al'ternativa', *Otechestvennaia istoriia*, 5: 19–25.

—— (1994) 'Po goriachim sledam (Men'sheviki ob Oktiabr'skoi revoliutsii)', *Kentavr*, 2: 70–73.

Mitrofanov, N. (1987) *Dni velikogo shturma. Povest'–khronika o sobytiakh pervykh dnei Oktiabr'skoi revoliutsii*, Moscow: Sovetskaia Rossia.

Naumov, V.P. and Kosakovskii, A.A. (eds) (1994) 'Kronshtadskaia tragediia 1921 goda', *Voprosy istorii*, 4: 3–21.

Protasov, L.G. (1993) 'Vserossiskoe Uchreditel'noe Sobranie i demokraticheskaia al'ternativa', *Otechestvennaia istoriia*, 5: 3–19.

Triumfal'noe shestvie sovetskoi vlasti, volume 1, Moscow: Akademiia nauk SSSR, 1963.

Zhuravlev, V.V. and Simonov, N.S. (1992) 'Prichiny i posledstviia razgona Uchreditel' nogo sobraniia', *Voprosy istorii*, 1: 1–18.

Primary sources in English

Ascher, A. (1976) *The Mensheviks in the Russian Revolution*, London: Thames & Hudson.

Brovkin, V.N. (1991) *Dear Comrades: Menshevik Reports on the Bolshevik Revolution and Civil War*, Stanford: Stanford University Press.

Browder, R.P. and Kerensky, A.F. (1961) *The Russian Provisional Government 1917: Documents*, 3 volumes, Stanford: Stanford University Press.

Buchanan, G. (1977) *My Mission to Russia*, 2 volumes, New York: Arno Reprint.

Bunyan, J. (1976) *Intervention, Civil War, and Communism in Russia, April–December 1918: Documents and Materials*, New York: Octagon.

Bunyan, J. and Fisher, H.H. (1934) *The Bolshevik Revolution 1917–1918: Documents and Materials*, Stanford: Stanford University Press.

Denikin, A.I. (1973) *The Russian Turmoil: Memoirs: Military, Social and Political*, Westport: Hyperion Press.

Gajda, R. (1919) 'Results of the Spring Offensive' (memorandum held in the Public Record Office), *PRO/FO538/2/14421.*

Golder, F.A. (ed.) (1927) *Documents of Russian History 1914–1917*, New York: Century.

—— (1992) *War, Revolution and Peace in Russia: The Passages of Frank Golder*, Stanford: Hoover Institution Press.

Howe, I. (ed.) (1963) *The Basic Writings of Leon Trotsky*, London: Mercury.

Kerensky, A.F. (1972) *The Prelude to Bolshevism: The Kornilov Rebellion*, New York: Haskell House Reprint.

—— (1977) *The Catastrophe*, Millwood: Kraus Reprint.

Kollontai, A.I. (no date) *The Workers' Opposition*, London: Solidarity.

Lenin, V.I. (1964–5) *Collected Works*, 20–29, Moscow: Progress.

McCauley, M. (ed.) (1984) *Octobrists to Bolsheviks: Imperial Russia 1905–1917*, London: Edward Arnold.

Meijer, J. (ed.) (1964; 1971) *The Trotsky Papers, 1917–1922*, two volumes, The Hague: Mouton.

Miliukov, P.N. (1922) *Russia Today and Tomorrow*, New York: Macmillan.

Sukhanov, N.N. (1984) *The Russian Revolution 1917: A Personal Record*, Princeton: Princeton University Press.

Trotsky, L.D. (1974) *My Life*, Harmondsworth: Penguin.

Tukhachevsky, M. (1995) 'The Red Army and the Militia', in A. Richardson (ed.) *In Defence of the Russian Revolution: A Selection of Bolshevik Writings, 1917–1923*, London: Porcupine Press.

Wade, R.A. (1991) *Documents of Soviet History, Volume 1: The Triumph of Bolshevism*, Gulf Breeze: Academic International.

—— (1993) *Documents of Soviet History, 2: Triumph and Retreat*, Gulf Breeze: Academic International.

Zohrab, I. (1991) 'The Socialist Revolutionary Party, Kerensky and the Kornilov Affair: From the Unpublished Papers of Harold W. Williams', *New Zealand Slavonic Journal*: 131–61.

Secondary sources in English

Acton, E. (1990) *Rethinking the Russian Revolution*, London: Edward Arnold.

Adelman, J. (1980) *The Revolutionary Armies: The Historical Development of the Soviet and Chinese People's Liberation Armies*, Westport: Greenwood.

Andrle, V. (1994) *A Social History of Twentieth-Century Russia*, London: Edward Arnold.

Asher, H. (1970) 'The Kornilov Affair: A Reinterpretation', *Russian Review*, XXIX, 2: 286–300.

Atkinson, D. (1983) *The End of the Russian Land Commune, 1905–1930*, Stanford: Stanford University Press.

Avrich, P. (1991) *Kronstadt, 1921*, Princeton: Princeton University Press.

Baburina, N. (1985) *The Soviet Political Poster, 1917–1980*, Harmondsworth: Penguin.

Benvenuti, F. (1988) *The Bolsheviks and the Red Army, 1918–1922*, Cambridge: Cambridge University Press.

Berkman, A. (1976) *The Russian Tragedy*, Sanday: Cienfuegos.

Bonnell, V. (1983) *Roots of Rebellion: Workers' Politics and Organisations in St Petersburg and Moscow, 1900–1914*, Berkeley: University of California Press.

Boyd, J.R. (1968) 'The Origins of Order No. 1', *Soviet Studies*, XIX, 3: 358–72.

Brinton, M. (1970) *The Bolsheviks and Workers' Control, 1917 to 1921: The State and Counter-revolution*, London: Solidarity.

Brovkin, V. (1985) 'Politics, Not Economics was the Key', *Slavic Review*, 44, 2: 244–50.

—— (1987) *The Mensheviks After October: Socialist Opposition and the Rise of the Bolshevik Dictatorship*, Ithaca: Cornell University Press.

—— (1994) *Behind the Front Lines of the Civil War: Political Parties and Social Movements in Russia, 1918–1922*, Princeton: Princeton University Press.

Brown, A., Kaser, M. and Smith, G.S. (eds) (1994) *The Cambridge Encyclopaedia of Russia and the former Soviet Union*, Cambridge: Cambridge University Press.

Buldakov, V.P. (1992) 'The October Revolution: Seventy-Five Years On', *European History Quarterly*, 22, 4: 497–516.

Burdzhalov, E.N. (1987) *Russia's Second Revolution: the February 1917 Uprising in Petrograd*, Bloomington: Indiana University Press.

Carr, E.H. (1964) *What Is History?*, Harmondsworth: Penguin.

—— (1966) *The Bolshevik Revolution, 1917–1923*, 2 volumes, Harmondsworth: Penguin.

Chamberlin, W.H. (1987) *The Russian Revolution, 1917–1921* (two volumes), Princeton: Princeton University Press.

Channon, J. (1992a) 'The Peasantry in the Revolutions of 1917', in E. Frankel, J. Frankel and B. Knei-Paz (eds) *Revolution in Russia: Reassessments of 1917*, Cambridge: Cambridge University Press.

—— (1992b) 'The Landowners', in R. Service (ed.) *Society and Politics in the Russian Revolution*, London: Macmillan.

Chase, W. and Getty, J.A. (1978) 'The Moscow Bolshevik Cadres of 1917: A Prosopographic Analysis', *Russian History*, 5, 1: 84–105.

Cohen, S.E. (1980) *Bukharin and the Bolshevik Revolution*, Oxford: Oxford University Press.

Dallin, D. (1974) 'The Outbreak of the Civil War', in L. Haimson (ed.) *The Mensheviks. From the Revolution of 1917 to the Second World War*, Chicago: University of Chicago Press.

Daniels, R.V. (1967) *Red October: The Bolshevik Revolution of 1917*, London: Secker & Warburg.

Davis, H.B. (ed.) (1976) *Rosa Luxemburg: The National Question – Selected Writings*, New York: Monthly Review.

Dukes, P. (1979) *October and the World. Perspectives on the Russian Revolution*, London: Macmillan.

—— (1992) 'From October 1917 to August 1991 and Beyond: Newer Thinking on the World Revolution', *European History Quarterly*, 22, 4: 569–95.

Engelstein, L. (1982) *Moscow 1905: Working-class Organisation and Political Conflict*, Stanford: Stanford University Press.

Feldman, R.S. (1968) 'The Russian General Staff and the June 1917 Offensive', *Soviet Studies*, XIX, 4: 526–43.

Ferro, M. (1980) *The Bolshevik Revolution: A Social History of the Russian Revolution*, London: Routledge & Kegan Paul.

Figes, O. (1989) *Peasant Russia, Civil War: The Volga Countryside in Revolution (1917–1921)*, Oxford: Oxford University Press.

Fitzpatrick, S. (1989) 'The Legacy of the Civil War', in D.P. Koenker, W.G. Rosenberg and R.G. Suny (eds) *Party, State and Society in the Russian Civil War*, Bloomington: Indiana University Press.

Gatrell, P. (1994) 'The First World War and War Communism', in R.W. Davies *et al.* (eds) *The Economic Transformation of the Soviet Union, 1913–1945*, Cambridge: Cambridge University Press.

Getzler, I. (1994) 'Iulii Martov: The Leader Who Lost His Party in 1917', *Slavonic and East European Review*, 72, 3: 424–37.

Giddens, A. (1979) *Central Problems of Social Theory*, London: Macmillan.

Gill, G. (1978) 'The Mainsprings of Peasant Action', *Soviet Studies*, XXX, 1: 38–62.

—— (1979) *Peasants and Government in the Russian Revolution*, London: Macmillan.

Gramsci, A. (1971) *Selections from Prison Notebooks*, London: Lawrence & Wishart.

Haimson, L.H. (1964; 1965) 'The Problem of Social Stability in Urban Russia', *Slavic Review*, 23, 4: 619–42; 24, 1: 1–22.
—— (ed.) (1974) *The Mensheviks. From the Revolution of 1917 to the Second World War*, Chicago: University of Chicago Press.
Hasegawa, T. (1981) *The February Revolution: Petrograd 1917*, Seattle: University of Washington Press.
Howard, M. (1992) 'The Vast Detour', *Times Literary Supplement*, November 6, 1992: 4–5.
Hughes, M. (1996) '"Revolution was in the Air": British Officials in Russia during the First World War', *Journal of Contemporary History*, 31, 1: 75–97.
Jenkins, K. (1995) *On 'What Is History?'*, London: Routledge.
Jones, S. (1992) 'The Non-Russian Nationalities', in R. Service (ed.) *Society and Politics in the Russian Revolution*, London: Macmillan.
Katkov, G. (1969) *Russia 1917: The February Revolution*, London: Fontana.
—— (1980) *Russia 1917: The Kornilov Affair*, London: Longman.
Keep, J. (ed.) (1964) *Contemporary History in the Soviet Mirror*, London: Allen & Unwin.
—— (1976) *The Russian Revolution: A Study in Mass Mobilisation*, London: Weidenfeld & Nicolson.
Knei-Paz, B. (1979) *The Social and Political Thought of Leon Trotsky*, Oxford: Oxford University Press.
Koenker, D. (1981) *Moscow Workers and the 1917 Revolution*, Princeton: Princeton University Press.
Kolakowski, L. (1992) 'A Calamitous Accident', *Times Literary Supplement*, November 6, 1992: 5.
Kolonitskii, B.I. (1994) 'Anti-bourgeois Propaganda and Anti-"Burzhui" Consciousness in 1917', *Russian Review*, 53, 2: 183–95.
Kowalski, R.I. (1991) *The Bolshevik Party in Conflict: The Left Communist Opposition of 1918*, London: Macmillan.
Krassin, L. (1929) *Leonid Krasin: His Life and Work*, London: Skeffington.
Lande, L. (1974) 'The Mensheviks in 1917', in L. Haimson (ed.) *The Mensheviks: From the Revolution of 1917 to the Second World War*, Chicago: University of Chicago Press.
Liebman, M. (1970) *The Russian Revolution: The Origins, Phases and Meaning of the Bolshevik Victory*, London: Jonathan Cape.
Lieven, D.C.B. (1983) *Russia and the Origins of the First World War*, London: Macmillan.
Longley, D. (1989) 'The *Mezhraionka*, the Bolsheviks and International Women's Day: In Response to Michael Melançon', *Soviet Studies*, XLI, 4: 625–45.
McCauley, M. (1991) *Bread and Justice. State and Society in Petrograd 1917–1922*, Oxford: Oxford University Press.

McKean, R. (1990) *St Petersburg Between the Revolutions*, New Haven: Yale University Press.

Malia, M. (1992) 'Why Amalrik was Right', *Times Literary Supplement*, November 6, 1992: 9.

Mandel, D. (1983) *The Petrograd Workers and the Fall of the Old Regime*, London: Macmillan.

Marot, J.E. (1994) 'Class Conflict, Political Competition and Social Transformation: Critical Perspectives on the Social History of the Russian Revolution', *Revolutionary Russia*, 7, 2: 111–63.

—— (1995) 'A "Postmodern" Approach to the Russian Revolution?', *Russian Review*, 54, 2: 260–4.

Mawdsley, E. (1987) *The Russian Civil War*, London: Allen & Unwin.

Melançon, M. (1988) 'Who Wrote What and When? Proclamations of the February Revolution in Petrograd, 23 February–1 March 1917', *Soviet Studies*, XL, 3: 479–500.

—— (1990) 'International Women's Day, the Finland Station Proclamation, and the February Revolution: A Reply to Longley and White', *Soviet Studies*, 42, 3:, 583–9.

Mendel, A. (1971) 'On Interpreting the Fate of Imperial Russia', in T.G. Stavrou (ed.) *Russia under the Last Tsar*, Minneapolis: University of Minnesota Press.

Moore, B. (1967) *Social Origins of Dictatorship and Democracy*, Harmondsworth: Penguin.

Munck, J.L. (1987) *The Kornilov Revolt: A Critical Examination of Sources and Research*, Aarhus: Aarhus University Press.

Nenarokov, A. (1987) *An Illustrated History of the Great October Socialist Revolution*, Moscow: Progress.

Nove, A. (1983) *The Economics of Feasible Socialism*, London: Allen & Unwin.

Patenaude, B. (1995) 'Peasants into Russians: The Utopian Essence of War Communism', *Russian Review*, 54, 4: 552–70.

Pearson, R. (1977) *The Russian Moderates and the Crisis of Tsarism 1914–1917*, London: Macmillan.

—— (1989) 'Privileges, Rights and Russification', in O. Crisp and L. Edmondson (eds) *Civil Rights in Imperial Russia*, Cambridge: Cambridge University Press.

Perrie, M. (1987) 'The Russian Working Class, 1905–1917', *Theory and Society*, 16, 3: 431–46.

—— (1992) 'The Peasantry', in R. Service (ed.) *Society and Politics in the Russian Revolution*, London: Macmillan.

Pipes, R. (1963) *Social Democracy and the St Petersburg Labor Movement, 1885–1917*, Cambridge, Mass.: Harvard University Press.

—— (1992a) *The Russian Revolution, 1899–1919*, London: Fontana.

—— (1992b) 'The Great October Revolution as a clandestine *coup d'état*', *Times Literary Supplement*, November 6, 1992: 3–4.

—— (1995) *Russian under the Bolshevik Regime, 1919–1924*, London: Fontana.

Rabinowitch, A. (1976) *The Bolsheviks Come to Power*, New York: Norton.

—— (1991) *Prelude to Revolution: The Petrograd Bolsheviks and the July 1917 Uprising*, Bloomington: Midland.

Radkey, O.H. (1950) *The Election to the Russian Constituent Assembly of 1917*, Cambridge, Mass.: Harvard University Press.

—— (1953) 'An Alternative to Bolshevism: The Program of Russian Social Revolutionism', *Journal of Modern History*, XXV, 1: 25–39.

—— (1958) *The Agrarian Foes of Bolshevism*, New York: Columbia University Press.

—— (1976) *The Unknown Civil War in Soviet Russia: A Study of the Green Movement in the Tambov Region, 1920–1921*, Stanford: Hoover Institute Press.

—— (1990) *Russia Goes to the Polls. The Election to the All-Russian Constituent Assembly, 1917*, Ithaca: Cornell University Press.

Raleigh, D.J. (1986) *Revolution on the Volga: 1917 in Saratov*, Ithaca: Cornell University Press.

Rogger, H. (1966) 'Russia in 1914', *Journal of Contemporary History*, 1, 4: 95–119.

—— (1983) *Russia in the Age of Modernisation and Revolution 1881–1917*, London: Longman.

Rosenberg, W.G. (1974) *Liberals in the Russian Revolution: The Constitutional Democratic Party, 1917–1921*, Princeton: Princeton University Press.

—— (1985) 'Russian Labor and Bolshevik Power After October', *Slavic Review*, 44, 2: 213–38.

Rosenberg, W.G. and Koenker, D. (1987) 'The Limits of Formal Protest: Worker Activism and Social Polarisation in Petrograd and Moscow, March to October, 1917', *American Historical Review*, 92, 2: 296–326.

Schapiro, L.B. (1985) *1917: The Russian Revolution and the Origins of Present-day Communism*, Harmondsworth: Penguin.

Serge, V. (1967) *Memoirs of a Revolutionary, 1909–1941*, Oxford: Oxford University Press.

Service, R. (1990) 'Lenin: Individual and Politics in the October Revolution', *Modern History Review*, September: 16–19.

—— (1991) *Lenin: A Political Life, volume 2: Worlds in Collision*, London: Macmillan.

—— (1995) *Lenin: A Political Life, volume 3. The Iron Ring*, London: Macmillan.

Shishkin, V.I. (1992) 'The October Revolution and *Perestroika*: A Critical Analysis of Recent Soviet Historiography', *European History Quarterly*, 22, 4: 517–40.

Sirianni, C. (1982) *Workers' Control and Socialist Democracy: The Soviet Experience*, London: Verso.

Skocpol, T. (1979) *States and Social Revolutions. A Comparative Analysis of France, Russia and China*, Cambridge: Cambridge University Press.

Smith, S.A. (1983) *Red Petrograd: Revolution in the Factories, 1917–1918*, Cambridge: Cambridge University Press.

—— (1984) 'Moscow Workers and the Revolutions of 1905 and 1917', *Soviet Studies*, XXXVI, 2: 282–9.

—— (1994) 'Writing the History of the Russian Revolution after the Fall of Communism', *Europe–Asia Studies*, 46, 4: 563–78.

—— (1995) 'Rethinking the Autonomy of Politics: A Rejoinder to John Eric Marot', *Revolutionary Russia*, 8, 1: 104–6.

Stone, N. (1975) *The Eastern Front 1914–1917*, London: Hodder & Stoughton.

Suny, R.G. (1994) 'Revision and Retreat in the Historiography of 1917: Social History and Its Critics', *Russian Review*, 53, 2: 165–82.

Swain, G. (1991) 'Before the Fighting Started: A Discussion on the Theme of the "Third Way"', *Revolutionary Russia*, 4: 210–34.

—— (1996) *The Origins of the Russian Civil War*, London: Longman.

Thurston, R.W. (1987) *Liberal City, Conservative State: Moscow and Russia's Urban Crisis, 1906–1914*, Oxford: Oxford University Press.

Tosh, J. (1992) *The Pursuit of History*, London: Longman.

Tukhachevsky, M. (1995) 'The Red Army and the Militia', in A. Richardson (ed.) *In Defence of the Russian Revolution: A Selection of Bolshevik Writings, 1917–1923*, London: Porcupine Press.

Uldricks, T. (1974) 'The "Crowd" in the Russian Revolution: Towards Reassessing the Nature of Revolutionary Leadership', *Politics and Society*, 4, 3: 397–413.

Volobuev, P.V. (1992) '*Perestroika* and the October Revolution in Soviet Historiography', *Russian Review*, 51, 4: 566–76.

Wade, R.A. (1969) *The Russian Search for Peace: February–October 1917*, Stanford: Stanford University Press.

Waldron, P. (1995) 'States of Emergency: Autocracy and Extraordinary Legislation, 1881–1917', *Revolutionary Russia*, 8, 1: 1–26.

White, J.D. (1979) 'The Sormovo–Nikolaev *Zemlyachestvo* in the February Revolution', *Soviet Studies*, XXXI, 4: 475–504.

—— (1994), *The Russian Revolution 1917–1921*, London: Edward Arnold.

White, S. (1988) *The Bolshevik Poster*, New Haven: Yale University Press.

Wildman, A.K. (1980) *The End of the Russian Imperial Army. The Old Army and the Soldiers' Revolt (March–April 1917)*, Princeton: Princeton University Press.

—— (1987) *The End of the Russian Imperial Army. The Road to Soviet Power and Peace*, Princeton: Princeton University Press.

—— (1992) 'Officers of the General Staff and the Kornilov Movement', in E.R. Frankel, J. Frankel and B. Knei-Paz (eds) *Revolution in Russia. Reassessments of 1917*, Cambridge: Cambridge University Press.

Wolfe, B.D. (1964) 'Party Histories from Lenin to Khrushchev', in J. Keep (ed.) *Contemporary History in the Soviet Mirror*, New York: Praeger.

Wood, A. (1992) 'The Bolsheviks, the Baby and the Bathwater', *European History Quarterly*, 22, 4: 483–95.

Zagorsky, S.O. (1928) *State Control of Industry in Russia during the War*, New Haven: Yale University Press.

Index